R.C. MACLEOD is a member of the Department of History at the University of Alberta.

The North-West Mounted Police were created in 1873 specifically to ensure that Canadian administration and settlement of the newly acquired North-West Territories were carried out in a peaceful and orderly manner. They did so with a remarkable degree of success. Contacts between the white and Indian societies were peaceful, and crime and violence among settlers remained under control at all times. Because of their efficiency and popularity with the public, the Mounted Police were able to make the transition from policing the frontier to maintaining law and order in a settled and developed community.

R.C. Macleod traces the evolution of the force and also investigates why it was so successful. He finds both structural and sociological reasons. The North-West Mounted Police had advantages not enjoyed by similar organizations elsewhere in the world. Its officers exercised extensive judicial powers; indeed, for its first decade or so of existence, the force carried out virtually all functions of government in the Territories. Sociologically, the élite nature of the force – it attracted a consistently competent group of men and officers – and public acceptance of the high social standing of its members freed them from the pressures of local opinion and power.

Above all, the NWMP was not an alien imposition, but a genuine expression of the society it served. Its members played so large a part in the creation of western Canadian society that by the time their original assignment was complete they were an important part of the way in which that society defined itself, and hence indispensable to it.

R.C. MACLEOD

The NWMP and Law Enforcement
1873–1905

For Andy
Best wishes.
[signature]

UNIVERSITY OF TORONTO PRESS
Toronto and Buffalo

Library of Congress Cataloging in Publication Data

Macleod, RC   1940–
  The NWMP and law enforcement, 1873 – 1905.
  Bibliography: p.
  Includes index.
  1. Canada. Royal Canadian Mounted Police – History.
  2. Law enforcement – Canada – History   I. Title.
  HV8157.M44   363.2′0971   76–3709
  ISBN 0-8020-5333-5

For my wife

Contents

Preface

This is not intended to be in any sense a definitive history of the North-West Mounted Police even for the limited period 1873-1905. I have approached the topic with one basic question in mind: why did the NWMP succeed not only in policing the frontier but in making the transition to maintaining the law in a settled and developed community? Aside from the fact that this question sums up what interested me most about the phenomenon under investigation, the question has the advantage of bearing directly on a number of themes which have over the years consistently attracted the attention of many historians – Turner's frontier thesis, the differences between Canadian and American society, the problem of reconciling order and liberty in a free society, to name only a few. It would be possible to approach the history of the NWMP from a large number of different points of view, given the massive documentation available for the force after 1885. Such studies will be essential before anything like a complete understanding of this remarkable organization is attained.

The most interesting feature of the Mounted Police, and one which makes it almost unique among police forces, is its consistent popularity, particularly in western Canada. At the time of writing I have just taken my children to the annual parade opening the Edmonton Exhibition which included a large Mounted Police contingent as part of the centennial celebrations of the force. City police participating in the parade were received by the crowd with indifference punctuated by occasional heckling and verbal harassment. Not so the Mounted Police who, judging from the applause, were easily the most popular of the ninety or so entries in the parade. In 1906 a small detachment of Mounted Police was called in by the BC government to capture some American train robbers who had found their way north of the border. The desperadoes were quickly rounded up and arrested after a gunfight in which one of their number was wounded in the leg. The wounded man later, on his way to serve a twenty-year jail term, paused to exchange a few words with the sergeant who had taken him prisoner. He thanked the policeman for the good treatment he had received while in custody and said, 'You may think it funny coming from me, but I certainly admire the way you boys do your work.'[1] Examples of Mounted Police popularity in the intervening years could be multiplied many times. In spite of the many difficult and unpopular tasks the force has had to face it continues to command admiration and respect.

The question which is the focus of this book rests upon the premise that the NWMP did succeed to an extent which justified their enormous reputation. During my research I made a point of looking for evidence to the contrary and found virtually none. There was certainly no lack of human weakness but for the most part the police were efficient, honest, humane and, when the occasion demanded it, heroic. Political patronage, of course, was very much a fact of life for the NWMP but it appears to have been a good deal less debilitating in its effects than in other branches of the public service at the time. The NWMP enjoyed powers unparalleled by any other police force in a democratic country and the most significant single fact about the history of the force is that they did not abuse those powers. They were used to the full to uphold the law but in no instance is there any record of their use for private gain or public tyranny. Newspapers in the North-West Territories occasionally published editorials objecting to such things as the judicial powers of the police but they always based their objections on principle and admitted that they knew of no cases of this authority being used improperly. The record of the police is the more remarkable when one considers that in every other branch of the Canadian government during this period corruption and inefficiency were accepted as unfortunate but inevitable side-effects of democracy. The wages of the police were never generous and they were almost always overworked, except perhaps in the period 1885-90 when they reached their peak strength of a thousand men.

The obvious place to look for an answer to the question of why the NWMP succeeded in spite of the obstacles in its path was in the methods and organization of the force. But it became apparent almost at once that the question could not be answered by investigating the police alone; the focus had to be on the interaction between the police and the rest of society. This is the emphasis of the last six chapters, and even the first five chapters, which outline the evolution of the force, are very much concerned with this interaction, since the changes in the structure and activities of the force were in part a product of changing social conditions. One of the more interesting things revealed by the NWMP records was that the force spent much, indeed most, of its time on activities not directly con-nected with law enforcement. These must also be taken into account since they had a great impact on relations between the police and the rest of society.

I would like to thank all the people who helped me at various stages of this study. Dr Donald Swainson of Queen's University first drew my attention to the absence of any scholarly study of the Mounted Police. My supervisor at Duke University, Dr Richard Preston, encouraged me to undertake the study as a doc-toral dissertation. During the research S.W. Horrall, the official historian of the force, offered many helpful suggestions. I would also like to thank the staffs of the Public Archives of Canada, the Public Archives of Manitoba, the Public Ar-chives of Saskatchewan, the Glenbow-Alberta Institute, and the RCMP Museum, Regina, for their co-operation and assistance. I am grateful to all my colleagues who teach Canadian history at the University of Alberta, especially L.G. Thomas and L.H. Thomas, who were always willing to share their knowledge of the his-tory of the Canadian West and to submit to discussions on the Mounted Police during the writing of the manuscript. My wife was a captive audience throughout the whole process of research and writing and words cannot express my appre-ciation of her patience and consistent interest in it. The office staff of the His-tory Department did their usual superbly efficient job of typing and attending to the thousand other details necessary to getting a book into print. The research for this study was made possible by a doctoral fellowship from the Canada Council.

This book has been published with the help of a grant from the Social Science Research Council of Canada, using funds provided by the Canada Council, and a grant from the Andrew W. Mellon Foundation to the University of Toronto Press.

PART I

THE GROWTH AND DEVELOPMENT OF THE

NORTH-WEST MOUNTED POLICE 1873–1905

1
Introduction

The North-West Mounted Police were an essential although usually unacknowledged part of Sir John A. Macdonald's famous National Policy. Development of
western Canada was the keystone of the National Policy and no development
could take place without a peaceful environment. Railroads could not be built,
capitalists could not be induced to invest, homesteaders could not be persuaded
to settle in an atmosphere of crime, disorder, and the threat of Indian warfare.
The Americans had proved that the West could be settled in spite of conditions
like this but at a cost that Canada could not possibly afford. By the 1870s the
US government was spending over twenty million dollars a year fighting the
Plains Indians.[1] Since the total Canadian budget at the time was just over nine-
teen million dollars, an Indian war of any kind would have been disastrous. Every
penny the government had at its disposal was committed to railway subsidies
and all the other expenses attendant upon opening an enormous tract of virgin
territory for settlement. As anyone familiar with the history of the Canadian
Pacific Railway knows, even with the absence of conflict it was a very near thing.
It is not an exaggeration to say that the only possible Canadian West was a peaceful one.

All this was generally recognized by all who thought about the problem in the
1870s. The question was, what, if anything, could be done about it? Many
rational and responsible Canadians sincerely believed that the undertaking was
inherently impossible. These included not only Liberal politicians such as Edward Blake and Alexander Mackenzie, but also Alexander Morris, the man chosen
by Macdonald to begin the process of extending Canadian control over the territories acquired from the Hudson's Bay Company.[2] If the Americans, with the

almost unlimited resources at their disposal, had failed to occupy the West peacefully, how could Canadians succeed? Only Macdonald knew, or thought he knew, the answer.[3] He would create a small force of three hundred men who would be both soldiers and police. They would be armed and trained as cavalry and could fight if necessary but hopefully they would not have to. Their main efforts as policemen would be to prevent crime and disorder from developing to the point where only military action could bring it under control. Such an organization was not quite unprecedented in the English-speaking world; Ireland and India had semi-military police forces which served as models for the NWMP. Circumstances in the Canadian West were vastly different, however, and even to many of the men who marched west in 1874 the NWMP seemed a forlorn hope.[4]

Events were to prove Macdonald correct and silence the doubters so effectively that their very existence has been forgotten. With unintentional irony the biographer of Alexander Mackenzie, who as prime minister almost succeeded in eliminating the Mounted Police shortly after they were formed, credits him with creating the force.[5] A few hundred men decisively influenced the development of the prairie West. By 1905 the RNWMP were so firmly established in their western base that they could evolve into one of our most important national institutions. This is an extraordinary sequence of events by any standard, an investigation of which should tell us a great deal about Canadian society then and now. None of the earlier studies of the Mounted Police raises the question of why Canada should have departed so abruptly from the British tradition in law enforcement when even revolutionary America continued the pattern.[6] The NWMP were, in fact, much closer to continental European law enforcement systems than those which evolved in the English common law tradition.

In countries whose legal systems derived from Roman law the police as a separate and recognizable institution of government not only pre-date the British police by several centuries but bear a fundamentally different relationship to other branches of government. In continental Europe the tendency was to identify police and administration (a tendency which can be seen in the word 'police' itself, which derives from the Greek *polis* and the Latin *politia*). In France, which is as good an example as any, the word *police* in medieval times meant all functions of civil government except the ecclesiastical. This very broad concept of the police function contracted steadily during the eighteenth century, but in 1791 a writer could still define *police* as that 'partie du gouvernement de l'état, qui a pour objet d'y maintenir l'ordre, la tranquillité et l'usage libre des choses publiques.'[7] The last phrase in this description is the important one. It meant not only what we would regard as the normal police functions of maintaining order and suppressing crime, but the administration of every sort of public facility from harbours to nurseries. Inevitably, given the nature of the French state in the eighteenth century, *police* also signified the more sinister purpose of gathering political intelligence. The use of *mouchards*, police spies, to neutralize potential threats to the régime reached a high level of development under the notorious Fouché, Napoleon's minister of police.

The identification of the police with the administration implied the other distinctive characteristic of European police, their control by the central government. The English, in contrast, both defined the police function much more narrowly and placed it in the hands of local government. The basic unit of law enforcement in Britain was, and still is, the county. When the forerunners of modern police began to emerge in London in the eighteenth century, they were officials of the magistrate's courts whose duties were confined to upholding the criminal law, a different set of officials being concerned with administering the civil law. A sharp distinction was thus maintained between police and administrative functions. This system was faithfully preserved by the United States and remains the backbone of the American law enforcement system in spite of the addition of state police forces and various federal agencies such as the FBI. Canada also followed the British precedent until the formation of the Mounted Police.

The NWMP, however, were a radical departure from the British pattern of law enforcement. They were centrally controlled, they had certain military characteristics like the French *gendarmes*, and in the period covered by this study they were very much involved in administrative activities and acted in the capacity of such functionaries of the civil law as bailiffs and sheriffs as well. In one very important respect the Mounted Police had powers which exceeded those of European police; they acted as magistrates and passed judgement on criminals as well as apprehending them. This study is an effort to explain why law enforcement in the Canadian West developed in this way and why it worked so well in terms of controlling crime and maintaining order without degenerating into a repressive police state.

This last point is stressed rather heavily because there is a very strong tendency among academics and other social critics to assume that structure dictates function; that because an institution enjoys wide powers, those powers must necessarily be abused. An examination of the treatment of minority groups by the police, of their handling of criminals of all types and of their approach to one particular problem, enforcement of the liquor laws of the North-West Territories, provide abundant evidence that the Mounted Police almost invariably used their authority wisely and well. In the absence of formal, structural checks upon their activities, it was necessary to look for informal controls. These are to be found in the political system and tradition within which the police operated, in the semi-military tradition of the force, and in the social structure of late nineteenth-century Canada.

The Mounted Police should have ceased to exist in 1905 when the new provinces of Alberta and Saskatchewan were created, or at least they should have retreated to the far North. One of the reasons Sir John A. Macdonald was willing to make such a departure from British law enforcement institutions was that he intended the Mounted Police to be a temporary organization which would be phased out once the West passed through the frontier stage. A federal police force operating in the provinces would be a constitutional anomaly since the BNA Act clearly gives the provinces control over and responsibility for law enforcement. Since 1905, of course, the Mounted Police have not only failed to disappear but have expanded into all but two provinces. The decision to allow the Mounted Police to continue operating in Alberta and Saskatchewan after 1905 as provincial police was of the utmost significance for the future of law enforcement in Canada. It established the pattern which exists today in all provinces except Ontario and Quebec and gave Canada a police system which is unique and highly successful. This system evolved in the two decades between 1885 and 1905, during which time the NWMP made the transition from a frontier force to one capable of coping with the problems of maintaining the law in a complex modern society.

The findings presented in this book will be disappointing to those who seek simple, universal solutions to complex social problems such as crime and its prevention. Police systems are not easily transferable from one society to another; they succeed in proportion to their ability to adapt to the peculiarities and subtleties of the societies they serve. To give only one example, the Mounted Police were much too élitist for American tastes but more egalitarian in their approach than the British (as many recruits of British origin discovered). Necessity forced the Canadian government to experiment in the case of the Mounted Police and the experiment turned out to be more satisfactory than tried and true precedents could conceivably have been.

2

The origins of the NWMP

Sir John A. Macdonald created the NWMP as a small but essential part of his grand design for a new Canada which would occupy the northern half of North America. Like so many of Macdonald's actions, the decision to establish a federal police force for the North-West Territories was taken reluctantly after years of deliberation. Like the other monuments left by that remarkable statesman, the Mounted Police, although not without flaws, proved to be a uniquely useful, flexible, and durable organization. That they did so is a tribute to Macdonald's profound understanding of the Canadian mentality; of the country's difficulties and limitations as well as its aspirations. The Mounted Police evolved through an effort to solve practical problems by application of the Canadian political tradition.

The problem was obvious – how was a small and as yet undeveloped country to extend its control over an enormous expanse of virgin territory separated from it by hundreds of miles of impassable wilderness? It was not simply a matter of expanding the frontier steadily westward as the Americans were doing to the south. The rocks and lakes of the Shield eliminated that possibility. If Canada could leap the barrier and hold the western interior until settlement and institutions bonded the region permanently to the rest of the country, the development that would ensure continued existence would surely come, but the hurdle was formidable indeed. It was one thing to purchase the area from the Hudson's Bay Company but quite another to hang onto it thereafter. Canadian claims to succeed to British sovereignty between the Great Lakes and the Rockies were well founded but such claims were worthless without effective occupation, as the annexation of the Oregon country by the US had proved a bare twenty-five years before. By the time Canada acquired the North-West Territories there were ominous signs that the events of 1846 might be repeated. Already the commerce of the south-western portion of the prairies was controlled from Montana.[1] An even more definite threat existed to the Red River area, which was rapidly becoming tributary to Minnesota.[2]

Macdonald was acutely aware of the implications of these developments in the North-West. Some sort of Canadian military presence in the region was necessary to discourage the Americans. The form this presence was to take is indicated by the instructions given to Captain D.R. Cameron, a Militia officer who accompanied Lieutenant-Governor William McDougall when he was sent out late in 1869 to take over the North-West from the Hudson's Bay Company.

I have no doubt, come what will, there must be a military body, or at all events a body with military discipline at Fort Garry. It seems to me that the best Force would be *Mounted Riflemen*, trained partly as Cavalry, but also instructed in rifle exercise. They should also be instructed as certain of the Line are, in the use of artillery. This body should not be expressly military but should be styled *Police*, and have the military bearing of the Irish Constabulary.[3]

Events caught up with the unfortunate Captain Cameron before he could put the plan into effect but the reference to it is of more than passing interest because it demonstrates that the Mounted Police were an integral part of Macdonald's overall scheme for governing the newly acquired territory.

The reference to the 'Irish Constabulary' was not accidental. Macdonald had decided that the Royal Irish Constabulary was the model which could provide a solution to the problem of cheap and effective law enforcement in the North-West Territories.[4] The RIC had come into existence during the Napoleonic Wars when it appeared that internal disorder in Ireland constituted an invitation to French invasion. The troops who normally assisted the civil authorities in maintaining order were in short supply because of the demands of the war and such troops as there were had to be concentrated to meet the threat of an invasion. Sir Robert Peel, who was Irish Secretary at the time, proposed to substitute a police force which would be armed, under military discipline, and controlled by the central government.[5] In the face of strong Whig opposition this plan was carried through and the RIC proved very successful in maintaining order in Ireland. By 1870 there were several other police forces in the British Empire, especially in India, modelled on the RIC and colonial police officers frequently received their training in Ireland.

One of the more interesting features of Macdonald's original plan for the Mounted Police was that it drew upon the British experience in India as well as

Ireland. Cameron was to recruit the bulk of his force at Red River and a substantial proportion were to be mixed bloods.[6] The Indian army and the various Indian police forces were recruited, except for officers, from the local population and this is clearly what Macdonald intended for the Mounted Police. The uprising of 1869-70 at Red River evidently convinced Macdonald that the mixed bloods were not sufficiently trustworthy because the provision for recruiting them does not appear in later plans for the police.

The 1870 rebellion affected not only the composition of the Mounted Police but also the government's timetable for organizing the force. The political furore in Ontario created by the execution of Thomas Scott made it necessary for the government to send a military expedition to Red River in the spring of 1870.[7] The expedition encountered no resistance but the two battalions of Canadian militia had been recruited for one year's service and remained at Fort Garry after the British troops had left. Macdonald decided that the country could not afford to maintain both troops and police in the North-West and the organization of the Mounted Police was postponed for a year. By the time the Militia enlistments expired it was hoped that Red River would have recovered sufficiently to be left to its own devices.

The rebellion, because it resulted in the formation of the province of Manitoba, had complicated the problem of law enforcement. Under the British North America Act the administration of justice, including law enforcement, is a provincial responsibility. A federal police force could not operate except in a very restricted way in Manitoba, whereas the Militia could. Between 1870 and 1873 the major, indeed almost the only, law enforcement problems of which the government was aware were in Manitoba. Until those problems were solved the rest of the North-West would have to wait. The uprising, however, had created tensions which were not easily dealt with. The continued unrest in Manitoba, although it prevented the immediate organization of the Mounted Police, served to confirm Macdonald's belief that a federal police force would be necessary for the peace, order, and good government of the North-West Territories.

The Manitoba government proceeded vigorously in an effort to re-establish law and order. The Militia battalions were their ultimate weapon but a provincial Mounted Police force was also established in the fall of 1870.[8] Courts were brought into being and a lieutenant-governor of ability and tact, A.G. Archibald, managed to keep a potentially explosive situation in hand. He was able to do so only with difficulty because of the hostility which existed between the French-speaking, Roman Catholic Métis and the rapidly increasing group of settlers from eastern Canada. The latter were overwhelmingly English-speaking, Protestant Ontarians, many of them members of the Orange Order. They regarded the Métis, whom they would have distrusted in any case for being French Catholics, as rebels and traitors for their part in the recent rebellion. The mutual suspicion between these two groups found an outlet almost immediately in politics; the Métis forming the backbone of the Manitoba Conservative party and the Ontario settlers for the most part joining the Liberals. The Conservatives easily won the elections for the first Manitoba Assembly and controlled it for several years thereafter. A Manitoba correspondent of the great fountainhead of Canadian Liberalism in the nineteenth century, the Toronto *Globe*, lamented just after these first elections:

It is a hard state of things, but at present we cannot help it, and we are so totally outnumbered. They can bring an overwhelming majority to any poll in the country; they have the money and are backed up by the whole influence of the Roman Catholic clergy in the province – and that in itself is no small item. Nothing here will save us but a heavy immigration from the yeomen of Ontario.[9]

The correspondent's heavy immigration of Ontario yeomen in fact materialized sooner than most people expected, bringing rapid changes in the political situation and adding to the difficulties of maintaining order. As important as the numbers of people involved was the fact that the new arrivals tended to be young, male, unattached, and concentrated in the city of Winnipeg. Here was a ready-made mob for whom the prospect of violence represented an agreeable diversion rather than a threat. The hostility of the mob was centred at first on the provincial attorney-general, J.H. Clarke, who, although he was neither Métis nor French was considered altogether too favourable to the former rebels. Clarke was so generally detested by the Ontario settlers that in May 1871, when word got around Winnipeg that he was returning from a trip to Ottawa, the mob collected to meet him at the steamboat landing. Clarke was able to come ashore only after he had collected a bodyguard of his friends and emerged from his cabin revolver in hand.[10]

Macdonald was kept fully informed of these events and they exerted a good deal of influence upon the decisions made with regard to future policy in the North-West Territories. What the Manitoba troubles revealed was that the first contacts between white settlers and indigenous groups, even so settled a people as the Métis, were bound to result in conflict if the government did not intervene with a firm hand. After receiving Lieutenant-Governor Archibald's reports on the Manitoba situation Macdonald suggested to his minister of militia, Sir George Cartier, that as an immediate measure Captain Cameron might be sent to Manitoba as deputy adjutant-general of the Militia. There he would be in a position to make plans for the police.

There must be organized ere long for the North West a Mounted Police. I quite agree with Cyril Graham and the Hudson's Bay authorities on that matter. With emigrants of all nations flowing into that country, we are in constant danger of an Indian war, and that commenced God knows where it may end. This may be prevented by the early organization of a Mounted Police.[11]

The Militia had by this time reduced from two battalions to two companies to clear the way for the police. Once again, however, events conspired to leave the unfortunate Captain Cameron out in the cold.

This time it was the threat of a Fenian invasion from Minnesota which postponed the formation of the Mounted Police. The Militia at Lower Fort Garry was entirely inadequate to meet an emergency of this kind and Lieutenant-Governor Archibald was forced to call for volunteers to defend the province. To his embarrassment, because of the delicate political situation, it was the Métis under the leadership of Riel, now returned from the United States, who responded most enthusiastically to the call. Archibald was forced to meet and publicly congratulate Riel for his people's demonstration of loyalty. Riel was officially a fugitive at this time since he had not been included in the general amnesty granted to the other Métis. Nothing could have aroused more fury among the Ontario settlers than the sight of Riel, the hated murderer of Thomas Scott, shaking hands with the lieutenant-governor.

The Fenian threat soon passed but by that time the political damage had been done. Archibald now replaced Clarke as the focus of anti-French feeling, so much so that within a year he had to be eased out and replaced by a man more acceptable to the Ontario settlers. The threat of invasion, although it did not materialize, also forced Macdonald to send reinforcements for the Militia. This did not mean that the Mounted Police were to be abandoned. Writing to the commissioner of the Dominion Police, who was in Winnipeg because of the Fenian threat, Macdonald again emphasized that his intentions remained the same. 'I am satisfied, however, that there must be a Mounted Police Force, say of 50 men, well selected and fully organized. Such a Force could be sent at a moment's notice at any time on the Plains where wanted.'[12] But for the time being attention remained focused on Manitoba rather than farther west.

The winter of 1871-2 was quiet in Manitoba. Anywhere in Canada winter is a powerful ally of the forces of peace and order and this is nowhere truer than in Manitoba, with the fierce extremes of its continental climate. The return of summer and a federal election in the fall promised to bring a renewal of tensions more serious than before. Among those concerned with the situation there were strong feelings of apprehension which turned out to be well founded. To help cool things off, Archibald resigned in April. The Ontario settlers celebrated this victory by burning both the former lieutenant-governor and Riel in effigy.[13] Commissioner McMicken reported that the Métis were restless as a result of the threatening mood of their antagonists.[14] In the House of Commons a Manitoba MP, Dr J.C. Schultz, requested that the Militia stationed in Winnipeg be further reinforced. Cartier, in reply, said that this was the intention of the government. He went on to say that Archibald had also recommended the formation of a constabulary force for the North-West, a project which the government was seriously considering.[15] This last remark is an indication of how closely the origins of the NWMP were connected, in the minds of those in power, with the situation in Manitoba. Many of those concerned, both in Ottawa and in Manitoba, seemed to assume that the two problems were one and the same; that a federal police force would help stabilize the situation in Manitoba before moving west.

This was not true of Macdonald, who always saw that for constitutional reasons the two matters had to be separated. He regarded the Manitoba turmoil as the sort of thing a Mounted Police force might have prevented had not the rising intervened and would prevent in the Territories. This view implied that the Manitoba situation had to be settled first and the approaching crisis there meant a further postponement of action on the police. Early in the spring of 1872 Macdonald had decided to go ahead with the police but he changed his mind during the summer.[16] It would have been pointless to make plans for the North-West if the essential gateway to the area was not secure.

The prime minister made some further moves in the summer of 1872 to calm the unrest in the tiny western province. The most important of these was the appointment of Alexander Morris as the first chief justice of the Court of Queen's Bench of Manitoba. The appointment was important because it would serve to strengthen the judicial system in the province, which was not fully organized. The new chief justice would also be in a position to act as a troubleshooter for the federal government. Finally there was the question of a replacement for Lieutenant-Governor Archibald. It seems certain that Macdonald had Morris in mind for this vital position, which included the appointment as lieutenant-governor of the North-West Territories as well. If Morris was able to cope with the political crisis and proved more or less acceptable to both major groups in Manitoba he was the logical choice for the post, provided that his health, which was poor, improved.

Morris was in many respects an excellent choice as the chief representative of the federal government in the North-West. Although he was a nervous and excitable man who tended to exaggerate the problems he faced, he had the intelligence and imagination necessary to grasp the essentials of a problem very quickly and accurately. He also thought in terms of the whole region and its long-term needs, refusing to be diverted by the immediate, short-term crisis in Manitoba. Macdonald knew his man well enough, Morris having been a Conservative of unquestioned loyalty and minister of inland revenue, to be able to discount his more hysterical outbursts, secure in the knowledge that if left to himself, Morris would successfully prevent most of his own dire predictions from coming true. Morris's most important credentials were his long-standing interest in and advocacy of the North-West as a field for Canadian expansion. Morris had been one of the more important early publicists of the idea of Confederation and western expansion had been his chief argument.[17] He was to confirm Macdonald's ideas about the Mounted Police and to exert a large influence on both the timing of the formation of the force and on its initial size.

Morris began writing lengthy and detailed letters to Macdonald almost as soon as he stepped off the boat in Winnipeg on 13 August 1872. All was quiet but Morris at once discovered a potential disaster. The enlistments of the men of the Militia battalion were due to expire soon and the majority did not intend to rejoin. If the government was to carry out its plan to retain the Militia for another year, more men would have to be sent at once.[18] Without the Militia the forthcoming election would dissolve into chaos. This time Morris did not exaggerate. The election which took place 19 September equalled any in Canadian history for violence. The Ontario settlers, much stronger than two years previously, took the initiative and the chief justice witnessed pitched battles involving forty men on a side armed with clubs and revolvers.[19] Fortunately there were no fatal casualties. Property damage, on the other hand, was extensive. The offices of the three Conservative newspapers in Winnipeg, the *Manitoban*, the *Gazette*, and *Le Métis*, were destroyed and the papers put out of action for three months.[20]

The conclusion which Morris drew from this incident and the continuing state of tension in Manitoba had a considerable influence on government policy. Macdonald had seen the Mounted Police as replacements for the Militia and had accordingly put off their introduction until the Militia could safely be dispensed with. Morris, on the spot, could see that the situation was not going to develop in the direction desired by the prime minister. For the foreseeable future the Manitoba authorities would require the assistance of the Militia, or at least their presence, in order to maintain the precarious peace that existed in the province. Action in the North-West Territories could not be postponed until Manitoba was able to guarantee its own internal security. Morris began to bombard Macdonald with letters urging that the Militia be retained and a police force be established as well. This was the pattern eventually adopted; one which had a great influence upon the direction in which the NWMP was to evolve. The continued presence of a military force west of the Great Lakes freed the Mounted Police from the necessity to concentrate all their men in a few locations and enabled them to disperse and thus function from the beginning as a true police force.

The insistent demands sent by Morris soon had their effect. Early in October 1872, Macdonald wrote to tell him that legislation for the establishment of the police would definitely be passed during the next session of Parliament.[21] Having convinced Macdonald of the necessity for action, Morris directed his energies to pressing for a larger force than the fifty men contemplated by the prime minister. Not even double that number would suffice. 'With regard to the Minute of Council about Police, I need not say that 100 men alone will not be sufficient.'[22] By the new year Morris was raising his sights still further.

The most important matter of the future is the preservation of order in the North West and little as Canada may like it she has to stable her elephant. In short the Dominion will have to maintain both a military and a police force in years to come. I do not think that you should diminish the military force below its present strength and the police should also be under military discipline and if possible be *red coated* – as 50 men in red coats are better here than 100 in other colours. You should get a statement of the American troops employed in the frontier, it [sic] is very large – the presence of a force will prevent the possibility of such a frightful disaster as befell Minnesota and which without it might be provoked at any moment.[23]

Three things gave Morris's latest advice added weight. He was now (since December) lieutenant-governor of Manitoba and the North-West Territories and thus directly responsible for making treaties with the formidable plains tribes and establishing order over the whole region. The stakes in this endeavour had been raised by the formation of the first (and subsequently abortive) Pacific railway company. Without a peaceful North-West this massive undertaking would have no hope of success. In the third place, Canada's top military man, the adjutant-general of the Canadian Militia, Colonel Patrick Robertson-Ross, had just completed a survey of the military requirements of the North-West. His report, which was in Macdonald's hands in December 1872, agreed very closely with the lieutenant-governor's estimate of the situation.[24]

The adjutant-general's journey was not the first reconnaissance of the prairies for this purpose. One of Lieutenant-Governor Archibald's first acts upon his arrival in Manitoba in 1870 had been to send Captain W.F. Butler, a British officer who had come west with the Wolseley expedition, on a tour of the former Hudsons's Bay Company territories to survey the state of affairs prevailing there and report on the measures necessary to establish control. Butler was a happy choice.

Not only did he carry out his assignment competently, but he recounted his experiences in one of the minor classics of Victorian travel literature, *The Great Lone Land.*[25] Butler was a man whose outlook was intensely humanitarian and who was unusually sensitive to the plight of the weaker peoples he encountered in a lifetime of soldiering throughout the British Empire. His army career in fact came to an end as a result of his strong attachment to these values when as commander of the British Army in South Africa in 1899 he attempted to block Lord Milner's effort to start what he considered an unnecessary war. In his report of 1871, Butler's sympathies were with the Indians and his concern was to recommend measures which would ease the inevitable shock of transition. His prescription was the establishment of effective control by the Canadian government through the use of special magistrates operating, as in Ireland and India, in close co-operation with a police force. Butler suggested a force of 100 to 150 men, one-third to be mounted.[26]

Two years later Robertson-Ross was not so optimistic. He recommended a regiment of 550 men, all mounted. The difference between the two estimates was not merely the result of two different readings of the same situation. Conditions in the North-West were changing rapidly and for the worse. The changes are reflected in the suggestions for distribution of the proposed force. Butler would have divided the force between two locations; Edmonton and the junction of the North and South Saskatchewan rivers near the present city of Prince Albert, a disposition which reflects a concern for keeping the peace between the Indians and the settlers who would soon be arriving. Robertson-Ross, on the other hand, would have stationed only 150 of his 550 men at these two locations.[27] The largest contingent of all, 150 men, he proposed to locate in what is now southern Alberta, close to the international boundary. The reason for this change in emphasis was growing concern over the activities of American whisky traders in this area. Butler had noted that the trade in illicit liquor between Fort Benton, Montana, and the south-western prairies was established and growing but he did not consider it much of a threat. By the time Robertson-Ross passed through, and he travelled a good deal farther south than his predecessor, conditions were much worse.

The sober military judgement of the adjutant-general added to the impassioned pleas of Morris finally tipped the balance and legislation was introduced in Parliament in the spring of 1873 to provide judicial machinery for the Territories and to enable the government to establish a police force by Order-in-Council.[28] The bill was received with massive disinterest in the House and passed without debate in April. The honourable members had more exciting things to occupy their attention by the time the police bill came up. The first stirrings of Canada's most celebrated political scandal of the nineteenth century were beginning to be felt. From 1 April, when the Liberals first made public their charges concerning a corrupt relationship between the Conservative leaders and Sir Hugh Allan's Canada Pacific Railway Company, the government's days were numbered. Only Macdonald's great political talents enabled him to prolong the struggle until November 1873 when the government finally fell. This was just long enough to encompass the actual organization of the Mounted Police and the dispatching of the first contingent of 150 men to Fort Garry.

Macdonald originally planned to proceed in a rather more leisurely fashion than this. The police would be recruited late in 1873 and would spend the winter of 1873-4 training in eastern Canada. This was not soon enough to suit Morris, who feared that further postponements might last indefinitely. He began searching for a lever which would budge the government from its preoccupation with the Pacific Scandal. As the summer of 1873 drew to a close Morris suddenly found the issue he had been seeking. Rumours had been circulating about a massacre of some Indians by American whisky traders on Canadian territory in the spring.[29] Late in August confirmation appeared in the form of newspaper reports in Montana and official notification through diplomatic channels from Washington. Morris lost no time in insisting that the massacre made immediate organization of the police imperative. The government, however, was not easily moved. Morris received a bland reply from Alexander Campbell, the minister of the interior, informing him that the government still did not consider the situation serious enough to warrant sending the police west immediately.[30] Morris, realizing that if the police were not sent at once they would have to wait until the following year because of the closing of the Dawson route for the winter, brought out his most powerful argument. News of the massacre, he said, had caused fear and unrest among both white settlers and Métis around Portage la Prairie and Qu'Appelle.

There is undoubtedly danger that the scene of 1869 may be repeated in the North West, but I believe it would be prevented by the presence of a force. Here it is impossible to dispense with the force we have as we are between two fires – we have a turbulent population of English, many of them fanatical Orangemen, and on the other hand an excitable, half-Indian French population.[31]

The governor-general now added his weight to Morris's pleas. He informed Macdonald that for diplomatic reasons it was desirable for the Canadian government to move vigorously against the perpetrators of the massacre.[32] The following day Macdonald announced that the police would be sent over the Dawson route at once to spend the winter in Manitoba.[33] On 1 October the hastily assembled first contingent left Ottawa and made its way, with numerous misadventures, to Lower Fort Garry where it spent the winter training under the supervision of Lieutenant-Colonel W.O. Smith of the Militia who had been appointed temporary commissioner of the force until the government could find the man it wanted to take over permanently.[34]

The importance of the fact that the Mounted Police were already in existence and in Manitoba when the Macdonald government fell and Alexander Mackenzie became prime minister cannot be overestimated. Had this not been so it is not at all unlikely that the force might never have been established. There are a number of reasons for believing this. The idea of a police force was Macdonald's own; an innovation not regarded with favour by many of his colleagues much less by the opposition. The Liberal party at this point in its history was very dubious about any kind of government action for western development. The Liberals as a party and Mackenzie in particular were even more passionately devoted to economy in government than Macdonald and the Conservatives. The great depression of the late nineteenth century was just beginning in 1873 and government expenditures in all departments were being cut.

An incident which occurred immediately after Mackenzie took office illustrates both his attitude to the West and the narrowness of the margin by which the NWMP survived. In 1873 the United States government had become concerned about suppressing the liquor traffic among the Indians of the northern plains. Interior Department officials complained that nothing could be done to halt the trade effectively so long as the traders enjoyed a sanctuary in Canadian territory.[35] These complaints were passed along to the State Department, which requested Canadian co-operation in eliminating the traffic. Macdonald, of course, had intended to use the Mounted Police for this purpose but Mackenzie when confronted with the same problem proposed a radically different approach. In a discussion of the matter with the governor-general, Lord Dufferin, Mackenzie said that the expense of an expedition to get rid of the whisky traders was too much for Canada. Could not some arrangement be worked out with the American authorities to allow the US Army to enter Canadian territory and round up the whisky traders?[36] Dufferin was horrified by this example of Mackenzie's naïve willingness to risk Canadian sovereignty in the North-West. He told Mackenzie that the Colonial Office would not tolerate such a course of action and persuaded him to change his mind.

I did not hold out any hopes to Mackenzie that his suggestion would be agreed to, as it involved a very important principle affecting our international relations, and in a subsequent conversation I suggested to him whether even though the expense might be considerable, an expedition organized by Canada itself would not have its advantages. In the first place the mere fact of putting forth her strength for the purpose of asserting her jurisdiction and repressing outrage in those wild districts, would flatter in a very legitimate manner the national pride of the Dominion and would evince the vitality of her executive functions – in the next place we would appear on the scene, not as the Americans have done for the purpose of restraining and controlling the Indian tribes, but with a view of ameliorating injuries inflicted on the Red man by the white...

On the other hand as the Americans are abhorred by the whole Indian people it might be a doubtful policy for us to become identified with them in anything like a military policy.[37]

Reluctantly Mackenzie agreed that the Mounted Police at Fort Garry, with an additional contingent of 150 which would join them in the spring, should move west as soon as possible in 1874 to deal with the whisky traders.

It is easy to understand why John A. Macdonald planned the Mounted Police in 1869. It is less easy to comprehend why he clung to the idea once the Red River uprising and its aftermath had changed conditions in the West drastically. Federal control over law enforcement in the only populated part of the West had been lost. The argument of economy also went out the window when it was found necessary to maintain both Militia and police west of Ontario. Would it not have been cheaper and more logical to send more Militia into the North-West Territories? The answer to this riddle lies in the failure of the traditional law enforcement system in Manitoba.

In settled communities like eastern Canada with well established political traditions the old English judicial system worked reasonably well. The magistrate with his court officials – sheriffs, bailiffs, and occasionally a few constables – could deal with most of the disputes and violations of the law that occurred from day to day, aided by custom and social pressure. If extraordinary violence threatened the Militia could be called out to back up the civil authorities.[38] These were relatively crude instruments of social control and on many occasions situations arose which were beyond the reach of either of these arms of the law. The election violence which was a common feature of the Canadian scene in the nineteenth century falls into this category. So do incidents like the so-called 'Shiner's War' which occurred in the Ottawa valley and the vendetta involving the Donnelly family in western Ontario.[39] Such outbursts, although they were beyond the control of the legal system, ran their course without doing any permanent damage to the state or threatening its continued existence.

In Manitoba, which had the same law enforcement system as eastern Canada while under the control of the Hudson's Bay Company, the same defects had much more serious consequences. Beginning in the 1820s the Company had erected an elaborate system of courts in Rupert's Land considering the sparseness of the population. There was also a series of experiments with police forces of various kinds; large and small, volunteer and paid.[40] None of these was very satisfactory but for three decades or so it did not greatly matter since the Company's authority rested upon its monopoly of the region's economic life and not on any general acceptance of its political legitimacy. In the late 1840s when an alternate outlet for trade to the south opened up, the weakness of the courts was quickly revealed. The famous Sayer trial of 1849, in which a mob led by Louis Riel, Sr refused to allow the accused to be tried, was only the most dramatic incident in the steady erosion of the Company's authority. By 1869 that authority was gone completely and the uprising of that year was a direct result of the Company's long-standing inability to enforce its laws. Governor McTavish had been unable to exercise the slightest influence on events, a state of affairs that was not lost on Sir John A. Macdonald. Writing to Sir John Rose, the Canadian representative in London, for details of the organization of the RIC in 1870 he explained his motives.

The reason why I telegraphed for the organization of the Irish Constabulary is that we propose to organize a mounted police force under the command of Captain Cameron, for Red River purposes. We must never subject the Government there to the humiliation offered to McTavish.[41]

For two brief periods, 1846-8 and 1857-61, British troops had been stationed at Red River. While the troops were there no difficulties were experienced in maintaining law and order. But between 1870 and 1873, with both a provincial police force and the Militia on hand, this was not the case. After the election violence of September 1872, Morris explained the reasons for the inadequacy of the system to Macdonald.

This affair brings up the question sharply, whether the authorities have enough to punish wrong-doers, and if the ringleaders are detected, they should be tried. Another thing established, is that the troops should be engaged for a definite and reasonably long period. Those here are just in thorough training and I believe would have been reliable. Now they are to be removed and a raw levy to take their place.[42]

A week later he added, 'you must have a force here engaged for a definite term, like the constabulary force. A smaller force such as that would be better than volunteers, who come here full of prejudice.'[43] The Provincial Police were even less useful in the lieutenant-governor's opinion. 'The Provincial Police, now reduced to six, are inefficient and are mainly recruited from the class who make up the roughs.'[44] The existence of hostile groups in the population of Red River clearly created a situation which could not be readily controlled by the local authorities alone. Farther west the even greater cultural and linguistic differences between settlers and Indians would create an even more serious problem. Significantly the Hudson's Bay Company had never tried to bring the Indians into the legal system. Company-Indian relations had rather been those between sovereign powers. This could not be the case under the Canadian government and the Mounted Police, it was hoped, could accomplish what the traditional system had never attempted.

3

The benevolent despotism of the NWMP
1874–1885

In terms of both politics and economics the period from 1874 to 1885 was one of transition in the North-West Territories. The Indians began the long and difficult adjustment to the advance of Canadian government and settlement. The economy of the region began to lose its complete dependence upon the fur trade and moved toward its new agricultural base. Both processes influenced the Mounted Police and were influenced by them.[1]

The evolution of the force in terms of its activities and preoccupations falls into three quite distinct time periods before 1905: the first dozen years in which the major concern of the police was to prepare the Indians for the painful adjustment to the advance of white society, the initial period of settlement from about 1885 to 1900 in which the force was concerned with developing techniques for dealing with the more complex kinds of criminality which accompanied settlement and the beginnings of urbanization, and the period of the great influx of settlers from Europe and the United States in which the police saw their most important role as agents for the assimilation of these newcomers. The division is, of course, a matter of emphasis and at any given time the force was engaged in all three kinds of activity. The year 1885 forms a natural dividing line because the Canadian Pacific Railway was completed at that time. The North-West Rebellion of the same year was to a considerable extent a product of the coming of the railway and of the social and economic changes that it brought in its wake. The coming of the railway also coincided roughly with the disappearance of the buffalo and the traditional economy of the Plains Indians which was based upon it. Prior to 1885 the NWMP served as the most important transitional institution; bringing to the North-West a money economy on a small scale with all its attendant cultural baggage and in this way preparing the Indians for changes on a larger scale. The inability of the Métis to secure any significant Indian participation in the 1885 rebellion is a measure of the success of the transition.

The nature of Mounted Police activities in the pre-railway era is revealed very clearly by a number of facts. The heavy concentration of the police at two points, Ft Macleod and Ft Walsh, shows the importance attached to the assimilation of the Plains Indians, who were considered the most dangerous and warlike of any tribal group in the country at the time. The economic and social impact of the presence of the force appears very graphically in the way police posts developed rapidly into centres of settlement. The present cities of Lethbridge, Ft Macleod, and Calgary as well as other less important urban centres owe their origins to the police. A record has survived from 1881 which lists the number of miles travelled that year by all members of the force stationed at Ft Walsh, then the headquarters.[2] The trips made were broken down into three categories according to their purpose; crime prevention, Indian affairs, and internal business. Nine trips for a total of 830 miles were made under the first category, sixteen trips for a total of 1283 miles under the second, and sixty-four trips amounting to 12,865 miles under the third.[3] These figures give a very clear idea of the nature of police activities. The last category is particularly interesting since it included all the administrative duties of the police except those having to do directly with the Indian population. Better than anything else it reveals the character of the force as an arm of the executive branch of the Canadian government.

The force which rode west in the summer of 1874 to assume these duties consisted of twenty-four officers, including two surgeons and one veterinary surgeon, and two hundred and ninety-five men. The authorized strength of the force was three hundred, a figure which it approximated until 1882 when an increase to a total of five hundred was granted. The police were organized into six troops designated A to F of approximately fifty officers and men each. There were four non-commissioned ranks; sub-constable, acting constable, constable, and chief constable. Each troop was commanded by a superintendent and inspector and included one or more superintendent and sub-inspectors. The headquarters staff included the commissioner and assistant-commissioner, the paymaster and adjutant, an acting paymaster and adjutant, and a quartermaster, as well as the three medical officers mentioned above. Except for the names of the ranks, the structure resembled that of a British cavalry regiment. Modifications were soon to be made to better adapt the police to their task but the initial organization reflected both the assumptions of the man who created it and the uncertainties of the situation in the North-West in 1874.[4]

The NWMP moved west in a body that summer, the only time in its history the entire force was to be assembled in one place.[5] The move west, known generally as the Long March, is one of the most famous and frequently described incidents in the history of the police. It is usually presented as a heroic tale of hardships endured and natural barriers overcome. No doubt these elements were present, but the most interesting point about the difficulties of the Long March is that they were largely self-inflicted. Instead of following the well-established northern fur trade route to Edmonton and then going south to the border region where the whisky traders were active the police marched in a more or less straight line closely paralleling the border all the way from Dufferin to the foothills of the Rockies. A more difficult route across the plains would have been hard to find. Not only was it virtually unmapped, but it lacked the water and grass necessary to sustain the expedition's horses. A great many animals were lost as a result, part of the command had to be detached and sent by an easier route to Edmonton, and those who did reach the original destination were in serious danger of perishing during their first winter from exposure or hunger. When they arrived the police were in no condition to meet any sort of resistance, Indian or white. They survived only with the aid of those whisky traders they had come prepared to fight. The state of the Mounted Police at the end of their thousand-mile journey is described in a number of diaries kept by members of the force.[6] In none is it described more vividly than in the account of Constable James Finlayson.

September 11. We are lost on the prairie. No one knows where we are. Council of Officers was held and decided to make for Three Butes [sic] or the Boundary Trail. Horses and oxen dying fast. Provisions getting scarce, things look very dark. No Buffalo seen today. Weather very cold.

September 27. No church parade. Most of us washing our clothes. Washed my clothes and had to go in my drawers and no shirt on until my clothes dried. If the people of Canada were to see us now with bare feet, not one half clothed, half starved, picking up fragments left by the American troops and hunting buffalo for meat, and have to pay for the ammunition used in killing them, I wonder what they would say of Col. French?

September 29. If Canadians knew what this expedition will cost I think Col. French would very soon get his discharge. He left here with the best wishes of the men. That he may never come back.[7]

Things were probably not quite as desperate as they appeared to Finlayson but clearly they were bad enough and it was fortunate for the police that neither the whisky traders nor the Blackfoot were as formidable as they had been led to believe.

The Long March was intended partly as a military expedition designed to impress the traders, the Indians, and the United States government by a show of force. The police went prepared to fight if necessary but not necessarily to fight. The reasons for the nearly disastrous choice of route were not military. The expedition was not a punitive raid to clear the area out and then leave. Commissioner G.A. French, the planner of the expedition, was very much aware of this, as his description of the column on the march shows.

To a stranger it would have appeared an astonishing cavalcade; armed men and guns looked as if fighting was to be done; what could ploughs, harrows, mowing machines, cows, calves, etc. be for? But the little force had a double duty to perform: to fight, if necessary, but in any case to establish posts in the far west.[8]

French, in organizing the force, had placed great stress on the non-military role of the police, suggesting that along with their other duties they should build roads and establish postal and telegraph communications.[9] The condition of his command at the end of their trek indicates that French had to a certain extent underestimated the difficulties of occupying a territory which lacked any kind of economic base but it does not change the fact that it was precisely this southern strip of country which had to be occupied in order to establish the Canadian claim. Posts had to be set up in exactly those areas whose locations made it most difficult. Some contemporary observers, like the missionary John McDougall, saw the march as a foolish error which was the product of inexperience; a view echoed by later writers as well.[10] But this criticism ignores the goals of the police. It also underestimates an organization which throughout its history was more interested in the ends it sought than in the narrowly technical means by which they were achieved. Although this fundamental attitude sometimes resulted in temporary or local setbacks, in the long run it was a major element in the success of the police.

It became clear at once that the police would not have to play a military role in the North-West. The Indians, who had been carefully prepared for the arrival of the police by a distribution of gifts and an explanation of the government's intentions, were not disposed to resist.[11] All accounts agree that the Indians welcomed the arrival of the police. The chiefs of the formidable Blackfoot Confederacy, decimated since 1869 by smallpox and impoverished by the whisky traders, had a very accurate idea of the weakness of their position.[12] Chief Crowfoot especially, paramount in the rather ambiguous hierarchy of the Blackfoot, was a statesman who saw that co-operation with the government was the only real hope for the survival of his people.[13]

The whisky traders proved even less of a problem. Except for isolated individuals they disappeared as the police arrived. Here again economic rather than military factors won the day. The traders, however flamboyant their way of life, were essentially small businessmen who had neither the resources nor the desire to challenge the Canadian government. Their motive was a fast dollar and if this was no longer possible they could either stay and accept the reduced profits of legitimate trade or go elsewhere. Many chose the latter alternative, to the distress of American officials, such as the Indian agent who wrote to his superior:

Driven out of the British territory, north, by the Mounted Police, many of these traders from Whoop-Up and Woody [sic] Mountain appear to be establishing themselves and pursuing their villainous avocations along the southern border of this reservation from the headwaters of the Marius River to the vicinity of Fort Peck.

Viewed from every philanthropic standpoint, these whisky traders are certainly an unmitigated curse to the Indian country. Their whole traffic is so extremely baneful that, if not checked, it is calculated to neutralize effectually every good influence which the government and the church can possibly exert in behalf of the Indian.[14]

No money was to be made fighting the police. The destructive and dangerous effects of the trade on the Indian population did not mean, as many Canadians assumed, that the traders were an equally formidable threat to the establishment of a Canadian administration. Merely by their presence the police removed the possibility of the very high profit margins which had enabled the independent whisky traders to withstand the competition of large established firms like I.G. Baker and Co. and T.C. Power and Co. at Ft Benton, Montana. The latter were happy to see the police arrive. With large fixed investments in the region, they were interested in its long-term trading prospects. They had made money before 1874 by financing the independent traders but they had no hesitation at all in welcoming a more stable economic situation and had no regrets about the disappearance of the whisky trade. I.G. Baker, Ft Benton's leading merchant, understood the situation very well and it was not with surprise that he wrote: 'The effect of the expedition was sudden and decisive: completely paralyzing the trade.'[15]

By the beginning of 1875 the police too were aware of the realities of the situation. They therefore broke up the command and began extending their network of posts, a process which was never to be reversed. In the first winter in the North-West posts were established at Ft Macleod in the south and at Ft Sas-

Table 1: Numbers of Men at NWMP Police Posts 1876-84[16]

Year	Total	Number of Men at:					
		Ft Macleod	Ft Walsh	Calgary	Edmonton	Battleford	Regina
1876	335	103	95	35	20	11	–
1878	329	76	139	30	22	33	–
1881	293	42	97	23	12	43	–
1884	557	68	–	66	19	103	96

katchewan near Edmonton. The detachment at Ft Saskatchewan was very small, consisting only of part of A troop under Inspector W.D. Jarvis. The rest of A troop along with B, C, and F troops were at Ft Macleod under the assistant commissioner. The other two troops, D and E, were at Dufferin and Swan River respectively. During the summer of 1875 additional posts were established at Ft Walsh in the Cypress Hills and at Ft Calgary. By 1881 sixteen major posts were in operation, most with a number of outlying detachments.[17] It would be tedious to list all new posts and the number of men in each one every year. Instead, by looking at the numbers stationed at several posts for selected years it is possible to get a clear idea of what the police considered their most important responsibilities in the period 1873-85 (Table 1).

The figures in Table 1, like all statistics, do not 'prove' anything; they illustrate with a greater degree of precision something already understood. Thus the process of decentralization can be seen in the percentage of the total strength of the force located at these six posts. In 1876 it amounted to 79 per cent. In 1878, because of the presence of Sitting Bull's Sioux at Ft Walsh, the percentage rose to 91 per cent. Thereafter it fell, to 74 per cent in 1881 and 63 per cent in 1884. Of greater interest are the changes in the distribution of the force among these major centres. Because the bulk of white settlement up to 1885 took place in the northern and eastern regions represented by the last three locations in the table whereas the first three posts were situated among the largest concentrations of Plains Indians, a glance at the table shows that these Indians were the chief concern of the police until nearly the end of the period. This concentration on the Indian problem reached a peak in 1878 and thereafter attention slowly began to shift to the settlement regions. (After the railway went through, the southwest also became a settlement region but this was not the case prior to 1884.) The sudden appearance in 1884 of Regina as a major post, the large increase in size of the Calgary detachment in that year, and the abandonment of Ft Walsh, all illustrate the profound effect of the arrival of the railway. The large concentration of men at Battleford in 1884 is a result of concern over the unrest among the Métis which was to find expression in the 1885 rebellion.

In their dealings with the Indians the police operated within the framework of the Canadian government's Indian policy. This policy envisioned three general stages in the process of assimilating the Indian. The first step was to sign treaties with the tribe to provide for cession of their lands in return for reserves and specified treaty payments. The second stage involved persuading the Indians to give up the hunt and settle on the reserves, since the treaties did not make this obligatory. The third stage was to try to integrate the Indian into the white man's economy and society, which at a minimum meant making the Indians self-supporting by teaching them agriculture. The first two steps were accomplished without encountering major problems, the third has yet to be completed with few real signs of progress after a century.

The police played a major part in the first stage, were almost entirely responsible for the second, and did what they could towards achieving the third. Their general approach to all three problems was simple but usually very effective. It consisted in giving the Indians first priority at all times. If the protection of the rights of the Indian demanded a policy that annoyed or interfered with the activities of the white settlers, that was unfortunate but it did not prevent the policy from being carried out. The police did not make promises they could not keep; and they did all they could to avoid the passage of laws they could not enforce.[18] They also firmly insisted that the law as it stood was to be obeyed, although in cases where ignorance was a factor they tended to be lenient. Horse stealing, for example, was in the nature of a sport among the plains tribes. The police only gradually introduced the idea that it was a crime, preferring to recover the stolen horses and return them with a warning to the thieves rather than make arrests. At the same time the police rejected the suggestion of an American Indian agent that horse stealing among Indians should be ignored because losses balanced out in the end.[19]

In the period 1871 to 1930 the Canadian government signed eleven separate treaties with the Indians of the North-West. The treaties which directly concerned the police were treaty number six with the Chippewyans, Crees, and Assiniboines of the northern prairies negotiated in 1876 and treaty number seven of 1877 with the Blackfoot, Bloods, Peigans, Sarcees, and Stonies of the southwest. In the case of these treaties, as with all the others, formal negotiations were carried out by the lieutenant-governor of the North-West Territories as the representative of the Canadian government. Before these negotiations could even be considered, however, a relationship of mutual trust had to be established. In the case of treaty number six this relationship had been established through the Indians' century-old contacts with the Hudson's Bay Company and later the missionaries.[20] The role of the police in this treaty was relatively small. They made all the preliminary arrangements, provided escorts (including the police band which the government had authorized in 1875 on condition that the men bought their own instruments),[21] and took care of the money and goods used for treaty payments. Their presence was necessary as well to inhibit the traders who arrived to relieve the Indians of their unaccustomed wealth.

The situation was quite different with regard to treaty number seven. In the south-west there were no established intermediaries between the Indians and the government with the single exception of the McDougall family, whose work had been among the Stonies, a small and isolated tribe. Here the whole burden of winning the confidence of the Indians rested with the police and within three years of their arrival they had been able to establish the necessary relationship of trust. When the formal negotiations took place at Blackfoot Crossing on the Bow River in 1877 they went very smoothly, more so in fact than the negotiations for the previous treaty. From the time of their arrival the police had devoted most of their energies to preparing the Indians for the treaty and its consequences. Their success may be measured by the insistence of the Blackfoot chiefs that the police, not the Indian department, distribute the annual treaty payments.

Once the treaties were signed the second stage could begin. It was made more difficult by a certain ambiguity in the treaties. Settlement on the reserves was voluntary and the Indians could not be legally compelled to stay there. Their hunting rights outside the reserves were to remain in force. But what if these hunting grounds were bought or leased by whites who disliked the idea of Indians on their land? The police realized that any attempt to force the Indians onto the reserves would be worse than useless. Persuasion was the only truly effective course open to them. Being professionals, the police were very much aware of the limitations of force, an awareness not always shared by Indian agents and other officials who dealt with the tribes. The police often found themselves in the position of warning these officials that they were pushing too hard. A typical case occurred in 1881 at Ft Walsh when a large number of Indians refused to accept their annual treaty payments until the government met some of their demands. An inspector of Indian agencies, T.P. Wadsworth, was very upset by the situation and wrote to his superior:

At present, however much we may dislike to confess it even to ourselves, we are not in a position to make a decided stand against the Indians – there are too many altogether to manage – and we are obliged to work with them quietly. Had there been a good force of policemen here today when the Indians would not accept their money when it was offered to them, I would have cut off their rations until they "came to time" – but upon consultation with Col. Irvine there was nothing to do but to accept the compromise offered by them.[22]

Fortunately the higher authorities in the Department of Indian Affairs tended to side with the police and respect their assessment of the best way to handle the Indians. When a volunteer force of settlers was proposed in 1884, Lawrence Vankoughnet, the deputy superintendent-general of Indian Affairs, dismissed the idea firmly.

The North West Mounted Police are quite sufficient to preserve order in the Territories as they have hitherto done; and it appears to me that any show of additional military force in that country would be attended with the same results that follow the presence of the United States Army in the portion of the North Western Territories across the border.[23]

If a rancher complained about Indians on his land the police would explain that according to the treaties the Indians had a right to be there.[24] At the same time a patrol would be sent to escort the Indians back to their reserve. This process was patiently repeated countless times. It was tedious and unglamorous but it worked. Even when the disappearance of the buffalo brought near starvation to the Indians, they respected the law and incidents of killing settlers' cattle for food were few. As Lieutenant-Governor David Laird reported in 1879: 'Altogether their conduct, considering their destitute condition, is more creditable than would be displayed by most men in civilized communities if suffering want to a like extent.'[25]

The Indians' respect for the law could withstand this severe test only because the police made certain that treaty rights were scrupulously observed. They were especially careful to keep squatters away from the reserves.[26] The relationship between the police and the Indians was governed by law and the Indians recognized it, even though force had to be used on occasion. In one or two cases Indians were killed by the police when they chose to fight it out to avoid capture. But these deaths provoked no general resentment because the Indians could be sure that force was used only as a last resort and that it was used against the individual as a lawbreaker, not because he happened to be an Indian.

The third stage of the process of absorbing the Indian into white society can only be considered a failure. The record of the Canadian government here is not inspiring. Farm instructors were too often political hacks who, in some cases, did not live on the reserves. The same was true of Indian agents and teachers in the 'industrial schools' established for Indian children. But this was not the essential reason for failure. Had the Canadian government poured massive quantities of money and effort into the reserves it would not have made a great deal of difference. Even today, as the experience of aid to underdeveloped nations and the literature on the subject demonstrate, no one is even close to understanding how to use the resources available to change a primitive society into a modern one. A century ago few people were able to recognize that a problem existed. If the Indian could not learn to farm in competition with his white neighbours, it was considered to be due to a natural laziness that doomed him to inevitable extinction. By the standards of the time the attitude of the police was enlightened. They protected the Indians from the more rapacious whites who were disposed to hasten the process of extinction. They fed the Indians if starvation threatened. They employed a few as scouts and special constables. Wherever possible they gave contracts for supplies such as hay, wood, and meat to the Indians.[27] Above all they acted as a check on the Indian agents and as an independent source of information for the government on conditions on reserves.

The most serious difficulty concerning the Indians experienced by the police was not a product of Canadian Indian policy at all. Following the extermination of General Custer's command at the Little Big Horn, Sitting Bull and his Sioux people fled to Canada, where they remained for four years. This incident has been described at length elsewhere and there seems little point in going into it in detail here.[28] It is sufficient to note that the police used the same techniques to control the Sioux that they had on the Blackfoot and other Canadian Indians, thereby avoiding even a single violent incident.

The Sitting Bull episode is mentioned here because of a curious by-product it produced which was to have an important effect on government policy regarding the police twenty years later. The officer placed in charge of the Sioux refugees was Superintendent James Morrow Walsh. From the first arrival of the Sioux, Walsh exerted a great deal of influence over Sitting Bull. Walsh, in fact, made himself indispensable because the Sioux trusted him as an individual. There is no question that Walsh was primarily responsible for resolving many tense situations and keeping the Sioux peaceful while they were in Canada. But the policy of the Canadian government was to get rid of the Sioux, who were not only a domestic problem but caused serious diplomatic complications with the United States, as soon as possible. By 1879 Macdonald, now back in office, had concluded that Sitting Bull's rejection of two American offers to take him back were the result of his being made too comfortable by the police. Macdonald had further decided that Walsh was deliberately keeping the Sioux in Canada because he enjoyed the publicity his association with Sitting Bull brought him. In November 1879 Macdonald confided his suspicions to the Governor-General. 'Walsh undoubtedly has influence with "Bull" which [sic] he tried to monopolize in order to make himself of importance and is I fear primarily responsible for the Indians' unwillingness to leave Canada.'[29] Unfortunately it was true that Walsh enjoyed publicity; Commissioner Macleod had reprimanded him previously for giving unauthorized interviews to American newspaper correspondents.[30]

Attitudes to publicity in this period were complex. As an organization the NWMP was always very much aware of the power and value of publicity and co-operated fully with writers and journalists who sought information about the force. On the other hand for an individual member of the force, especially an officer, to attempt to publicize himself was regarded with extreme distaste. One could believe almost anything of such a man. By 1881 Macdonald had convinced himself that Walsh was wholly responsible for the Canadian government's embarrassment over Sitting Bull. Walsh was given extended leave to remove him from the scene but Macdonald was still worried.

I greatly fear, that Major Walsh is pulling the strings through Thompson, the deserter from the Mounted Police, to prevent 'Bull' from surrendering. Walsh is still at Brockville and I have given him two months more leave to keep him there lest he might return and personally influence Sitting Bull. I regret much being obliged to play with this man Walsh, as he deserves dismissal. But if he were cashiered, he would (for he is a bold and desperate fellow) at once go westward and from mere spite urge the Indians to hostile incursions so as to cause an imbroglio. When this is over I shall recommend Your Exy. to dismiss him most summarily.[31]

Macdonald had found a scapegoat and Walsh, although not dismissed summarily, was forced to resign in 1883, after Sitting Bull was safely back in the United States.

The whole incident would have been unimportant to anybody except Walsh had it not been for the fact that upon leaving the force Walsh went into business in Brandon, Manitoba, and became friendly with the rising Liberal politician, Clifford Sifton. When the Liberals came to power in 1896 Walsh submitted a memorandum on the police which was very influential in determining government policy regarding the police. Naturally enough Walsh was less than enthusiastic about the force which had expelled him (his superiors had sided with Macdonald and entertained the same suspicions). Yet by any reasonable standard he had a legitimate grievance. Walsh had his personal shortcomings but he was not, at least at this stage of his career, an irresponsible man. His responsibility for the Sioux involved two assignments which were ultimately contradictory; to keep them peaceful and to persuade them to leave. In the circumstances of 1876, with some four thousand Sioux and only three hundred police in the entire North-West Territories, Walsh could only give priority to the first. This in turn meant treating the Sioux well and naturally the Sioux preferred this to an uncertain welcome in the United States. It is abundantly clear from the tone and content of Walsh's reports that he developed a genuine affection for his charges and a concern for their welfare. By 1880 however the situation had changed. Inaction, hunger, and disease had reduced the military potential of the tribe to the point where the Canadian government felt able to pressure them into leaving. Walsh was obviously not the man to put this new policy into effect and there seems to be little doubt that his efforts to do so were less than successful. But it is equally certain that Walsh did not deliberately prolong the crisis. He was understandably bitter about the way he was treated and in later years wrote several drafts of a book justifying his conduct.[32] Walsh's bitterness was nearly disastrous for the police since his memorandum of 1896 came close to bringing about the dissolution of the force.[33]

The actual business of the suppression and prevention of crime, as we have seen, occupied the police for only a relatively small proportion of their time. It should not be surprising to find also that law enforcement was very much oriented to the Indian problem as well. The liquor laws were the chief concern of the police because they had a direct bearing on the behaviour of the Indians. Crime statistics are available only from 1880 and these are not always complete, but those extant reveal that in every year after 1880, violations of the liquor laws made up the largest single category of offences.[34]

The reports of arrests and cases tried do not tell the whole story. Much of the time the police were involved in preventive activities which did not end in arrests. This type of police activity was not determined by criminal actions reported to exist but by what those in command of the force perceived as their most serious problem. Beyond all question liquor was regarded as the most serious threat. Nor was this idea without foundation. The Indians of North America were one of the few peoples in the history of the human race who did not invent some sort of alcoholic beverage. The effects of liquor sold by the traders were devastating to a people who had developed no cultural devices for dealing with it. This is revealed over and over again in the history of the fur trade. When the Indians became drunk they were totally unmanageable. Even before the police arrived, therefore, the North-West Territories Council had passed legislation which forbade the manufacture, sale, or importation of liquor into the North-West Territories.[35] Smuggling, especially from the United States, was the largest source of illegal spirits and the police spent much of their time trying to prevent it.

A very vivid account of the methods used by the police to prevent smuggling has survived in the diary of Constable R.N. Wilson. His description of a successful patrol is worth quoting at length.

February 20 [1882]. Warned to go on special duty with Constables Callaghan, Leader and Jerry Potts the Guide. Started at 8:30 P.M. and rode all night excepting about two hours which we spent at Standoff where Const. Leader remained. At daylight we were near Lees Creek, later in the day we crossed the St. Mary's River and met Corp'l. La Nauze who is on the same duty as ourselves. We rode to the Boundary line and cached ourselves in a coulee. From a small hill near by we could watch the gap in the Milk River Ridge through which the Sun River trail runs. In the afternoon with the aid of field glasses we could distinguish two objects coming towards us through the gap. We laid low for a couple of hours and a man on horseback rode past us, we at once rode out and made him prisoner, we then waited a few minutes longer and a man with a team and wagon drove up, this man we also made a prisoner of, and upon searching the waggon found over twenty gallons of pure alcohol in five-gallon coal oil cans. The owner was an old expoliceman named Cochrane who had been smuggling for some time, but always managed to avoid the men who were watching for him. The mounted prisoner was an American named Davis who was riding ahead as 'Scout' for Cochrane.

Drove back to St. Mary's and camped. The night was bitterly cold and we had no blankets but those under our saddles. The two prisoners and Jerry were soon howling drunk and the rest of us managed to keep from freezing by taking frequent doses of alcohol diluted in water which Jerry called "mix." About midnight a priest who was camped not far from us came over and was persuaded to take a drink for his stomach's sake, it was not too long before he and Tom La Nauze became very jolly and were toasting each other drinking out of two old fruit cans and touching them together at every sip. Callaghan had long retired, crawling in between David and Cochrane who were to [sic] drunk to prevent him and before morning I had the honour of being the only sober man in camp although I must admit that I took quite enough to keep the cold out.[36]

Penalties for liquor law violations were stiff. The smugglers in this case, a first offence, were fined a hundred dollars each and lost their team and waggon. But for every successful patrol there were many unsuccessful ones and the problem of enforcing the liquor laws absorbed a great deal of time and effort.

A whole range of other varieties of crime occurred as well and these were not allowed to go unpunished. There was no pattern to the normal run of assaults and petty theft; and for these the police had to await complaints. Crimes of violence always took precedence when they occurred but even in murder cases the emphasis tended to be on the Indian problem. The police were concerned above all to demonstrate to the Indians that they would be protected. The classic instance of this attitude was the capture and trial of the perpetrators of the Cypress Hills Massacre.[37] The police went to quite extraordinary lengths to search out the suspects in order to make an example of them, only to find that they did not have sufficient evidence either to extradite those suspects living in the United States or to convict those captured in Canada.

But what of the other activities, those classified under the heading 'internal business,' which occupied most of the force's time? To a great extent in the early years these were housekeeping duties necessary to ensure the bare survival of the police. They had to build their own posts when they arrived in the West.[38] They were also forced to be as self-sufficient as possible in their food supply. Vegetables were grown in large quantities at all posts. Experienced farmers chosen from among the constables were given the opportunity to plant gardens in their spare time. The force would then purchase their crops at fixed rates.[39] Basic food supplies like meat and flour could be purchased but that did not entirely suffice. As Commissioner French soon discovered, the force had to bake its own bread, kill and cut its own meat, and cut wood for fuel. The latter was a sizable task in itself, amounting in 1875 at the relatively small post at Swan River to about one hundred cords a month.[40]

The care and feeding of horses took up almost as much time. At the start the police grew and harvested their own oats and hay, but this practice was abandoned as soon as it became possible to buy it. Farms were established at most major posts to take care of horses not actually in use. This operation was centralized in 1880 at the police farm at Pincher Creek, an outpost of Ft Macleod. Two years later the police turned over operation of the farm to the Stewart Ranch Company. The farming operations were to a certain extent experimental farms as well, with the police testing varieties of plants under western conditions for the Dominion Experimental Farm in Ottawa. Farming operations were abandoned in the early 1880s for the most part because they made such heavy demands on the time of the force. They had proved to be subversive of discipline as well. Many constables objected to heavy manual labour and several mutinies occurred as a result.[41]

Farming operations did have certain advantages, however. Knowledge of local agricultural conditions and the willingness of the police to lend settlers such equipment as sawmills and threshing machines made relations with settlers much closer than they might otherwise have been. The settlers saw the police as practical men who understood the problems of the country. This attitude persisted long after the police ceased to do any farming. In 1897, for example, when plans to reduce and perhaps to replace the police became public knowledge there was a wave of protest in the west. In a typical letter one G.F. Guernsey of Ft Qu'Appelle wrote to Frank Oliver, a leading western Liberal, to register a protest. He objected particularly to the idea of replacing the police with militia which, unlike the police, would be useless and expensive; 'not to mention the number of Colonels and Majors running around loose.'[42]

As time passed administrative duties made up an increasing proportion of the category of internal business. Those connected with the Indians have already been mentioned. In addition the police provided the first postal service in many areas. They acted as Customs officers and took the census. Before local boards of health were established the police proclaimed and enforced such things as quarantine regulations. Police surgeons and hospitals were often the only medical services available. The police gathered a great variety of information for various departments; meteorological records, crop reports, and corrections in government maps. In the administrative sphere the attitude of the force was as important as the actual duties it was assigned. Generally speaking if an officer felt that the performance of a given task was in the public interest, he saw that it was done and worried about authorization later. In 1876, for example, Commissioner French wrote to Ottawa:

I have the honour to inform you that, believing it to be in the interest of the public service, I have during the past five months furnished supplies and afforded assistance to the telegraph construction party working eastward from this point.[43]

French also convinced the local representative of the Department of Public Works that he should do the same without waiting for instructions. The most important action of this sort taken by the police was the issuance of relief supplies to the destitute – white, Métis, and Indian.

Relief was provided, either in the form of food or employment, to all who asked for it. The procedure was entirely informal with the funds sometimes even coming out of the officers' own pockets.[44] An effort was made to end the practice in 1891,[45] but without complete success as this reply to a request for relief some months later indicates.

There is no Parliamentary appropriation from which the expense for relief to destitute Half-Breeds can be paid, and it is very desirable that no issues should be made, but Mrs. Le Jour and her children must not be allowed to starve. You are authorized to issue a limited quantity of provisions to this family if absolutely necessary, sending the account therefor to me.[46]

The most important non-police activities of the force were its judicial duties. These were very extensive. All officers of the force were *ex officio* justices of the peace. The commissioner and assistant commissioner were, in the early years, given the higher judicial rank of magistrate. In any case two JPs sitting together could try all but the most serious offences. This meant that the police themselves tried the great majority of the suspects they apprehended.[47] The force was also well represented in the legislative branch of government. From 1874 until the North-West Territories Council became the Legislative Assembly in 1888, the commissioner was always one of the appointed members. In an informal sense the force had double representation after 1880 since Colonel Macleod, the former commissioner who had resigned in that year to become a magistrate, was also a member of the Council.

There can be little doubt that the administrative activities of the force greatly increased its effectiveness as a law enforcement agency. From the point of view of the Indian or the settler the police were, for all practical purposes, the government. For a developing community this system had a good many advantages; it was cheap, simple, and efficient. As far as dealings with the Indians went it worked very well indeed. There were none of the misunderstandings that divided authority could create. As a Blood chief put it in 1888 when the structure of government had become much more complex: 'The Bloods are talking for their country as Judge Macleod used to talk for his. Why is he not here?'[48] The police were just as aware of the advantages of their position. In discussing the problem of handling the refugee Sioux in 1878 Macleod wrote urging that no Indian agent be appointed. 'A divided authority would be attended with the most serious results – they would be pitched from the Police to the Agent and from the Agent to the Police in a vacuum which would be anything but satisfactory.'[49]

It is obvious that the NWMP up to 1885 occupied a position of power rarely, if ever, equalled by a police force in a free society. The question naturally arises; did the inhabitants of the Territories chafe under this despotism, however benevolent? The answer would seem to be a definite no. There is little evidence that the population feared the powers of the police and much evidence that they entirely approved. Paul F. Sharp finds this difficult to explain. He noted that newspapers in Montana brought the question up and considered such concentration of power in the hands of the police intolerable. Sharp explains this apparent anomaly as follows:

Frontiersmen, whose social and political views were libertarian by eastern standards, were impressed by the effectiveness of the Mountie's power. But this concentration of authority was feasible only because the Whoop-Up country was virtually uninhabited by white settlers. A handful of traders comprised the region's population familiar with Anglo-American legal codes. Later when settlers poured into the region, mounting criticism forced an end to the policeman's dual role.[50]

This explanation would perhaps be adequate if Sharp's last sentence was a statement of fact, but investigation shows it to be incorrect. As chapter five below will show in more detail, the efforts of the police to divest themselves of their judicial role, which they found onerous, were unsuccessful. They continued to try cases in large numbers as late as 1905 because civilian Justices could not be found. This state of affairs can only be explained by abandoning all Turnerian assumptions about the influence of the frontier. Canadians in the West, exposed to the same environmental influences as American frontiersmen, demonstrably possessed very different ideas about politics and society. The political culture of the Canadian North-West was derived almost entirely from eastern Canada and in fact was partly the creation of the police themselves.

The outline of what the police had accomplished in their first dozen years is clear. The territory had been prepared for settlement; the 1885 rebellion occurred because the Métis recognized this fact and feared its consequences for them. The railway was complete and there was no longer any question as there had been in 1870 of Canada's ability to occupy the area effectively. The police had established themselves very firmly in a position to meet the next phase of western development. A tradition of orderly government had been created which would reinforce the political ideas of new arrivals.

4
The organization man:
Commissioner L.W. Herchmer's reforms

Under the leadership of its third commissioner, Lawrence William Herchmer, the NWMP passed beyond its initial heroic phase and became in the period 1886-1900 an institution capable of coping with the complex demands of an increasingly technological society. The police made this transition largely by adopting a technological approach themselves. That is, they began to look for methodological solutions to the problems they faced. The assumption that there are such solutions is, of course, one of the fundamental beliefs which have shaped western civilization in the last century. The NWMP adopted this attitude earlier than most institutions and rapidly became one of the most efficient police forces in the world. We are now beginning to have doubts about the ultimate efficacy of the technical approach to human problems; solutions often seem to create more serious problems than those they were intended to solve. There is considerable support for such a view in the history of the Mounted Police from 1886 to 1900. The efficiency of the force increased vastly in this period but at the end of it, although some problems had been solved, new ones had appeared and the force itself was in serious danger of passing out of existence.

The author of most of these changes, L.W. Herchmer, entertained no doubts about the unlimited possibilities of the technical approach. If he had been bothered by such doubts he could not have achieved what he did. His dilemma, the great shortcoming of all technicians, was that in order to isolate specific problems and reduce them to manageable proportions, it was necessary to ignore the larger political and constitutional framework within which the police existed and to concentrate on improving the efficiency of the daily routine. When contradictions appeared between technical efficiency and political-constitutional imperatives the whole structure came close to collapsing. Looked at in this way, Herch-

mer's important contributions to the development of the police, hitherto ob-
scured by his unfortunate personality, can be placed in their proper perspective.
Herchmer indeed deserves much more attention than he has received since, in
terms of the innovations he introduced, he was the most influential of the early
commissioners of the force. In order to understand why his technical improve-
ments had such a mixed outcome it is necessary to look at the political and administrative framework within which the police operated. This can best be done
by briefly reviewing the careers of Herchmer's predecessors.

Gilbert and Sullivan's famous line about the policeman's lot certainly applied
to the commissioners of the Mounted Police. Every one of the first four left the
force involuntarily in unhappy circumstances. Yet the police were on the whole
very fortunate in the men who led them. With the exception of A.G. Irvine
(1880-6) the early commissioners were men whose talents moulded the force in
exactly the manner the times required. The first commissioner, George Arthur
French, provided the organization, the discipline, and the link with the long traditions of the British Army which gave the NWMP a pride and *esprit de corps* it
never lost. His successor, James Farquharson Macleod, was a man whose legal
training and distinguished service as a Militia officer gave him an ideal background for his post. More important still he was a man of iron integrity and great
sympathy for the Indians. At a time when relations with the tribes were of the
utmost importance he established a pattern of friendship and fair dealing between police and Indians which lasted nearly a century. A.G. Irvine is the odd
man out in this group. He appears to have been intelligent enough but he lacked
the force of character necessary to maintain control within the force and to
make his advice, which was often sound, heard by those in power.

French, after organizing the police and presiding over their first ventures in
the north-west, resigned in 1876 in an atmosphere of considerable bitterness. Experience had led him to believe that certain changes in the organization of his
command were essential, but he soon discovered that the government was entirely uninterested. Relations between French and the Mackenzie government
had been quite strained almost from the beginning. The commissioner had been
reprimanded for his refusal to spend the winter of 1874-5 at Swan River.[1] As an
appointee of the Macdonald government, French was automatically suspect on
political grounds and the Liberals were prone to regard any opposition on his
part as a deliberate attempt to sabotage their policies. Distance, and Ottawa's
general ignorance of western conditions, provided all too many opportunities
for misunderstandings. Inevitably French became suspicious in his turn and
by the spring of 1876 these suspicions had brought him to a state of mind that
only a change from the isolation of Swan River could cure. In an extraordinary
letter French confided his view of the situation to his immediate superior in
Ottawa.

I am at the present time in receipt of reliable information which discloses an organized conspiracy for vilifying officers of this Force, mainly carried on by scur-
rilous letters in disreputable newspapers, these statements being backed up
regardless of truth by private letters to subordinate officials at Ottawa with the
design that the contents should be mentioned to higher Authority. I have the
best reasons for believing that in at least one instance a private letter from a very
subordinate Officer of this Force finding fault with my methods of conducting
the affairs of this Force, was successfully brought to the notice of one if not two
Ministers of the Government. I expect ere long to be in a position to bring
charges home to the individuals concerned, but in the meantime I beg to request
that this letter may not be allowed to fall into other hands than your own.[2]

After the government had denied five urgent requests for permission for him to
come to Ottawa, at his own expense if necessary, French resigned. He had been
rather shabbily treated by the government and the whole incident was unpleas-
ant; but the departure of French did no harm to the police as an institution. This
can be said with equal truth about the resignations of each of the commissioners
who followed French down to the end of the nineteenth century. Conditions
changed so rapidly that no one man could cope with all of them over an extended period of time. Once the police were well established and it became clear
that there would be little if any fighting a different type of man was required to
undertake the very different task of dealing with the Indians.

Assistant Commissioner Macleod was promoted to fill the vacancy left by
French's resignation. The fact that he was a Canadian was regarded with general
approval.[3] Morale among the officers was strengthened.

It has long been felt that there is sufficient talent and ability of Canadian growth
to obviate the supposed necessity of resort to the Imperial military service for
every important military command and the selection of Lieut.-Col. Macleod not
only redounds to the credit of Mr. Mackenzie's Government, but must be emi-
nently satisfactory to the large number of his old comrades of all ranks who love
and appreciate him.[4]

In his brief tenure as commissioner Macleod lived up to the expectations of his
admirers. Yet he too was forced to resign after four years. This time the reasons
do not appear to have been entirely political. Sir John A. Macdonald was back in
power in Ottawa and he had given Macleod his original appointment in the police. Macleod's Conservative credentials were impeccable. He had articled in the
law office of Alexander Campbell, a member of Macdonald's cabinet and former
law partner of the prime minister. Upon his resignation Macleod received the

equally important post of stipendiary magistrate and remained a member of the North-West Territories Council.

The ostensible reason for Macleod's removal from command was that he was spending too much money.[5] Macdonald professed to be shocked at the extravagant manner in which Macleod in his concern for the efficiency of the police was depleting the public treasury. There was probably a good deal of truth in the accusation. Macleod certainly exhibited no talent for financial management in his personal affairs. He received a salary which was entirely adequate for the day and did not live in an expensive manner, but he died a poor man. This being the case it was desirable to move Macleod into a position where the government could make use of his talents without having to worry about his handling of large sums of public money. Macdonald however had more than this in mind. Macleod had been overly independent in refusing to accept political appointees as officers in the police.[6] Macdonald was determined to reorganize the force so that it could be more effectively controlled from Ottawa, both politically and financially. As an administrator of great experience Macdonald knew that to be effective the change in structure would require a change in personnel. Macleod had to be replaced by a more pliable man who would accept the new arrangements without too many questions.

The new arrangements consisted of the addition of a new office, that of comptroller of the NWMP. The functions previously performed entirely by the commissioner were divided. The commissioner retained control of operations in the field while the comptroller was given full responsibility for the financial arrangements of the police. He also had an important voice in matters of broad policy since he was in the position of interpreting the requirements of the force to the cabinet minister responsible and interpreting the wishes of the government to the commissioner.[7] The power of the office was further enhanced throughout the period under consideration because of the individual who held the position.

Frederick White became comptroller in 1880 and held the post until 1912. Commissioners and governments came and departed but White was always there. Fred White had been a clerk in the Justice Department, where he attracted the attention of Sir John A. Macdonald, probably because White was then working under Hewitt Bernard, Macdonald's brother-in-law. In 1878 he became the prime minister's private secretary and he remained one of his most trusted associates as long as Macdonald lived. In 1880 Macdonald appointed White comptroller of the NWMP, an appointment which made sense since White had been responsible for the force as a clerk in the Justice Department since 1876. White came very close to being the ideal civil servant. He was highly efficient, tactful, discreet, courteous but firm with his subordinates, friendly but distant with his equals, and never presumptuous with his superiors. His great contribution to the force was to insulate the commissioner at least partially from the vagaries of politics and so allow him to devote his time to running the day-to-day operations of the force. White was a master of the art of explaining the activities of the police to eastern politicians in terms they could understand. What the worthy legislators understood best was money and White's favourite ploy was to demonstrate that it cost only half as much to keep a Mounted Policeman in the field as a trooper in the US Cavalry. Everyone loves a bargain and this helps to account for the fact that the police attracted very little parliamentary criticism.

In his reorganization of the police Macdonald had sought a more pliable man as commissioner. In Acheson Gosford Irvine he found such a man. Like his predecessor, Irvine was a former Militia officer, a member of the Red River expedition, and an original member of the force. But even though Irvine was commissioner for longer than either Macleod or French and directed the force during a period in which it weathered a rebellion and increased from three hundred to a thousand men, he failed to leave his mark on it in any significant way. Irvine's personality was so bland that to the historian he is almost invisible. The effect on his contemporaries was much the same. Irvine knew what was happening in his jurisdiction but he reported his belief that rebellion was imminent in 1884 with exactly the same emphasis that he used in reporting the amount of hay the force had in stock. The result was that no one paid much attention to anything he said.

The great crisis of Irvine's term of office was the North-West Rebellion of 1885. Macdonald chose in this case to ignore warnings from the NWMP and listen to those who told him there would be no trouble.[8] In one sense Irvine's forced retirement immediately following the rebellion was unjustified in that the commissioner was a victim of the government's mistakes.[9] At the same time it must be admitted that it would have been an even more serious error to leave Irvine in command. The commissioner of the Mounted Police occupied a position of such importance that it was essential he be a man with the force of character to ensure that his voice was heard.

The rebellion had seriously damaged the reputation of the police and vigorous new leadership was required to restore it. Accordingly, this time Macdonald devoted a good deal more thought to the delicate problem of choosing a new commissioner. In order to rebuild the image of the force and restore discipline the new commissioner would have to be an outsider with a military background. He would also have to be politically and socially acceptable. This narrowed the choice down to two categories; either an officer from the Imperial forces whose social standing would be unquestioned and who would be politically neutral, or a member of the eastern Canadian élite with sound Conservative affiliations. Macdonald was inclined to prefer the former alternative and offered the position first to Lord Melgund and then to Colonel E.T.H. Hutton.[10] Both declined. At least two former senior officers of the Canadian Militia with experience of the west, Colonel W. Osborne Smith and General T. Bland Strange, asked for the job but were rejected.[11] Why Smith was considered unsuitable is not known but Macdonald's reasons for turning down Strange are worth quoting. 'Strange is too old altogether and too much of a mere gunner to have control of the Police force, besides his crazy fear of the Indians which almost amounts to semi-insanity.'[12]

When Macdonald finally chose L.W. Herchmer for the position it must have been with some misgivings. Although Herchmer had an extensive military background he had never seen action and lacked the reputation that might have gained him a readier acceptance by the officers of the force. In other respects however Herchmer fitted the requirements very well and Macdonald presumably hoped that time, Herchmer's abilities, and steady political support from the prime minister's office would remove any initial problems. Political support was something Herchmer could definitely count on since Macdonald was not a man who forgot his friends. Herchmer's father had gone to school with Macdonald in Kingston and was more than a casual acquaintance.[13] After his ordination as an Anglican clergyman the elder Herchmer left Kingston and moved to England to serve in some capacity at Oxford. Here he married (a niece of the great landscape painter, Turner) and although he returned to Canada, always insisted that his children be born in England. Both his sons went into the British Army but the ties of the family with Canada must have remained strong because both returned to Canada before long. They always considered themselves Canadians.

The older son, L.W. Herchmer, received a commission in the 46th Regiment of Foot in 1858 at the age of eighteen. After serving two years in Ireland and two years in India he sold his commission and came to Canada. For the next ten years his activities are unknown except for his marriage in 1864 to Helen Sherwood, daughter of the first attorney-general of Upper Canada. In 1872 when Macdonald began seriously planning the Mounted Police he offered both Herchmer brothers commissions.[14] The police did not materialize that year as expected and L.W. Herchmer joined the International Boundary Commission as commissariat officer instead. In 1878 he joined the Indian Affairs Department as an Indian agent and by 1885 had risen to the position of Inspector of Indian Agencies.[15] By the time of his appointment to the police as commissioner Herchmer was as well equipped for the job in terms of experience as any man could be.

Herchmer needed all his experience and skill to deal with the problems, internal and external, which confronted him when he took over. Internally discipline and morale were at a low ebb as a result of the rebellion. The police had been forced to fight a holding action with the fraction of the force that could be spared from detachment duty until the Militia arrived. Reverses in this situation were inevitable and it was doubly unfortunate that in the first engagement of the rebellion, at Duck Lake between the Métis and a mixed force of police and civilian volunteers, the battle should develop in such a way that the civilians took most of the casualties. This was pure chance but combined with the fact that the police were forced to withdraw from the field and later abandon Ft Carlton it led to a good deal of misinformed if understandable criticism. Had the police been allowed to redeem themselves in a later battle the situation might have improved but once the Militia arrived the police as a body took little further part in the fighting. To add to this disappointing record the force had been hastily increased to a thousand men on the eve of the rebellion. Many of these had joined because of the prospect of action and they became very restless after hostilities ended.

As an experienced military man Herchmer knew the remedy for this kind of situation – as much drill and training as possible. Fortunately the increased size of the force made it feasible for the first time since the formation of the police to carry out extensive training. Herchmer toured the major posts and personally supervised these activities. Cavalry drill was abandoned and the Mounted Infantry regulations of the British Army adopted in their place.[16] Superintendent R. Burton Deane was detailed to prepare a handbook for the force.[17] Undesirables were quickly weeded out and replaced by steadier men, a process which was easily accomplished when peace returned and there was again a waiting list to join the force. Morale and discipline improved rapidly.

The most serious external difficulty facing the police in 1886 was the prevalence of horse stealing in the border regions. Horse theft by Indians had been a problem since the tribes on both sides of the border had discovered that the line afforded them a considerable measure of immunity if they carried out their raids in other than their country of residence. Because the Indians stole mostly from each other, losses tended to balance out. The police tried to stop it but it was not of great concern. But by about 1884, when organized gangs of white horse thieves made their appearance, horse stealing developed from a minor irritant into a major problem.[18] Naturally these men found Canadian horses just as acceptable as American ones. By 1885 farmers who lived south of the CPR main line found it necessary to sleep in their stables and the police themselves lost several horses.[19] Commissioner Irvine seemed at a loss to think of any better way to handle the situation than increasing the number of men in the border area. More men were certainly necessary but the use made of them was more important. If horses could be stolen from the police themselves, more men would mean more horses to steal.

The other great problem, more potential than actual in 1886, was the increase in crime which was bound to accompany the increased settlement brought by the railway. The days when the police could have a divisional post at every important settlement were rapidly coming to an end. It would no longer be possible for a detachment to keep track of all people and events in the area informally as had been the case previously. The demands on the force caused by the construction of the railway had foreshadowed these new challenges.[20] Another indication of the future course of events was the rapidly increasing difficulty of enforcing the liquor laws among the white population.[21] Macdonald, who never lost sight of the fact that one day control of law enforcement would pass to local authorities in the North-West Territories, continued to cherish his illusion that settlement would reduce the necessity for police but the annual reports of the commissioner revealed an opposite trend.

Herchmer, who had observed all these conditions at first hand in his travels as inspector of Indian agencies, had very definite ideas about how the police should be organized to meet them. He immediately instituted a system of regular patrols to cover the entire North-West Territories and especially the border areas.[22] All main trails which crossed the boundary were patrolled constantly and Indian scouts were assigned to patrol to ensure that lesser trails were not overlooked. This system was extended year by year in an effort to cover every corner of the Territories. The results were highly satisfactory with the number of cases of horse stealing dropping from forty-eight in 1885 to nine in 1887.[23] There was, of course, nothing new about patrols as such as far as the police were concerned. Herchmer's contribution lay in his recognition of the importance of a systematic approach. As long as one gap existed in the patrol network the rest were ineffective. The systematic regularity of the police patrols which Herchmer introduced was a highly effective deterrent to potential horse thieves for the simple reason that horses are very difficult to conceal. The thief could still make off with horses from an isolated farm or ranch but the problem of moving the stolen animals undetected through the patrol network was almost insuperable.

As the patrol system was expanded and improved in the late 1880s and early 1890s other advantages became apparent and new uses for it were discovered. Almost every farm and ranch was visited regularly. Constables were issued with patrol books which would be signed by each settler they visited on patrol and complaints recorded.[24] These visits not only helped to keep the police fully informed about all that went on in the district but provided the settler with a welcome relief from the isolation of his farm or ranch. The exchange of information was two-way and the police used the patrol system to prevent the growth of unfounded rumours which could be potential sources of trouble. The most frequent rumours concerned Indian uprisings. The police took great care to let settlers know that these were false.[25]

At its greatest extent, in the period 1888 to 1892, the patrol system covered not only the entire North-West Territories but the border regions of southern

Manitoba and the Kootenai district of southern British Columbia as well.[26] In these years the police averaged about 1,500,000 miles annually on horseback.[27] To avoid the danger that criminals might try to use the regularity of police patrols to their advantage, all divisions were ordered in 1890 to maintain two flying patrols at all times. These would have no fixed route to follow and would cover whatever parts of the district seemed to require it.[28]

After 1892 the patrol system began to be cut back. The police had reached a high point of a thousand men during the 1885 rebellion and remained at that strength until 1893. In that year the force was reduced to eight hundred and fifty men and ordered to cut a further hundred as soon as possible.[29] The force remained at a strength of seven hundred and fifty men for a decade but after 1895 more and more men were withdrawn from the North-West Territories for duty in the Yukon to maintain order on the gold diggings. By 1898 there were two hundred and fifty police there, leaving only five hundred in the Territories.[30] The best and most experienced men went to the Yukon, leaving the Territories with a high proportion of raw recruits who had to be trained before they could take over the heavy responsibilities of patrol duty. While the strength of the police was declining, the population of the area was increasing. New settlements were springing up and after 1893 it was never possible to make the patrols as inclusive as they once were. The effects of the reductions in strength did not appear immediately in the crime statistics. Rural crime had been almost eliminated by 1892 and a strong tradition of order established. This tradition and the reputation of the police sustained them until the boom conditions of the early twentieth century brought a new wave of rural crime in the West, this time in the form of cattle rustling.

The period from the rebellion to the turn of the century was not without its moments of excitement for the police but generally speaking it was very quiet. The level of criminal activities will be dealt with statistically in a later chapter. Statistics, however, do little to convey the flavour of the period, how it felt to the participants; an aspect of reality as essential to understanding as the other. The diary of a small rural detachment gives some idea of the day-to-day activities of a more or less typical police post. Such a post was the one at Nanton, some fifty miles south of Calgary on the railway line to Lethbridge, in the heart of the ranching country of southern Alberta. In 1899 it was an outpost of Ft Macleod and consisted of a sergeant and for about half the year a constable as well. Crime was almost nonexistent. The detachment encountered only one lawbreaker during the year, a rancher who violated the quarantine regulations by shipping a load of cattle without having them inspected.

Daily patrols were carried out to ranches in the district and occasionally the police would stay overnight at one of these. The sergeant met all trains which stopped at Nanton, noted the movements of travellers through the village, and spent his weekends in an effort to keep the rather ramshackle police post, which leaked copiously every time it rained, in order. Nothing varied the routine except the occasional prairie fire and the annual inspections of the post. The life would have been unbearably monotonous except for the constant stream of visitors who stopped for a meal or just to break the tedium of a long journey with a little conversation.[31]

Life at a large divisional post offered a little more variety but generally the combination of hard work and routine was much the same. The following report of a flying patrol from Prince Albert in 1892 was typical.

I have the honour to report that, in accordance with your instructions I left Prince Albert on Tuesday the 31st January for Kinistino, with Constables Carter, Conway and team. The trails were fairly good as far as the Dunlop's ranche, where we stopped over night. I visited several settlers along the road. No one had any complaint to make, they all appeared to be in fair circumstance. On Wednesday morning we left Dunlop's with a strong wind blowing and the thermometer at 45 below zero. The trails were very heavy. I called at all the houses along the road. The half breeds seemed to be quite contented and had evidently lots to eat. Several of the white settlers seemed to be in poor circumstance, judging from the look of their shacks. We arrived at Mr. Meyer's place about 5 P.M., having taken eight hours to drive the 20 miles the trails were so bad. On Thursday there was a strong wind and Mr. Meyer's thermometer registered 55 below zero. We didn't take the team out that day, but I visited all the settlers I could in the Carrot River district on snowshoes. I found them all contented and doing very well. One settler named Craig, a new arrival from Dakota has lost about 20 head of cattle, part of a band that he drove into the country with him. I couldn't get to his place, as it was fifteen miles away and there was no trail, but the settlers around Kinistino say that owing to the representations made to him by the Immigration Agents that cattle could paw out their own living in this part of the country during the winter, he neglected to put up any shed or shelter of any kind, and very little hay and that the deaths of his cattle resulted wholly from starvation and cold. On Friday the 3rd instant, I left Kinistino to return to Prince Albert. The cold was intense. We reached Dunlop's ranche that evening and stayed there for the night. The next morning (Saturday) we left Dunlop's and reached the Barracks at Prince Albert at 5:30 P.M. The trails were very heavy and we had great difficulty in getting through at all.[32]

Inspector Strickland's patrol report quoted above illustrates another key aspect of Herchmer's system; the emphasis on complete and accurate information about everything which might in any way affect the public order. It has been asserted that the mere presence of the police, their visibility as a symbol of the authority of the Canadian government, accounts for their success.[33] Visibility was unquestionably one of the force's most important attributes but it was only one of several interdependent factors which explain their effectiveness in this period. Herchmer, as we have already seen, recognized that more was necessary and along with a systematic approach he added a new emphasis on information. A vital element in the functioning of any institution is its system of communications. This is perhaps especially true of a police force which must not only gather reliable information about threats to the political order but communicate them effectively to the political authorities. Herchmer improved both these dimensions of police communications.

Explicit instructions were issued as to the kind of information the police were expected to include in their patrol reports:

These patrols should visit isolated ranches and settlements and report on everything that has come under their observation, the police outfits they have met, freighters, travellers, movements of doubtful characters, condition of crops, prospects of hay, the ownership of any particularly fine horses they may see and to each report a rough map should be attached.[34]

The ideal which the police sought to attain was for the superintendent to know, at least by reputation, every person in his district. This was a goal which could never be reached in practice but the police were very serious about making the effort. In 1890 Superintendent Steele recommended that a man by the name of George Irish be granted a liquor permit. Irish subsequently used the privilege illegally and the lieutenant-governor complained to Herchmer that the man's background had not been properly investigated. It turned out that there had been two men of the same name living on the same ranch and Steele had confused them. He received a stiff reprimand from the commissioner which Comptroller White felt was excessively harsh. Reporting the matter to Macdonald, White wrote: 'Commissioner Herchmer considers that Superintendent Steele should be familiar with the history of every man living in his District.'[35] Training in the techniques of observation was carried out at the larger posts where constables attended weekly lectures on police duties.[36] While the force was at its greatest strength it was also possible to send constables to Regina for a two-month training course on their promotion to non-commissioned rank.[37]

Patrol reports and reports from detachments were made to divisional headquarters every week. Any of these which recorded anything out of the ordinary were passed on at once to the commissioner. Routine reports were summarized in the regular monthly reports of each division. These in turn were the basis of the commissioner's annual report. The information in the reports can be analyzed into three types, each with a distinct purpose. The routine reports presented a picture of the 'normal' state of society in western Canada at that point in time. They represent the collective judgement of the force as to the type and extent of change society could tolerate and still remain in equilibrium. They were the backdrop against which aberrations could be measured. At the other end of the scale was information concerning obvious anti-social behaviour, clear violations of the Criminal Code. These activities had been defined through legislation as dangerous to the social order and could therefore be dealt with at the local level. If they were serious enough they were reported at once.[38]

Much of the information in the police reports, however, falls somewhere in between these two categories. This third type of information was passed on to higher authorities for decision and consisted principally of recommendations for government action to control the development of undesirable situations. Here was the main thrust of the force's attempt to prevent crime. It included such things as reports of new settlements which required police attention, deficiencies in the Criminal Code which left offences unpunished or made enforcement unnecessarily difficult and reports on unusual increases in the incidence of particular types of crime. From this more or less factual data the reports shaded off into speculative areas such as the possible effects of adverse economic conditions or the use of American school textbooks by immigrants from the United States.[39] For any police force in a democratic state, the manner in which it handles this type of information is crucial. The police must deal with potential threats to the public order and at the same time must be careful to avoid the systematic invasion of privacy which characterizes a police state. The success of the Mounted Police derives to a great extent from their consistent ability to make this kind of distinction.

The police were quick to recognize the usefulness of the technological advances which would improve communications and enable them to make better use of limited manpower. The typewriter was adopted in the late 1880s, well before it came into general use in other government departments. The telephone was welcomed eagerly and greatly increased the usefulness of what had been isolated one-man posts.[40] Although their artillery was of ancient vintage, the police adopted the Maxim gun when it came on the market in the 1890s. Fingerprinting was begun shortly after the turn of the century and the use of photography dates from about the same time.

Herchmer was highly successful in his attempt to establish a system for controlling crime and keeping order in the rural parts of the North-West Territories. He was much less successful in the urban areas. There were very few towns of any size in the Territories before the turn of the century, of course, but they were the foci for almost all political, social, and economic activity. They were also the centres of criminal activity and could not be ignored by the police. Unfortunately for the police no direct approach to urban law enforcement was possible. Political and constitutional barriers stood in the way of the creation of a simple and effective solution such as the rural patrol system. This is not to suggest that the problem was unique or that it could have been solved by changing the political framework. In a federal state such compromises are essential. The problem of conflicting responsibilities for law enforcement had been inherent in federal control of the North-West Territories from the beginning. It had been glossed over at first by Macdonald's vague theory of a gradual evolution of law enforcement institutions as the Territories developed. The difficulty was that nobody in the North-West showed the slightest interest in taking over law enforcement. The people of the Territories had sought and obtained a measure of responsible government by 1892 but law enforcement was specifically excluded from the list of governmental functions they sought to control.[41]

This rejection by the citizens of the Territories of a constitutional right to which they were entitled left the federal authorities baffled and frustrated. They were now confronted with the task of setting limits to federal involvement in law enforcement and of persuading the territorial governments to shoulder the burden. For the purpose of central government policy the limit of police responsibility was taken to be the unincorporated town. As a matter of policy incorporated towns were responsible for organizing their own police.[42] This distinction was purely artificial because it was based not on social reality but on political considerations. In practice only a few of the larger towns organized their own police and in most cases they were too few or too incompetent to handle the job.[43]

The structural differentiation imposed by political necessity did not correspond to any division in function; the problem of maintaining law and order in the Territories was indivisible. Whether or not the towns chose to hire their own constables, the NWMP remained responsible for the entire region. But because they had to operate on the assumption that their presence in the towns was at best temporary, they were prevented from taking steps which would have increased their effectiveness. Herchmer, for example, realized almost as soon as he took over the force that the urban situation required a detective service with specialized training. The plan to organize a detective service got as far as the appointment of Inspector Charles Constantine, who was brought in from the Manitoba Provincial Police to supervise the training of the detectives. At this point the prime minister seems to have realized that such a step implied a permanent urban commitment. No detectives were appointed and nothing more was heard of the scheme for fifteen years.[44] A proposal the following year to set up a special railway police branch met the same fate.[45] Similarly efforts to move the headquarters of the Edmonton district to that city from the small neighbouring town of Fort Saskatchewan were blocked. White was expressing government policy when he wrote:

Fort Saskatchewan has been the Police Headquarters of that District for the last 18 years. It has been found the most convenient centre from which to control the Police scattered throughout the District, and I certainly could not endorse a recommendation for a transfer of the Headquarters to Edmonton which has become an Incorporated Town and within which there is now very little necessity for Mounted Police.[46]

Although the government frustrated attempts to set up a formal police structure in the towns, public demand was so great that they were prepared to allow an informal police presence in urban areas on the condition that the NWMP constables assigned to town duty were in no way under the control of the town authorities and were not responsible for enforcing municipal by-laws.[47] These provisos were a legal fiction to maintain the constitutional proprieties. In 1900, for example, the Town of Lethbridge requested that the Mounted Police corporal on town duty be allowed to act temporarily as town constable and enforce the local by-laws. His superior persuaded the commissioner to agree, arguing that the work in no way interfered with NWMP duties and in any case: 'A portion of the work would be required of him by the officer commanding "K" Division.'[48] Although a separate detective branch was not formally established, staff-sergeants of long experience were assigned more or less permanently to detective duties.[49] If there were signs of serious disorder in any town which it appeared the local police were unable to control, the NWMP moved in immediately.[50] Once there they often remained for years.

By the turn of the century the commissioner and the comptroller, while still loyally paying lip service to the theory of the disappearing police, were well aware of the true state of affairs. Their exasperation occasionally came to the surface in their communications with their political chiefs. In a memo of 1898 White wrote: 'An impression appears to prevail that the construction of Railways and the advance of settlement reduces the necessity for Police, but this theory is not supported by the actual condition of affairs.'[51] Commissioner Herchmer was even more explicit the following year:

I have on previous occasions recommended the withdrawal of detachments from well settled districts, but after long experience I find this will not do, as when crime does occur, too much valuable time is lost in getting a constable on the ground, and the expense is greater in the long run than that of keeping a constable permanently in the vicinity.[52]

With the reductions in manpower in the 1890s pressures on the force in two opposite directions became particularly acute. Demands for the services of the police became so insistent that White believed the old informal system of policing urban areas was no longer viable. He requested a clear statement of policy from his superiors. A particular incident brought matters to a head. It had been decided in 1899 to eliminate the divisional headquarters at Lethbridge in order to save money and men. The citizens of Lethbridge reacted vigorously to the proposal and their protests induced the minister of the interior, Clifford Sifton, to order the move postponed.[53] Confronted by contradictory orders, to save money and at the same time maintain the level of services, White outlined his view of the situation and asked Sifton for further instructions:

The Memorial of the Town of Lethbridge revives in a forcible manner the difficulty we have been endeavouring to combat during the last three or four years, viz. – the reduction of Police expenditure in settled Districts. Our estimates have been cut down to the lowest point in anticipation of being able to withdraw Police from many small outposts which ought to be self-sustaining and reducing the numbers in others, but the invariable result has been protests and pressure to withhold action, or, if reductions have been started to return to the old condition of affairs.

If the policy of the Government is to extend Provincial government to the Territories in the early future, it might perhaps be well to let matters jog on as at present, otherwise the undersigned would suggest that a distinct policy be laid down which will enable definite replies to be given to the constant application for the establishment of new police detachments, or the retention of Police at places where their services could be dispensed with if the settlers could be induced to realize that they ought to rely upon their own resources.[54]

Presumably Sifton agreed with White's suggestion to let matters ride. The document contains a marginal note in his handwriting: 'In abeyance. C.S.'

The police were at this point facing a crisis which put their continued existence in jeopardy. In part this situation had come about as the result of political and constitutional factors beyond the control of anyone in the force. Paradoxically it was also partly due to the very success of Herchmer's system. Had the police been ineffective, the people of the North-West Territories would have been anxious to get rid of them. To a certain extent, however, the crisis was a product of Herchmer's personal shortcomings and his political connections. By 1896 Herchmer had become a distinct liability to the force he had served so well. To the Liberal government which took office in that year Herchmer, as a friend and appointee of Sir John A. Macdonald, was highly suspect. No constructive changes could be made in the force while it was commanded by an officer the government did not believe it could trust.

When Sir John A. Macdonald was alive Herchmer enjoyed a large measure of immunity from political pressures. But even in this period Herchmer was making enemies who would be alive when Macdonald was dead. Herchmer was not a man who got along well with other people even under the best of circumstances. His rigid sense of duty was not tempered in any way by tact; an unfortunate combination of personality traits which made him appear harsh and arrogant. Even if Herchmer had enjoyed a more winning personality he would have found it difficult to avoid controversy. Three years before he took over as commissioner his brother, Superintendent W.M. Herchmer, had the misfortune to run afoul of the Territories' noisiest politician, Nicholas Flood Davin. Davin was an expatriate Irishman, publisher of the Regina *Leader* and the most prominent Conservative MP west of Winnipeg. He was a superb and colourful orator who saw himself as a crusader for the rights of the underdog, a view which was not entirely without foundation. His defects, however, were as large as his virtues and included a tendency to get frequently and uncontrollably drunk.

Returning by train from Ottawa in the summer of 1883 Davin overindulged and ended his spree by wandering through the first class coaches with his trousers off. Unfortunately for all concerned Superintendent W.M. Herchmer was also on the train along with his wife, the wife of Lieutenant-Governor Dewdney, and a member of the North-West Territories Council.[55] The ladies were, of course, unspeakably shocked and Herchmer was forced to bring charges against Davin. He considered charging him with indecent exposure but settled for the lesser offence of illegally bringing liquor into the North-West Territories. Davin was tried and convicted. Another man might have been grateful to let the matter drop there but not Davin. He vigorously maintained his innocence, claiming that he had merely fallen out of his berth when the curtain gave way.[56] Although Davin took the matter all the way to Sir John A. Macdonald, nobody believed him and the full force of his rage fell upon Superintendent Herchmer. Vowing to drive him out of the force, Davin began a campaign against Herchmer in his newspaper. It took the combined efforts of Sir John A. Macdonald and Lieutenant-Governor Dewdney to make him abandon the campaign and smooth over relations.[57] Davin was a man who cherished his grudges. The matter was dropped but not forgotten. He remained hostile to Herchmer as long as he lived.

When W.M. Herchmer's brother, L.W. Herchmer, joined the force as commissioner in 1886 he inherited this feud. The idea of a vendetta was not displeasing to a man of Davin's temperament. The fact that the older Herchmer brother held a much more important post simply made it easier for Davin to see himself as a victim of tyranny. Had the commissioner been a popular leader who commanded the complete loyalty of his subordinates, Davin might never have had the opportunity to seek his revenge. But Herchmer was not popular. His appointment had been strongly resented by the officers of the force because he was an outsider brought in over their heads. Because he was without tact and lacked any vestige of a sense of humour Herchmer quickly transformed this initial hostility into a positive detestation. The situation was made to order for Davin, who collected the grumblings of discontented policemen and waited. He found a valuable ally in C.E.D. Wood, a prominent lawyer and publisher of the Ft Macleod *Gazette*. Wood was related by marriage to Superintendent R. Burton Deane, the officer commanding 'K' Division at Lethbridge. Deane had already had several acrimonious disputes with the commissioner.[58] Wood thus absorbed all the anti-Herchmer stories which circulated in the force. By 1889 Wood and Davin felt they had collected enough evidence and launched an all-out attack on the commissioner in their respective newspapers, accusing him of a long list of misdeeds ranging from interfering with the judicial decisions of junior officers to incompetence to prejudice against French Canadians.[59] Macdonald ordered a confidential investigation of the charges and this was carried out by White. The investigation confirmed Macdonald's suspicion that the charges lacked substance and were grounded largely in the malice of Wood and Davin.

Macdonald's death early in 1891 left the Conservative party, the country, and the police under the dubious leadership of a succession of Conservative party hacks. Macdonald was scarcely cold in his grave before Davin succeeded in forcing a judicial inquiry into the commissioner's conduct. A judge of the North-West Territories Circuit Court, E.L. Wetmore, conducted the investigation. It was very thorough. Advertisements inviting anyone who cared to complain to come forward were inserted in every newspaper in the Territories. The result was a total of 137 charges against Herchmer. Eighty-nine of these were laid by Wood, four by Davin, thirty-eight by members or ex-members of the force, and six by other citizens of the Territories.

Twenty-one of the charges were so flimsy they were withdrawn by the complainants before being considered. Of the remaining hundred and sixteen, nine were proven, all having to do with violations of the internal disciplinary regulations of the force.[60] None of the more serious charges proved to have any foundation in fact. Judge Wetmore's summary of his findings was unequivocal:

It will be seen that some of the matters of complaint brought home to the commissioner were the outcome of too much zeal on his part; some arose from mistakes of the law or from misapprehension of his powers. These mistakes and misapprehensions are such as any person in his position might be likely to make, and do not strike my mind as being of such a character as to amount to misconduct in office. The most learned and experienced of judges make mistakes at times and misconceive the extent of their powers, and it is not a matter of surprise that the commissioner has sometimes done so. As to the remainder of the charges brought against him I have nothing to add beyond this: that a very large proportion of them are attributable to infirmity of temper, brusqueness of manner or hasty conduct.[61]

Herchmer had been cleared but the whole affair damaged the reputation of the police at a time when the force was vulnerable. The Conservative government drifted aimlessly after Macdonald's death, able to think of no more constructive policy than a general cutback of government expenses. This was not done on the basis of any estimate of national priorities but wherever the least opposition was likely to be encountered. The Herchmer scandals, as the newspapers of the day called them, left the police open to attack and had a good deal to do with the cutbacks in manpower of the 1890s. Even White, who was a friend of Herchmer's and recognized his considerable abilities, realized that the commissioner was now a liability to the force. Following the inquiry he wrote to Dewdney, then minister of the interior: 'If it could be found possible to provide for Herchmer in some other branch of the public service where his unfortunate infirmity of temper would be less taxed, a better feeling would prevail throughout all ranks of the police force.'[62] The inquiry, however, had left the government no excuse to demand Herchmer's resignation and he had no intention of submitting it voluntarily.

With the victory of Sir Wilfrid Laurier's Liberals in 1896, Herchmer's position became even worse. Because he had been a personal friend of Macdonald, the Liberals could not bring themselves to trust him. Yet Herchmer's general administrative competence gave them no opportunity to get rid of him. This awkward situation continued until 1900 when the South African War unexpectedly brought it to an end. The war aroused intense enthusiasm among all Canadians who had any military pretensions and Herchmer, although he was sixty years old, was no exception. He had always felt his lack of combat experience keenly and he saw the war as his last chance for the kind of glory he craved. He immediately applied for permission to go to South Africa with the Canadian contingent and the government was happy to oblige.[63] On his return he was informed that his services were no longer required and he was to be pensioned off at once.[64] Like his predecessors he retired in an atmosphere of bitterness, believing that his services had not been recognized. There was a good deal of truth in this view. Herchmer's personality problems and the rapidly changing circumstances of the North-West Territories had trapped him in a hostile environment that had prevented a graceful exit for the man who had prepared the Mounted Police for the twentieth century.

5

Commissioner A. Bowen Perry
and the survival of the NWMP
1900–5

The retirement of Herchmer and his replacement by a man who was both more adept at handling people and a good Liberal did not at first seem to mark any significant change in government policy concerning the police. Provincial autonomy was only a matter of a few years away in 1900 and the federal government was determined to end its responsibility for law enforcement on the prairies as part of the transfer of power. These were years of uncertainty for the police. The new Commissioner, A.B. Perry, believed as late as 1905 that he had been chosen to preside over the disappearance of the force from the scene of its earliest triumphs. Indeed, when the autonomy celebrations were held in the new capitals of Regina and Edmonton in September 1905, a special effort was made to collect 200 Mounted Police in full dress to participate, because the police authorities believed the force would shortly withdraw to the far north.[1]

These expectations were never fulfilled. Instead, in late 1905 and the first months of 1906, a constitutional compromise was worked out which allowed the force to continue its work in the new provinces. The federal government had at last yielded to the social and political realities of law enforcement in western Canada and in doing so had laid the foundation for the eventual creation of the Royal Canadian Mounted Police in 1919. The Mounted Police were simply too useful to be thrown away at this point. They had made themselves indispensable, if not to the government at Ottawa, then to the people of the North-West Territories. It was popular pressure from the West that forced the Laurier government to abandon its plans to do away with the force.

The margin of survival for the police had been very narrow throughout the decade from 1896 to 1905. The force was saved from extinction only by such extraneous events as the discovery of gold in the Yukon and the outbreak of war in South Africa. When the Liberals came to power in 1896 they brought with them the belief that the force was a nest of Conservatives. Frank Oliver, a leading western Liberal, voiced these suspicions in a letter to Laurier:

The commanding officer is everything that a person in his position should not be and is nothing that he should be. The officers and men who are like minded with himself are the ones who receive advancement at his hands. Your deputy controller White is competent only in crookedness and in conjunction with Herchmer is deliberately doing all that he can by improper advice to yourself and improper action in the Territories to injure your Government and those who support it. I have written plainly because I think it is right that you should understand the situation. I have written without prejudice except for the well-being of the country.[2]

Laurier also inherited the policy of reducing the strength of the force from the previous Conservative government. The new cabinet quickly determined to carry the policy to its logical conclusion of phasing out the police altogether. There were a number of other reasons why the Laurier government was receptive to the idea of eliminating the Mounted Police. After eighteen years in opposition the Liberals were prone to overestimate their ability to put into effect what appeared to them to be rational decisions. The Liberals were at this time the party of provincial rights and had emphasized this plank in their 1896 campaign. One of their basic assumptions was that provincial governments wanted to increase their powers in all fields. This ideological commitment was reinforced by the dependence of the Liberals on Quebec for their parliamentary majority. French Canadians at that time regarded the division of powers set forth in the BNA Act as the chief guarantee of their national survival. It would therefore have been injudicious of the Liberals to have appeared to be tampering in any way with the constitutional division of powers. The Liberals were also in the nineteenth century the party most insistent upon economy in government. What better way to save money than by eliminating an organization staffed almost entirely by loyal Conservatives?

All these attitudes were focused by a memorandum sent to Laurier after the election by James Morrow Walsh, who had been driven out of the police by Sir John A. Macdonald in 1883. Walsh had waited thirteen years to repair his self-esteem by humbling the organization which had rejected him.

I have claimed for some time that the large sum expended on the force for the last ten years, for the duty it had and now has to perform, was, and is, a waste of money and an injustice to the tax payers and that the force should be reduced in number and reorganized.

This I said to Sir Richard [Sir Richard Cartwright, Laurier's minister of trade and commerce] previous to our general elections five years ago and said it to Ives about a year and a half ago. Ives asked what reduction I would suggest, I replied to cut the force in two, that five hundred men were sufficient to perform the duties and maintain law and order quite as well as it was being done. Since that time the force has been reduced and Ives informed me last winter that it was the intention of the Government to bring it down to five hundred men.

The force should be reduced and reorganized for two reasons if for no other. 1st – In the interest of economy and the discontinuing of a wasteful expenditure. 2nd – It has for eighteen years been under Tory rule and become what no force of its kind should ever be permitted to be, a political partisan machine which has to a great extent destroyed its usefulness.[3]

The Walsh memorandum was to form the basis for Liberal policy toward the Mounted Police for the next five years, not only because it reflected the government's preconceptions but because it came from a politically reliable source, a friend and confidant of Clifford Sifton, Laurier's minister of the interior, and the party's chief organizer. Laurier delegated all matters concerning western Canada to Sifton as a matter of course. Hence the influence of Walsh's view of the police.

Sir John A. Macdonald had established the tradition that the police reported directly to the prime minister. Officially the situation remained the same under Laurier, but in practice Laurier delegated almost complete control of the force to Sifton. Until his resignation from the cabinet in 1905 all authorizations for action came to the police from Sifton's office. The prime minister had, however, the final word in matters of high policy. The situation was peculiar in some respects. It is not at all clear to what extent Laurier was aware of the control over the police exerted by Sifton. In 1902 the governor-general, the Earl of Minto, recorded a conversation with Laurier which included the following passage:

I also alluded to the manipulation of the Mounted Police by Mr. Sifton, as regards the moving about and billeting of detachments for political purposes. He said as regards any accusation against Mr. Sifton in respect of the manipulation of the Police, he was quite certain that nothing of the sort existed – that the Police was [sic] in his own hands under Fred White his Comptroller, in whom he had the most perfect trust, and that nothing was ever done in connection with the Force except under Fred White's direction. (I did not think it wise to contradict him, but Fred White has assured me on more than one occasion most positively that the manipulation of the N.W.M.P. is absolutely in Sifton's hands – that Sifton takes no advice whatever – and that he himself has almost despaired of being able to carry on the control of the Force. In fact Fred White has to me expressed his utter despondence at the consequences of Sifton's unjustifiable interference). The Force is directly under the Prime Minister's control and legally Sifton has nothing to say to it whatever, but it has been allowed to drift under his influence.[4]

The fact that it was Sifton rather than Laurier who controlled the police was of the utmost importance. As Liberal organizer he was the member of the cabinet most sensitive to public opinion and it was public pressure which ultimately proved the salvation of the police.

Sifton began his term of office with a determination to reduce the size of the Mounted Police as quickly as possible and eventually to eliminate them altogether. The only question was how to do it? Two spectacular murder cases involving Indians had occurred in 1896, reviving fears of an uprising.[5] Public confidence was involved and if the police were to be withdrawn some replacement had to be found. The logical solution seemed to be to replace the police with a military force of some kind. The military was unquestionably a federal responsibility and the constitutional problem would in this way be eliminated. In addition the military already possessed a good deal of experience in aid to the civil power in Canada. By March 1897 it had tentatively been decided to extend the Militia system to the North-West Territories by raising a regiment of five hundred volunteer cavalry.[6] These plans proceeded slowly but by 1899 locations had been chosen for the company headquarters of the volunteer regiment and details of its organization worked out.[7]

At this point, late in 1899, war broke out in South Africa. The men, funds, and equipment set aside for the expansion of the Canadian military into the North-West were immediately diverted into organizing and equipping an expeditionary force. It would appear that even the organizational structure set up for the North-West Territories became the basis for a private regiment of cavalry raised for the South African War, Lord Strathcona's Horse. The majority of the regiment's men were recruited in the Territories and most of the officers came from the Mounted Police, a pattern which the proposed volunteer force would have followed. The war postponed the introduction of the military into the North-West Territories for a few crucial years. By the time the Militia Department had recovered from the effects of the war government policy concerning the police had changed. In 1904 the minister of militia and defence, Sir Frederick Borden, asked White for the plans of the police barracks at Calgary, which he understood were to be turned over for military use. Laurier instructed White to keep the plans and informed Borden that the arrangements had been altered.[8]

The change in policy and the changed attitude on the part of the Liberal government which it reflected were the products of a variety of influences. Even without the intervention of the war it would have been difficult for the government to carry through the planned elimination of the Mounted Police. The plan to replace the police with a military force was based on the false assumption that the role of the police in the Territories was primarily a military one; that the police existed as a deterrent to an Indian war. The assumption was not shared by the residents of the Territories and their protests combined with the lessons of experience gradually converted the government to their point of view. An editorial writer for the Regina *Standard* expressed the general opinion of the people of the Territories when he wrote: 'We would mildly hint to the government the necessity there is for all policemen (this would include officers) being policemen first, and not soldiers doing useless things.'[9]

As soon as the Liberal government took over in 1896 it was confronted by several practical administrative reasons why the police should be retained. The most important of these was the problem of the Yukon. With the discovery of gold in that remote territory in 1894 the Canadian government once again faced a situation similar to the one which had resulted in the creation of the North-West Mounted Police in 1873. Sovereignty had to be asserted and effective administrative control established over an area far from the populated regions of Canada and subject to strong American pressures. It was logical that the Mounted Police should be given the initial responsibility for asserting Canadian control in the Yukon. The pattern of the early years of the force was repeated, with the police functioning as an embryonic government until the regular government departments could establish themselves.[10] In the first months of 1897 there were fifty police in the Yukon. This proved to be only the beginning of the rush and in the summer of that year the number of police had to be increased, first to a hundred, then to two hundred and fifty.[11] The importance of this new field of operations might have seemed an ideal opportunity to withdraw the force from the North-West Territories but in fact it had the opposite effect.[12] Withdrawing from the Territories would have meant transferring training operations to the Yukon and this would have been prohibitively expensive. It cost exactly twice as much to maintain a policeman in the Yukon as it did in the more southerly parts of the country.[13] The lure of the gold mines affected the members of the force who were sent to the Yukon and very few re-enlisted there. The police in the North-West Territories were necessary to provide a pool of trained and experienced men who could cope with the extra difficulties of the gold rush. To train these men and keep them under supervision in the Yukon would have meant tripling or quadrupling police expenditures, a situation the government was not prepared to contemplate.

At the time the Liberals took office the Canadian economy was beginning to come out of a twenty-year depression. The West in particular was entering an equally long boom period. One of the first manifestations of economic recovery in the West was a renewal of railway building on a large scale. The Canadian Pacific built new branch lines, including a major one through the Crow's Nest Pass into southern British Columbia. Two completely new transcontinental systems, the Canadian Northern and the Grand Trunk Pacific, also began to take shape. The railway builders, recalling the part played by the Mounted Police in the building of the original CPR line, requested their assistance once more. The government was anxious to encourage railway construction for both economic and political reasons. They found it impossible to refuse police help for the new lines.[14] Other large business enterprises in the North-West Territories made similar demands. Mining and ranching operations required no new efforts on the part of the police but the owners exerted pressure on the government to maintain the police at their 1896 level. In the fall of 1897, for example, the owner of a coal mine at Anthracite, west of Calgary, found to his consternation that the police were being withdrawn from the town. He wrote to Archibald Stewart, an Ottawa contractor with Liberal connections, to have him use his influence with the government:

We have found the Mounted Police system a God send to us from the start. By its help our camps have been orderly, life and property have been safe, and both Canmore and Anthracite as pleasant places to live in, so far as law and order are concerned, as the best policed city in the Union.[15]

This kind of pressure was effective. Stewart got in touch with Laurier and a month later White wrote to Stewart assuring him that the prime minister had promised co-operation. The mine could count on at least a man or two. 'He instructed me to say to you that, whilst reductions in the strength of the force are absolutely necessary, care will be taken to provide adequate police supervision for the preservation of law and order.'[16] Requests of this kind from men who could be expected to contribute to party funds made it very difficult for the government to withdraw the police from specific locations across the Territories.[17]

The most effective pressure for the retention of the police came from neither special interests nor administrative necessity but from grass roots political sources. Governments in nineteenth-century Canada frequently ignored administrative problems if they were too costly or likely to prove embarrassing to the government. If circumstances were sufficiently compelling they would also occasionally risk offending the business interests which were their sources of campaign funds. But no democratic government, then or now, could afford to ignore the authentic voice of the people, particularly when it spoke with such rare unanimity as in the case of the Mounted Police. Between elections the voters of the North-West Territories made themselves heard by means of such organizations as chambers of commerce, through letters to the editor and newspaper editorials, through the North-West Territories Assembly and, most important of all, through members of parliament and party workers of the party in power. All these sources of information relayed the same message; the government should, if anything, increase the numbers of the police. It would reduce them at its peril. Members of Parliament found it especially hard to resist requests for police detachments from their constituents. Frank Oliver, an important western Liberal and later minister of the interior in Laurier's cabinet, had been one of the most strident critics of the police on political grounds prior to 1896. Within months after the election Oliver was urging Laurier to heed a resolution of the Edmonton Liberal Association asking that no reduction be made in the Mounted Police.[18] This was only the beginning of a steady flow of similar requests from Oliver.[19] Other Liberal politicians followed suit.[20]

The chorus of protest against the attempt to phase out the police was to grow louder every year. Even in 1897 it was of sufficient volume to make the Liberal leaders begin to hedge their bets. They began to look around for a candidate to replace L.W. Herchmer as commissioner. If the opposition died down and it proved possible to eliminate the police, nothing would be lost. If it became apparent that the police would have to be retained Herchmer could be replaced by a politically reliable commissioner. Strangely enough, considering the long reign of the Conservative party, the ideal candidate to replace Herchmer was easily discovered. There were very few adherents of the Liberal party in the force in 1897 but almost by chance one of this small minority had come to Laurier's attention. Shortly after taking office he received a letter from a political confidant in Regina describing the situation of a Mounted Police inspector by the name of Aylesworth Bowen Perry.

Perry was on the point of resigning his commission, Laurier's correspondent reported:

Ce Monsieur est un de nos rares amis parmi les officiers de la police Montée. Tout en restant fidèle à ses principes politiques, il n'en a pas moins réussi, grâce à ses talents et une conduite absolument irréprochable, à commander l'estime et la confiance des chefs de son Département. Il est ancien élève de l'Ecole de Kingston, il a près de 15 années de service dans la police, et est actuellement en charge du poste à Regina. Il a 35 ans; est marié et père de trois enfants.[21]

He went on to say that Perry had studied law in his spare time, passed the bar examination with distinction and wished to resign to practise law. Perry, he recommended, should be appointed crown prosecutor at Ft Macleod since the Liberals needed someone there to look after the interests of the party. A few inquiries would have revealed to Laurier that this description was accurate. There were even one or two points in Perry's favour that the correspondent had omitted. In addition to his other talents he possessed sufficient tact to avoid quarrels with Herchmer, a fact which in itself made him almost unique in the force. He had also graduated first in his class from RMC.

It seems clear that Perry was encouraged by Laurier or Sifton to stay with the police, but there is no direct evidence of it. Perry was promoted to superintendent a few months after the Liberals took office. The following year he was given the choicest assignment the force had to offer, command of the police contingent sent to London to take part in Queen Victoria's Diamond Jubilee Celebrations. Herchmer was bitterly resentful at being deprived of this plum which clearly indicated that Perry was marked as his replacement.[22] In 1899 Perry was given command of the large and semi-independent police contingent in the Yukon.[23] When the South African War began almost all the officers of the police volunteered for service there. Perry's name was not on the list of those who indicated a desire to go.[24] Commissioner Herchmer decided to go to South Africa and he was barely out of the country when Sifton ordered Perry back from the Yukon to take command of the police.[25]

A crucial point had been reached. The decision to appoint Perry commissioner marked a definite change in the Liberal government's policy concerning the police. Early in 1900 was the only time when a decision to withdraw the police from the North-West Territories would have been politically possible. The government could have pleaded that the men of the force were urgently needed in South Africa. As it was, so many of the force volunteered that police strength in the Territories sank to three hundred and forty-nine all ranks, the lowest it had been since 1884.[26] The difficult problem of what to do with several hundred unemployed policemen would also have been solved since most of them could have been absorbed into the Canadian contingents for South Africa. The uncertainty of the situation was expressed by White in a letter to a former officer of the force who had volunteered his services to the police for the duration of the war:

I am unable to say what will be done with the Force, or rather the remnant that will be left after Steele has taken the men he wants; the Government may possibly decide to avail themselves of the opportunity of reducing the strength. Personally I think this is unlikely, but so far I have received no instructions.[27]

The order placing Perry in command came exactly a month after this letter was written. It included instructions to recruit men to fill the vacancies left by the South African volunteers.[28] The government had committed itself to the continued existence of the police at least until provincial autonomy came along.

The future of the Mounted Police now rested with the new commissioner. He would either preside over its dissolution or see it become a permanent part of the Canadian scene. By the time he retired twenty-three years later the latter alternative had become an accomplished fact. The old North-West Mounted Police with its regional identity had become a national police force, the Royal Canadian Mounted Police. Most of Perry's career as commissioner is beyond the scope of this study but the first five years, culminating in the agreements to continue the services of the police in the new provinces after 1905, is central to it. Perry carried out a more difficult assignment in the years 1900-5 than any of his predecessors. With a force which was under strength he managed to cope with the enormous influx of settlers to the prairies and the corresponding increase in crime. The magnitude of his achievement and that of the police under his command can be seen in the fact that while the number of police remained the same, the number of criminal cases handled rose from less than a thousand in 1900 to over four thousand in 1904.[29]

For the most part the increase in crime was due to the increase in population and caused no essentially new problems for the force. The increased number of cases could be dealt with adequately by overhauling existing procedures. To improve the effectiveness of the limited number of men available, Perry increased the proportion of non-commissioned officers to constables.[30] The old plan for a detective branch was revived, this time with success. The government went so far as to authorize extra pay for men on detective duty.[31] This was an important step. The few men initially assigned duty as detectives developed eventually into the Criminal Investigation Branch of the force. Perry also made some important changes in administrative procedures. Several types of regular reports were eliminated.[32] Reporting of individual criminal cases was dropped from the monthly reports and replaced by a system of crime reports with an individual file for each case.[33] These changes all helped the police cope with the increased number and complexity of cases.

Inevitably new problems appeared along with the intensification of the old ones. One such new task which the police considered of primary importance was the assimilation of settlers who arrived from outside the country. The majority of those who took up land in the North-West Territories during the great wheat boom fell into this category. Eastern Europeans (mostly Ukrainians, always referred to by contemporaries as 'Galicians') and Americans made up the two largest immigrant groups. The police were particularly careful to impress upon new settlers that the laws of their adopted country were different from those they had left behind and that obedience to Canadian law would be strictly enforced. In the case of European settlers the police emphasized explanation of the rules because they believed that the laws of most eastern European countries provided their citizens with an imperfect grasp of what Canadians considered right and wrong. In settlements where Americans predominated the emphasis was on enforcement. Describing two such settlements in the District of Assiniboia an officer reported:

The settlers and residents of Carlyle and Arcola are chiefly Americans, a large proportion of them being single men, who are imbued with the American western idea of law and order, and consequently will have to be taught that they cannot do as they like on this side of the line.[34]

The police felt, rather smugly, that American law might be all right but that Americans were not used to seeing it properly enforced. The technique for impressing these facts of western Canadian life upon new arrivals is well illustrated in the instructions issued by the commissioner for handling the Barr Colonists, a group of English immigrants who founded the present city of Lloydminster:

The Government is anxious that advice and assistance should be given to these colonists. The police must be especially active in aiding the new settlers to overcome their difficulties. They must establish friendly relations, carefully explain the law without resorting to harsh measures, and give them general advice.[35]

The police had no doubts about their ability to convert immigrants into satisfactory Canadian citizens. Reporting on a small American settlement on the Canadian side of the international boundary, Superintendent R.B. Deane wrote:

They live in Canada but get everything from the United States and most likely they still believe they are American citizens and do not intend to abide by Canadian laws unless they are told to. No doubt a detachment of N.W.M. Police at that point will soon settle the matter.[36]

In communities where immigrants mingled with previous arrivals cultural differences often produced misunderstandings. In these cases the police took pains to expose accusations based on nothing firmer than national stereotypes.[37] It is hard to assess the extent to which the police influenced the attitudes of the newcomers to law and order. There is little evidence, however, that immigrant groups were anything but law abiding. The police watched their progress carefully and were convinced they would make good citizens.

The other major problem of the first few years of the new century was in fact the reappearance of an old problem – stock theft. Livestock came into the North-West Territories at this time in very large numbers. In May 1901 Superintendent Deane reported that 3095 head of cattle were brought into Lethbridge district from Manitoba and 1440 from the United States.[38] The opportunities to steal a cow or a horse increased enormously at a time when the patrol system was being cut back for lack of men. There were additional complicating factors. Homesteaders were beginning to crowd the large ranchers in southern Alberta and a state of considerable tension developed between the two groups.[39] No violence occurred but the mutual hostility found expression in cattle and horse stealing by both sides.

Evidence was exceedingly difficult to gather in cases of stock theft. If a man was found in possession of horses or cattle bearing another man's brand he could claim that they had strayed into his herd. Legally this did not absolve the possessor of the missing animals but if the police refused to accept this explanation the accused could almost always find several friends or employees who would swear in court that this was the case. The efforts of the police to enforce the law strictly were hampered in the case of stock theft by the attitude of Judge Charles B. Rouleau. Rouleau took the curious position that the police should treat all cases of farmers and ranchers appropriating stray animals as misunderstandings and leave them to be settled out of court by the parties involved.[40] The judge, whose intention was undoubtedly to try to ease the burden on the police and on the courts, should have been able to see that such an attitude would have the opposite effect. Cases became longer and more complex and a climate of fear and uncertainty developed. There was talk in the newspapers of the possibility of vigilante justice and lynchings.[41] Even White wrote despondently to Sifton: 'At times I think a Vigilance Committee, shorn of all the sinuosities of legal technicalities, is the only effective court of trial for cattle and horse thieves.'[42]

Fortunately none of Rouleau's colleagues on the bench shared his views on the proper approach to the problem of stock theft.[43] Rouleau himself evidently changed his attitude shortly afterward. White requested that Sifton speak to him about cases of this kind and perhaps this is what changed his attitude.[44] Perhaps he was overruled by his judicial colleagues. Whatever happened the problem eased somewhat after 1901 and there was no further talk of lynchings. Short-handed as they were in 1901 because of the South African War, the police had come uncomfortably close to losing control of the situation.

The new problems encountered by the police after the turn of the century had a good deal to do with the government's decision not to withdraw the force from the North-West Territories. Those members of the cabinet who were directly concerned with the police came gradually to the realization that getting rid of the force would create more serious problems than it would solve. Sifton's attitude in particular underwent a marked change. Up to the end of 1901 his communications with White were confined to direct orders, issued in a suspicious and almost harsh manner. They were concerned almost entirely with manipulating the police to obtain the maximum political advantage. The following message to White is typical of the period 1897-1902:

I have been out visiting Lethbridge and the Mormon settlements there and have decided to withdraw order for withdrawal of men from Mormon settlements. Telegraph the Commanding Officer to allow the men to remain as they are until I get to Ottawa when I will decide what is to be done.[45]

By about 1902 Sifton was beginning to take an interest in the operations of the police and to consult White and Perry about them. He became less and less concerned with the patronage side of police affairs. When White asked permission to establish some new detachments north of Edmonton in 1904 Sifton replied:

I am quite satisfied to let you go on and exercise your own judgment. I think it is necessary that a good deal should be done in the direction suggested. The keeping of order is the first consideration, and I shall not censure you for extravagance in doing anything you conceive to be necessary.[46]

Sifton had gained an appreciation of the value of the police apart from their narrowly political uses. In 1904 he recommended to Laurier that the police establishment in the North-West Territories be increased by one hundred men.[47] This is not to say that political considerations were no longer in the mind of the minister of the interior. He had discovered that the long-term political advantages of retaining the police outweighed any possible advantages to be derived from withdrawing them. In a letter to Sifton a Liberal senator, L.G. Power, summed up this view of the police:

If I may be permitted to trespass on territory which is regarded as yours, I wish to say that I feel very strongly that it is desirable that the N.W. Mounted Police should be increased to its original strength – one thousand. Looking at the vast influx of strangers into the territories, at the increase in the duty to be performed by the Police and the absorption of 300 men by the Yukon, I think that everyone who knows about the existing conditions in the North-West must feel that the addition of 200 to the existing strength would be about the least that could be made. I am satisfied also that the strengthening of the forces of law and order to this extent would be exceedingly popular in the region directly affected and would not be the subject of criticism elsewhere.[48]

This sort of political calculus was Sifton's speciality and it was obvious that there was much to gain and little to lose. The increase in the numbers of the police took place in time for the general election of 1904.

The increase in strength takes on added significance when it is realized that by this time the Liberal government was fully committed to granting provincial autonomy by 1905.[49] The subject had been debated more or less seriously for five years but the actual negotiations between the federal government and the government of the North-West Territories did not begin until 1905. The basis for the discussion was the contention of the territorial government, accepted in principle by the federal government, that the new provinces should be given institutions and powers analogous to those granted by the British North America Act to the original provinces. Within this general framework both governments had specific and to some extent contradictory aims, which meant that a good deal of hard bargaining would take place. Laurier wanted two things above all from the negotiations; continued federal control of the public lands in the North-West and school legislation which would allow a tax-supported Roman Catholic separate school system. The concessions he could offer in return for the achievement of these aims included the continued services of the Mounted Police.

As it turned out the negotiations did not mention the police at all, although the North-West Territories government always acted on the assumption that the police would continue as before. It is true that other aspects of the negotiations, especially the schools question, may have distracted the attention of the public, but this does not fully explain why the question of the police, involving as it did a fundamental constitutional right of the new provinces, received so little attention. From the available evidence it would appear that the subject was avoided by mutual consent. The Territorial delegates were reluctant to bring it up for fear that a discussion might force the federal government to take a firm position and find reasons why the police should not be maintained. The federal government also wished to avoid raising thorny constitutional points. Perry reported to White a conversation with Sifton to this effect. 'In his [Sifton's] opinion there is no solution which will be satisfactory. He thought the whole subject bristled with difficulties. He offered no solution but expressed himself as opposed to the establishment of a large force of Mounted Infantry.'[50] The Alberta and Saskatchewan Acts which created the new provinces made no specific mention of law enforcement.

Once elections were held and the new provincial governments formed the police waited expectantly to be relieved of their duties in the Territories. The provincial governments, however, remained silent until Laurier tired of waiting and took the initiative. In identical letters to premiers Walter Scott and A.C. Rutherford, Laurier announced that he was sending White to arrange an understanding on the transfer to the provinces of the responsibilities handled by the North-West Mounted Police:[51]

particularly in relation to the administration of justice and the maintenance of prisoners. ... We at Ottawa are anxious to meet you in as generous a spirit as may be found possible, but you must gradually, if not immediately, accept the natural and constitutional heritage of all Provinces, and pay the cost thereof.[52]

The last phrase is the key to the whole letter. What it signified was that Ottawa was willing to maintain the police in Alberta and Saskatchewan but the provinces must pay. If they did not, other provinces would soon demand similar concessions.

Once this point was clearly understood it was not at all difficult to reach an agreement which would evade the barriers raised by the British North America Act. Only two changes in the existing situation were necessary. The attorney-general of each province replaced the federal minister of justice as the source of legal authority and advice for the police. The two new provinces agreed to pay $75,000.00 annually for the services of the force. This sum amounted to about one-third of the actual cost of maintaining the police. It was more than a token payment but certainly a bargain by any standards. The federal government agreed to maintain the police at a strength of at least five hundred men in the provinces. The initial agreement was for a period of five years. This was not a deadline in any sense and the agreements were renewed every five years until 1917 when they were cancelled due to the shortage of recruits caused by the war. The arrangement worked very well on the whole with little friction between the two levels of government over the police. For fifteen years after 1917 the provinces maintained their own police. In 1932 and 1933 the Royal Canadian Mounted Police absorbed all the provincial police forces except those of Quebec, Ontario, and British Columbia. Newfoundland in 1949 and British Columbia in 1956 abandoned their provincial police forces in favour of a contract arrangement with the RCMP. The pattern which had evolved during the first thirty years of the history of the North-West Mounted Police had reasserted itself.

PART II

SPECIFIC PROBLEMS AND RESPONSES

6

'The feelings and manners of a gentleman': Social class in the NWMP

The traditional distinctions in military organizations between commissioned and other ranks originated in the social gulf between the classes from which the leaders and the led were recruited.[1] Military bodies, at least until class lines began to blur in the last century or so, reflected in an exaggerated way the societies from which they were drawn. The officers were gentlemen in the eighteenth-century meaning of the term while the other ranks were drawn from the lowest reaches of the social order and often were, in Wellington's phrase, the scum of the earth. A study of the social background of the officers and men of the North-West Mounted Police reveals that to a considerable extent the traditional military pattern was followed. Officers and men were by and large drawn from different social classes, and ideas about class played an important and explicit part in the training and organization of the force. The major difference between the police and most military organizations of the day was that because of the élite nature of the police, constables and non-commissioned officers did not represent the lowest element of the Canadian social hierarchy. In the three decades after the founding of the police significant changes took place in the social composition of the force. An examination of these changes reveals a good deal, not only about the police, but about the society of which they were a part.

From a numerical point of view the officers of the Mounted Police were an insignificant group. At no time in the period under consideration did they number more than fifty-five men and during the first decade of the existence of the force there were scarcely more than two dozen at any one time. Even these figures are slightly padded by the inclusion of medical officers.[2] Yet few groups of similar size have been as influential in any period of Canadian history. In 1887 a doctor from Ft Macleod wrote to a government official asking to be appointed surgeon in the Mounted Police. The doctor then indicated his second choice:

If there is no hope to entertain as Surgeon for the Mounted Police I beg as a favour that you will assist me in preparing the path for the place as Senator; which position I dare say I can fulfill to the satisfaction of all classes of the population of the Territories.[3]

This unusual set of priorities, while it no doubt exaggerates considerably, conveys some of the prestige which surrounded officers of the Mounted Police in the North-West Territories. That the officers enjoyed power commensurate with their influence should be clear from previous chapters. They not only controlled law enforcement but exercised a powerful influence on the entire range of administrative policy in the North-West. Because of their power and prestige they were a potent force in moulding the political and social ideas of the people of the Territories. It is therefore important to examine who they were in order to assess the way in which they influenced the social and political development of the Canadian West.

Upon examination, the officers of the police emerge as a fairly cohesive group in the sense that it is possible to speak of a typical officer of the force. The typical officer of the period 1873-1905 was Canadian-born, drawn from the governing élite of eastern Canada, Anglican or Roman Catholic in religion, almost certainly with military experience and training, and frequently with a legal background. A survey of the nationalities of officers as of May 1894, showed that thirty-eight of fifty were born in Canada. Of the twelve non-Canadians, six had been born in Britain, five in India, and one in Jamaica. One of the latter group had come to the country as an infant and probably should be considered as one of the Canadian group. Most of the other non-Canadians had spent a number of years in the country before joining the police. Only two had come directly from England to take up their commissions.[4] It may safely be said that at least eighty per cent of the officers were Canadian at any one time in the first three decades of the Mounted Police. This fact contradicts a belief widely held at the time and perpetuated by some historians of the force that many, if not most, of the officers were English gentlemen. It is easy enough to see how such a tradition could develop. Most people in the upper levels of Canadian society at this time looked to English society as a model for their life style. Few police officers would have been offended at being mistaken for a member of the English gentry.

The myth of the English officer was not due to a disproportionate number of non-Canadians in senior positions. In 1894 three of the eleven superintendents and seven of the thirty-one inspectors were British.[5] The assistant commissioner at this time had been born in Jamaica but had lived in Canada since early childhood. Three of the five commissioners of the police to 1905 were born in the United Kingdom. These three, French, Macleod, and Herchmer, all played very important parts in shaping the character of the force but it would be misleading to think of the last two as British. Macleod came to Canada at an early age and, as we have seen in an earlier chapter, his appointment was welcomed on the grounds that he was a Canadian. There is perhaps more reason to assume that Herchmer, educated in England and for a time an officer in the British Army, should be grouped with the non-Canadians. But Herchmer's family background appears to have been a more important influence than his place of birth. There is no indication that Herchmer ever thought of himself as other than Canadian. Even more significant is the fact that when Herchmer was under attack in the 1890s his enemies made no mention of his English origins. Had Herchmer been generally considered to be British there is no doubt that his attackers would have attempted to use it against him.

Canadian attitudes toward Britain in this period were ambivalent but very pronounced. On the one hand most English-speaking members of the Canadian élite were fiercely attached to the connection between Canada and the mother country. But their imperialism was a manifestation of an intense nationalism which sought a position of equality for Canada within the Empire.[6] On the practical level these complex attitudes meant that although Britain remained the model in most areas of life, individual Englishmen in positions of authority in Canada were frequently the objects of a deep resentment and suspicion. Canadians tended to regard such people as a threat to their status as first class citizens of the Empire. In 1888 an immigration officer of the Canadian government who acted as a recruiting agent for the police at Winnipeg, W.C.B. Grahame, offended Canadian sensitivities by suggesting that the police should recruit in England. To this suggestion the Ottawa *Free Press* replied:

one would imagine that Captain Grahame could find plenty of recruits in Canada without importing English dudes. If we are to have "Canada for the Canadians" why send to England for troopers when Canadians can be obtained? The recruiting of the mounted police force with strangers who have no sympathy with Canada, who know nothing of the country and who imagine that all their follies and vices should be condoned because "they are English don't cher know" has been a fruitful cause of trouble in the past, and if the management of the force is left to Captain Grahame and Mr. Herchmer the outlook for the future is not promising.[7]

A similar attitude lay behind Nicholas Flood Davin's several attempts in Parliament to limit the choice of officers for the police to promotions from the ranks and graduates of the Royal Military College, Kingston.[8]

When the government in 1894 did make one of its rare appointments of an Englishman to a commission in the police the reaction was immediate and vigorous. The *Canadian Military Gazette* objected to the appointment on the grounds that it was due to the influence of the governor-general, Lord Aberdeen. Such appointments were bad for morale. 'We could have understood the appointment of a graduate of the Royal Military College or of an officer with a record in the Militia; but for this appointment of a rank outsider there can be no excuse.'[9] These sentiments were echoed by the Toronto *Telegram*:

Inspectorships in the Mounted Police ought not in a country like Canada to be the reward of individuals whose possession of political influence is no proof of merit. Outsiders who have just been boosted into positions of command on the force may be all that officers should be, but they reach their positions by the wrong road. Most of the policemen are Canadians and many of them must be at least the equals in education of the political favorites sent up to control them. The force could develop men to fill vacancies in the upper ranks, but influence at Ottawa is now the key to inspectorships that should be within the reach of merit.[10]

The language of these protests would appear to leave them open to the interpretation that the writers objected to the use of political influence as such. This was not the case. It was well known that all appointments involved political influence and objections were raised only in those cases involving the appointment of Englishmen.

These strong public prejudices had the effect of keeping the leadership of the Mounted Police Canadian. The original group of officers appointed on the formation of the police in 1873 contained a higher proportion of non-Canadians than at any time in the subsequent history of the force. Appointments made after 1873 were almost entirely Canadian. The police caught the public imagination very quickly, partly as a result of the publicity received during the 1874 march westward. The public recognized the Mounted Police almost at once as something uniquely Canadian and governments were well aware of the political dangers involved in giving commissions to outsiders. By the early 1880s a definite policy regarding recruitment and promotion of officers had taken shape, a policy which was to last until the end of the period under discussion and beyond. In order of priority, officers were to be drawn from among graduates of the Royal Military College, officers of the Active Militia of Canada, and the non-commissioned officers of the force itself.[11] Of these three sources the Militia was at first the most important. The Militia represented the old pattern of political and social influence and declined steadily as a source of police officers. With the passage of time more and more officers came from the other two groups, reflecting the major socio-political trends of Victorian times. Royal Military College graduates represented technical excellence and ability whereas promotions from the ranks were a response to the growing emphasis on democracy.

These tendencies were strengthened by the operational experience of the force. RMC graduates and officers promoted from the ranks proved themselves more effective than others in the day-to-day duties of the police. The Royal Military College attracted many of the best of the country's youth and gave them an education of very high quality. Successive commissioners of the force were enthusiastic about the performance and potential of the RMC graduates in the police.[12] By 1900 there were seven representatives of the school among the officers of the police. Their influence was greater than their numbers would suggest since the seven included the commissioner and three superintendents, none of the thirteen officers drawn from the Militia at this time holding a rank above that of inspector.[13] By 1903 the number of RMC graduates had risen to eleven, almost a quarter of the officers of the force.[14]

Those officers promoted from the ranks had the advantage of long experience with the problems encountered by the police in the North-West. Some possibility of promotion within the force was necessary to sustain morale and the commissioner and comptroller exerted all their influence to ensure that as many officers as possible were chosen from the ranks.[15]

The fact that new criteria for officer recruitment tended to replace the old did not mean a change in the social standing of the officer corps as a whole. RMC graduates were gentlemen by training and were drawn from the same élite social group as Militia officers. Furthermore, the police always attracted a fairly large number of well-educated men of good family into the ranks as constables. It was from this group that promotions generally came. Recommending a man for promotion in 1875, Commissioner French wrote:

Staff Constable Norman is a B.A. of Trinity College, Dublin, (his father being a Q.C. there) – he left a good situation in the G.T.R. offices at Toronto to join this Force, in the hope that attention to duty and good conduct combined with a good education might eventually lead to promotion to a position more in accordance with his birth and education...[16]

Those officers promoted from the ranks therefore had no difficulty adapting themselves to the social standards required of an officer of the Mounted Police. By the first years of the twentieth century promotions from the ranks had become the norm and appointments to commissions from outside the exception. As early as 1896 the largest single group of officers, seventeen of forty-one, had entered the force as constables. In 1902 Sifton ordered that several vacancies were to be filled by promotions from the ranks and wrote to White: 'If recommendation comes from Sir Wilfrid on any other lines I wish you would acquaint him with my views and ask him to let the matter stand until I have seen him.'[17]

One final consideration governed the composition of the officer corps of the Mounted Police. This was the ever-present necessity to provide representation for all those regional, ethnic, and religious groups which were important in Canadian politics. The balance among these groups in the police bears a strong resemblance to that achieved in federal cabinets in this period, indicating that the same sort of political forces were at work. A report of 1894 showed that of the officers in the force at that time; twenty-five were from Ontario, ten from Quebec, three from Nova Scotia, two from New Brunswick, one from British Columbia, seven from Manitoba, and two from the North-West Territories.[18] The over-representation of the western provinces is natural considering the nature and location of the police. Within the regional groups there were other subtleties to be considered. English-speaking Roman Catholics, for example, had to be represented. In 1895 one Father McDonagh wrote to John Costigan, Minister of Marine and Fisheries in Mackenzie Bowell's government, to remind him that a commission in the police had been promised to a Catholic. 'Would you kindly as the representative of our people see that we get fair play which means at least in this matter the promised appointment.'[19] In this case the appointment did go to the man recommended by Costigan.

Inevitably the question of French-Canadian representation on the force was a delicate problem. Representation there had to be but how many? The police found it useful to have a few French-speaking officers to cope with Métis communities where the population was predominantly French-speaking also. Three or four French-Canadian officers sufficed for these purposes and those in charge of the police seem to have been reluctant to include any more. About half the officers listed as being representative of Quebec were English-speaking. With this token representation French-Canadians appear to have been satisfied. In the early years of the police there was some pressure to increase their number but once the pattern was firmly established, Quebec politicians were content to keep the number of commissions the same.[20] The number of commissions held by French-Canadians was directly related to the amount of pressure exerted by Members of Parliament and cabinet ministers from Quebec. There was little public demand in the province to encourage them to exert more pressure.

Relations between French and English-speaking officers within the police appear to have been good. A French-Canadian officer, who was one of the original members of the force and whose career in the police lasted almost thirty years, Superintendent Sévère Gagnon, left a diary of the 1874 expedition which reveals something of this. In spite of the fact that many members of the force were Orangemen and ostentatiously displayed Orange emblems on 12 July, Gagnon did not feel out of place. When the expedition split into two groups Gagnon expressed his regret at parting with many good friends.[21] In 1890 when Commissioner Herchmer was under attack, one of the charges made against him in the newspapers was that he was anti-French Canadian. He indignantly rejected the charge, which is perhaps only to be expected.[22] More significant is the fact that the charge was not repeated in the exhaustive catalogue of misdeeds attributed to Herchmer before the commission of inquiry.

The end result of all the factors which affected the recruiting of police officers was a group of men who had rather definite ideas about the structure of society in western Canada and their place in that structure. The idea of a classless frontier society was completely foreign to the officers of the Mounted Police. They saw the Canadian West as having a definite upper class. This élite was most readily identifiable in the larger urban centres where such institutions as gentlemen's clubs existed to give concrete expression to ideas about social leadership. Police officers considered themselves very much a part of the upper class of western Canada. In 1905 Superintendent G.E. Sanders, the commanding officer at Calgary, wrote to the Commissioner to ask if the force would pay his membership fees in the Alberta Club which he intended to join, 'because I think it would be beneficial to the service.'[23] Sanders was already a member of the Ranchmen's Club, Calgary's oldest and most exclusive, because the Mounted Police officer in command at Calgary automatically received an honorary membership. The Comptroller sympathized with Sanders but told the Commissioner he could never get such an expediture past the Auditor-General.[24] Police officers expected, and were expected by the community, to be social leaders. In 1897 Commissioner Herchmer complained that officers without private means found it impossible to do the entertaining expected of them.[25] On another occasion one of Laurier's political correspondents wrote to ask that Inspector F.J.A. Demers, in charge of the detachment at Battleford, be promoted to superintendent. 'The position he holds, commanding the force, makes it much more expensive for him as he has to stand the expense of entertaining as an officer in command is expected to do.'[26]

Indications of the social attitudes of the officers of the police appear in many other places. After his inspection of the force in 1875, Major-General Selby-Smyth recommended distinctive uniforms for the officers. 'I think a neat full-dress uniform should be adopted, not costly, but such as they could feel becoming their position in society. I believe the officers desire this improvement.'[27] The general made several other recommendations but this was the only one the government was prepared to put into effect immediately.

The issue which most clearly revealed the social ideas of the police officers was that of officers' servants. When the force was organized it was intended that each inspector would be entitled to one servant and each superintendent two. The servants were to be constables who would receive extra pay and other privileges in return for this duty.[28] This system worked well enough until about the turn of the century when increased demands on the police made it impossible to divert constables from their regular duties. The matter came to a head in the Yukon, where Assistant Commissioner Z.T. Wood began the practice of enlisting Japanese servants as special constables. The government, under pressure from anti-oriental agitation in British Columbia, put an end to the practice.

The inability to secure enough constables as servants was partly due to the rising spirit of democracy and partly to the élite nature of the force. Most constables felt that this kind of duty was beneath their dignity. None of these considerations altered the views held by the officers about their rightful position in society. In 1907 a board of officers was convened to consolidate the rules and regulations of the force. The board made the following report on the servant question. 'We consider that it is neither desirable, reputable nor even possible for an officer to perform his duty to the public unless he is provided with some sort of domestic assistance.' The board recommended hiring special constables for this purpose. 'There are precedents for this in the case of the Royal Irish Constabulary and the Royal Engineers, whose men are too valuable to be diverted from their regimental duties.'[29] A year later the comptroller, always a keen judge of which way the political winds were blowing, pronounced upon the board's recommendation. In a letter to the commissioner, White said that while he sympathized with the officers, he saw no solution to the problem:

I have given the subject a good deal of thought, and, whilst I do not think we shall be able to return to the status of detailing a constable to each officer for domestic purposes, I hope we may find it possible to recommend a cash allowance.[30]

Social and political trends were running contrary to the thinking of the police officers and officers' servants quietly disappeared from the force in the first decade of the twentieth century.

Most officers who joined the police remained with the force for the remainder of their active lives. Those officers who left to take up other pursuits generally moved into high-status occupations, a fact which tends to support the ideas of the officers themselves about their social position. Superintendent James Walker left the police to manage the giant Cochrane Ranch in southern Alberta. Commissioner Macleod left about the same time to become a judge. Superintendent Sam Steele transferred to the British Army during the South African War and retired as a major-general. Superintendent G.E. Sanders, who left the police in 1908, served as magistrate in Calgary until 1932 with time out for service during the First World War as commanding officer of the Second Canadian Pioneer Battalion. He ended his career as a member of the Unemployment Relief Commission from 1932 to 1936.[31] Even Superintendent J.M. Walsh, who left the police under a cloud during the Sitting Bull episode, prospered in business and maintained his social standing to the point where Clifford Sifton appointed him commissioner of the Yukon during the gold rush.

As a group the officers of the Mounted Police were élitist, sure of their position in society and, as such men tend to be, secure in their strongly held opinions and attitudes. They came to the North-West determined to mould it according to their image of what Canadian society should be. For these men the frontier environment was not an active force in the shaping of the social order, but a passive framework within which social ideas could be worked out. The frontier was a blank slate upon which men could trace the lines that pleased them. The existing state of things in the early years of settlement was not as important a reality as the one which would eventually be created; it existed largely as a series of obstacles to be overcome and then forgotten. General Selby-Smyth noted in his 1875 report that the men of the Mounted Police were contented in spite of the primitive conditions under which they lived. He felt that their satisfaction came from their future hopes. 'above all they have the conscious knowledge that they are pioneers in a rich and fertile territory, magnificently spacious though still strangely solitary and silent, which at no distant time will re-echo with the busy life of a numerous and prosperous population...'[32] The police did not celebrate the conditions of frontier life but spent most of their time trying to ensure that they disappeared as soon as possible. The officers of the force were never inhibited in their determination to do what they considered to be the right thing by considerations of democracy in the sense of the absolute will of the majority. Thus the native peoples and other minorities could be protected. The emphasis instead was on equality before the law, a concept which is not necessarily democratic. It was this concept which allowed the police to combine an élitist view of society with a responsiveness to a democratic political system.

The figures in Table 2 reveal some significant differences between the national backgrounds of the non-commissioned ranks and those of the officers. The proportion of British-born was much higher in the ranks. The percentage of British recruits rose steadily to a high point of 50 per cent in 1890 where it remained for the balance of the decade. The sharp drop in the number of British recruits after 1900 was due to the demands of the South African War, although there are indications that a decline was beginning before the war broke out. Unfortunately,

Table 2: Birthplace of Recruits 1873-1902

	1873[a]	1877-8[b]	1887-8	1889	1890-1	1895-7	1900-2
Maritime Provinces	14	18	17	8	29	5	139
Quebec	34	48	5	9	8	6	23
Ontario	115	163	92	38	55	16	119
Manitoba, BC, and NWT	4	10	11	14	18	12	9
Total Canadian	167	239	125	69	110	39	290
Percentage of total	69	65	55	46	41	42	81
UK	65	70	90	69	133	45	56
Percentage of total	27	20	40	46	50	48	16
Other or unknown	13	41	11	12	24	8	12
Total	245	350	226	150	267	92	358

[a] GAI, Papers re North-West Mounted Police compiled by Eleanor Luxton
[b] PAC, RG 18, B-4 (all figures 1877-1902)

figures on the number of men from different national backgrounds who remained with the force are more difficult to find. But returns are available from 1888 and 1895 which throw some light on the question. These figures show that the percentage of non-commissioned officers and constables born in the United Kingdom rises from 33 per cent in 1888 to 61 per cent in 1895 while the percentage of Canadians in the same period drops from 56 per cent to 33 per cent.[33] British-born recruits evidently tended to stay longer with the police than those from Canadian backgrounds.

Why this should have been the case is not entirely clear, but some possible reasons might be advanced. Almost none of the British-born recruits came to Canada with the specific idea of joining the police and none were recruited in Britain. Those who joined the force some years after emigrating to Canada undoubtedly saw it as something of a refuge from a society which was much more mobile and egalitarian than the one to which they were accustomed. The police could provide what most other Canadian occupations lacked in the eyes of someone from the British Isles, an assured status in society. To many Canadian recruits, on the other hand, the police probably represented an opportunity for change and adventure before they settled down, a free ride, and paid introduction to the North-West.

The police were characterized at all times by a very high turnover of personnel in the ranks. Two years after the formation of the force Commissioner French noted that only sixty-eight of the original one hundred and fifty members of the police remained.[34] A pattern had been established which was to last for the first forty years of the history of the police. In the early years a constable could serve out his term and on leaving the force receive a free land grant. Government policy was to encourage the settlement of ex-policemen and in many cases regulations were relaxed to allow constables an early discharge to enable them to put in the year's crop.[35] Substantial numbers of policemen took advantage of this policy and a total of two hundred and seventeen land grants were issued in the first four years of police operations in the West.[36] It was also possible, except for a few years after 1900 when a severe shortage of recruits developed, for a constable to purchase his discharge before his term of engagement in the force was completed.[37] The police had no interest in keeping discontented men as long as there was a plentiful supply of new recruits.

The same philosophy applied to deserters. Deserters accounted for a considerable proportion of the number of men who left the police in any given year. A report on desertions in the decade 1879-89 lists a total of four hundred and eighty-eight in that period. On the average during those years just over 6 per cent of the force left illegally every year although percentages varied from year to year according to changing conditions.[38] Over the whole period from 1873 to 1905 the average desertion rate was probably a little lower since the decade for which figures are available includes the period of the rapid expansion of the force during the 1885 rebellion. The police were less selective in their recruiting at this time and many men who entered the force during the expansion were unsuited to the rigorous demands of Mounted Police life.

The police made no great effort to prevent desertions. The penalties for the offence were not severe, amounting in most cases to a fine or at the maximum a year in prison, and legal action of any kind against deserters was rare. The police only proceeded actively against those deserters who remained within the North-West Territories. Most deserters fled to the United States and many found their way back to eastern Canada. These cases were not prosecuted unless the deserter was incautious enough to brag publicly about his escape. In such a case the deserter's actions might jeopardize future recruiting and the police moved to silence him. The policy regarding deserters was outlined in a memorandum for Laurier by Fred White in 1905:

Your letter to Mr. Macdonald describes exactly the position we have always taken with regard to deserters from the force. Unless (1) a deserter has committed a serious crime, (2) attempts to return to the North West and flout the fact of his being a deserter in the face of members of the force who have loyally continued in the service, or (3) does not [sic] on returning to his home in Eastern Canada abuse the service and boast of his having succeeded in getting out of it by desertion, he is never molested.[39]

The rapid turnover of personnel in the Mounted Police acted as a very efficient process of selection. Incompetents and those who were unhappy in the police were weeded out in short order. The legendary ability of the Mounted Police to accomplish great things with very few men is partly a result of this selection process. Ultimately, of course, the police could be selective in recruiting only because of the number of potential recruits almost always exceeded the requirements of the force. The founding of the North-West Mounted Police coincided with the beginning of the great depression of the late nineteenth century, which lasted until 1896. This meant that for the first twenty-five years of its existence the force was recruiting in a labour market in which jobs of any kind were hard to find. The police could afford to be particular about the type of man they recruited. In a typical recruiting drive in the Maritime provinces in 1900, only one hundred and forty men were accepted out of three hundred and thirty-five applicants.[40] Even in 1903 with recruiting generally suffering from high wages in the West because of the wheat boom, only five of the thirty-five applicants at Winnipeg that year were accepted.[41]

The legally established requirements for entrance to the force were minimal. In theory anyone over the age of eighteen who was physically fit, five feet ten inches or taller, literate in either French or English, and able to ride a horse could join the police. In practice the requirements were much higher. Applicants under the age of twenty-one were rarely accepted and all were well above the level of bare literacy. The majority of those whose applications were rejected were turned down on medical grounds. In fact the percentage of medically unfit, impossible to calculate exactly, was appallingly high, well over half those who applied; an indication of the low standards of diet and medical care common at the time. As was the case with the officers, patronage played a major role in recruiting, although it was less strictly applied in the recruiting of constables. If recruiting had to be undertaken in eastern Canada, politics dominated the proceedings. Government Members of Parliament submitted lists of acceptable candidates in their constituencies and it was from these lists that recruits were selected.[42]

The requirements of patronage did not apply as strongly to recruits who made their own way west and joined at Winnipeg or Regina. The police consequently tried to fill as many vacancies in the ranks as possible in this manner. By

1883 it had become established policy that applicants should make their own way to Winnipeg or Regina.[43] In 1903, faced by a severe shortage of recruits, White was still reluctant to recruit in eastern Canada if it could be avoided. He expressed his reasons in a letter to Perry. 'If we commence we shall have to make a circuit of the country by counties and, as you know, it generally happens that the most undesirable candidate has frequently the strongest influence.'[44] Recruiting in the West had additional advantages. It was cheaper, it discouraged triflers and potential deserters, and it meant that those who joined the police were disabused in advance of some of their more romantic notions about life on the frontier.

Motives for joining the force varied widely but the desire for adventure was undoubtedly a prominent one. Fred Bagley, who enlisted as a trumpeter in 1874, spoke for many when he wrote:

I had always been a close student of the works of James Fenimore Cooper, and imagined that life in the N.W.M.P. would be one grand round of riding wild mustangs (I was always an expert horseman), chasing whisky traders and horse thieves, potting hostile savages, and hobnobbing with haughty Indian Princes and lovely unsophisticated Princesses. Alas! A few years in the service of the force sufficed to dissipate much of this glamour.[45]

That many of Bagley's less articulate contemporaries shared his motives is indicated by the high proportion of recruits from urban and essentially sedentary backgrounds (Table 3). The police consistently regarded farm boys as the most desirable type of recruit but there were never enough of these to fill more than a fraction of the requirements. The great merit of farmers' sons in the eyes of the police was that they understood the care and management of horses and were generally accustomed to a rural life. In his report on the police in 1875 General Selby Smyth had strongly recommended recruiting men with farm backgrounds for this reason and, he added, 'The decayed gentleman is a failure.'[46] The general need not have worried on this score. Most of the recruits came from a class that was increasing in its vigour and importance in the social scheme. As Table 3 shows, most recruits came from occupations that were rising in the scale of social and economic importance in late Victorian times. If the nineteenth century was the great age of the middle class, the twentieth was to be the age of the lower middle class. In the period under consideration the lower middle class was expanding to include the two groups from which a majority of the police were drawn. These were clerks and skilled workers, whom the Victorians always referred to as 'mechanics.' The growing social and economic importance of these groups and the increased self-confidence that accompanied this growth were re-

Table 3: Former Occupations of Recruits 1873-1902[a]

	1873	1877	1887-8	1889	1890-1	1895-7	1900-2	Average Percentage
Farmers	9	57	61	56	102	33	98	27
Clerks	46	59	13	16	32	12	65	15.6
Police or military	13	37	25	20	15	15	12	10
Skilled workers	43	130	81	41	73	14	123	29
Unskilled workers	–	30	18	–	24	4	23	6
Students or professionals	–	16	20	7	16	10	32	6
Miscellaneous or no previous occupation	39	19	5	1	2	3	8	1
Total	150	348	223	150	264	91	361	100

[a] Figures for 1873 are from GAI, Papers re NWMP compiled by Eleanor Luxton. The figures for the years 1877-1902 are from PAC, RG 18, B-8.

flected in such developments as the extension of the franchise and the rise of the trade union movement. Much of the success of the Mounted Police and their reputation for energetic and impartial law enforcement stemmed from the aware-ness, subconscious perhaps, that they represented the direction in which society was moving.

This awareness was deliberately fostered by those in charge of the police. Heavy stress was laid upon the differences between a Mounted Police constable and a private soldier in the Militia or regular forces. Thus Commissioner French in organizing the police rejected military punishments as degrading. Fines and the threat of discharge he felt were sufficient.[47] French expressed this attitude even more explicitly in one of the first General Orders he issued. 'The Commis-sioner hopes that Sub-Constables of the force will consider themselves policemen, and not Militiamen, and that a proper notion of self-respect will prevent them committing offences which it should be their province to apprehend others for.'[48]

A handbook for the guidance of constables issued in 1889 offered the follow-ing advice:

Towards the attainment of complete police efficiency, it is essential that the members of the force should cultivate the good opinion of the country at large, by prompt obedience to all lawful commands, by pursuing a steady and impartial line of conduct in the discharge of their duties, by their clean, sober and orderly habits, and by a civil and respectful bearing to all classes.[49]

The same kind of admonition appears in a similar volume issued in 1904. 'It should be remembered that the manner of performing small things is what demonstrates the difference between the members of a regular corps and those of an irregular one.'[50]

The efforts of the officers of the police to instill in their men ideas about their social standing were generally successful although the results were sometimes unexpected. In the early years of the force constables were often reluctant to perform the many menial chores necessary for survival. In 1875 a state of near mutiny existed in some divisions because the men objected to spending their time cutting hay and cleaning stables.[51] The reluctance of constables to act as officers' servants reflects the same attitude.

The ideas of police constables about their proper station in life can be seen in their off-duty activities. Requests for recreational equipment included not only such items as footballs, boxing gloves, and baseballs, but cricketing, tennis, and fencing equipment as well.[52] Divisional posts had reading rooms with substantial libraries of books and subscriptions to periodicals. The list of periodicals sent to all posts included about ten Canadian newspapers as well as the *Canadian Illustrated News*, *Punch*, the *Illustrated London News*, the London *Times, Field,* and *Graphic*.[53] Constables and non-commissioned officers frequently organized their own annual balls, which were quite as formal and correct as those of the officers.

There is every indication that the population of the North-West Territories shared the view of the social standing of the police held by members of the force. Every town council which applied for the services of the police gave as a reason the fact that Mounted Police constables commanded greater respect than a man hired locally as town policeman. To some extent this respect was due to the status of the constables as representatives of a powerful law enforcement agency. But it would be a mistake to overlook the fact that the police uniform symbolized a certain minimum social standing as well. The policy of the force was to transfer men quite frequently to prevent undue involvement in local issues; but, even so, ex-policemen, especially non-commissioned officers, moved easily into positions of responsibility in western Canadian communities (see Table 4).

Biographical details are relatively rare for those below the rank of inspector but a few cases for which information is available will serve as examples. Frederick D. Shaw was a Nova Scotian who had worked as a railway clerk for some years and later studied and practised dentistry. Shaw joined the police in 1880 and served until invalided out in 1884, rising to the rank of staff sergeant. On leaving the police he resumed the practice of dentistry at Ft Macleod and later became customs collector and coroner for the area.[55] A.J. Redmond, a sergeant who served in the force from 1899 to 1908, bought the Maple Creek *News* when he left the police and published it until the 1930s. Redmond also served three terms as mayor of Maple Creek between 1914 and 1932.[56] Another expoliceman

Table 4: Occupations of Ex-Mounted Policemen 1893[a]

Occupation	Number	Percentage
Civil servants	23	6
Farmers or ranchers	147	38
Clerks	19	5
Skilled workers	74	19
Small businessmen	32	8
Unskilled workers	50	13
Professionals	13	3
Unknown	31	8
Total	389	100

[a] PAC, RG 18, A-1, vol. LXXX, no. 262

had been mayor of Maple Creek from 1910 to 1913 and still others in the town in this period included the postmaster, the town clerk, a hotel owner, a general merchant, and the owners of both the local lumber-yards.[57]

Social class in the North-West Mounted Police was important, and was perceived as being important at the time, because of the generally accepted beliefs about the relationships between class and criminality. Attitudes toward class in the Mounted Police rested upon twin assumptions: that criminality was largely a lower class phenomenon and that it was important that law enforcement officers be the social superiors of those who broke the law. These were widely-held public assumptions in the age of Victorian respectability. The frontier was assumed to be lawless not because of its physical or economic characteristics, but because it was peopled initially by the lower social groups. Hence Sir John A. Macdonald's expectation that the need for the police would disappear once large-scale settlement took place. The ability of the Mounted Police to live up to the social standards expected of them by the public was a major factor in their success and helps account for the rapid growth of their reputation. The Mounted Police caught the imagination of the public because they were, in terms of social class, close to the popular image of what an ideal police force should be.

7
Patronage and public service: The NWMP and politics

The social standing of the members of the Mounted Police was a product of the way they were recruited and this in turn was linked to the political system of the time. The relationship between the police and political system is a crucial one for any democratic society. This is so because the role of the police is to some extent contradictory. The police control some aspects of public behaviour and yet ultimately the public must control the police. Law enforcement officers must be responsive to the changing demands of the political system and therefore to the elected representatives of the people. But to give politicians in power too much control over the police is to risk having them use law enforcement as an excuse to stifle opposition. In theory police are part of the administrative structure whose only function is to enforce laws and regulations made by others. In practice this remains an ideal situation which can never be fully realized although, other things being equal, a police force is successful to the degree it approaches the ideal. The law is subject to interpretation at several levels and the manner in which the police choose to interpret it is often more important than the provisions of the law itself.

In addition there are many areas of public behaviour not explicitly regulated by law with which the police must concern themselves. Those in charge of the police can manipulate law enforcement in a negative manner without interfering with the way in which the police perform their duties, simply by making police available for some areas and not for others. The question of the proper relationship between the police and the rest of the political system is inevitably a dilemma which can never be solved to the entire satisfaction of all parts of society. A balance must be struck in which the contradictory demands of different parts of society are reconciled as far as possible. In this situation a great deal depends upon the police themselves and what they consider their proper role to be. They must be sufficiently independent to resist the constant pressures from both public and politicians that would destroy their usefulness. On the other hand the police must not become so self-sufficient that they can be unresponsive to legitimate demands. To function effectively the police must represent a broad consensus, not so much of public ideas about the way things are, but of the way they should be. The North-West Mounted Police managed to meet most of these criteria as well as was humanly possible given the prevailing crudities of the Canadian political system in the nineteenth century.

Because the force was a creature of the federal government, its involvement with municipal politics was minimal. The general policy of withdrawing from incorporated towns and cities whenever possible, combined with that of frequent transfers of personnel, discouraged the development of ties between the police and local politics. Municipal politics in the North-West Territories was to a large extent free from close connections to the party system, which also made it easier for the police to remain detached. There is no indication that the force ever took sides in a local election. Requests for police action in a municipality often came from higher levels of government.[1] The tendency was, if anything, for the police to act as a check on the power of the little oligarchies which often ran municipal affairs. In a number of cases this produced conflict between the force and the local power structure.

This was certainly the case in the anti-Chinese riots in Calgary in 1892 (chapter 11). The mayor and the chief of the municipal police used the riots as a test of strength against the Mounted Police; and they lost. The mayor would have liked to allow the riots to run their course and he tried to hinder the attempts of the force to control them. During the smallpox epidemic which gave rise to the riots quarantine camps had been established outside the city limits by the Mounted Police. The town police chief, in an attempt to assert his control over the residents of the camps, blatantly ignored the quarantine regulations. When the Mounted Police tried to stop him, he assaulted the sergeant in charge and dared him to arrest him. The sergeant accepted his challenge and threw him in jail.[2] He was released when the mayor promised to take disciplinary action, although he had no intention of so doing. Instead he threatened to remove prospective witnesses to the incident from the town's welfare rolls if they testified against the police chief.[3] The mayor also refused to prosecute the rioters.[4] He was finally forced to back down when the town's Police Commission requested that the Mounted Police take over law enforcement duties. The Mounted Police did not move into the town but the significant part of the whole incident is that they were available as an alternative for that part of the population of Calgary which did not want to go along with the mayor's high-handed actions.

The attitude of the police in the Calgary case was to avoid becoming embroiled in local politics unless some serious threat to public order was involved. The same attitude came to the surface in rather different circumstances in Ft Macleod in 1900. Sergeant (later Inspector) E.J. Camies had been carrying out the duties of town constable in Ft Macleod in addition to his regular Mounted Police responsibilities. This arrangement was terminated when the town solicitor, one Harris, tried with the co-operation of the town council to use Sergeant Camies to further a case of technically legal, but still blatant, extortion. It began when the sergeant was asked by the council to gather evidence against a well-known prostitute in town. This Camies did with great thoroughness and the woman was prosecuted by Harris on behalf of the town. Harris asked for, and got, a sentence of five months in prison without option of fine.

To this point there was nothing exceptional about the case. But a few days later the woman appealed her sentence to a higher court with Harris now acting as her lawyer. Sergeant Camies then discovered that Harris had not only collected $1600.00 in legal fees from the unfortunate woman for the appeal, but that she had receipts to prove it. Harris also held the mortgage on the house she occupied. Sergeant Camies reported these unsavory proceedings to his superior officer and declined to have anything further to do with the town authorities of Ft Macleod.[5] The officer in charge, Superintendent Howe, was equally disgusted and asked the commissioner for permission to end the arrangement by which the Mounted Police carried out town duties, adding, 'I feel sure that you will agree with me that it is quite impossible for any Constable of the NWM Police who possesses the least degree of respect for himself, or regard for his Corps, to associate with, much less carry out the instructions of such a caricature of a Town Council as this.'[6] The commissioner agreed wholeheartedly and ordered that the enforcement of local by-laws by members of the force should cease. He also made it clear that the town should not be left entirely to the tender mercies of Harris and the council. 'You are therefore requested to instruct Sergeant Camies to carry out the duties placed upon us by the [Police] Act. If to carry out those duties you require to station a detachment in the Town of Macleod you will do so.'[7] The council made several subsequent attempts to renew the old arrangement but were refused.

The police also managed to offend the locally powerful Gaetz family in the town of Red Deer. On two occasions members of the family charged the sergeant in command of the Red Deer detachment with not protecting the respectable portion of the citizenry, by which they meant themselves.[8] In the first instance an investigation revealed nothing improper, but the sergeant in charge was transferred out of deference to local feelings. When the charges were repeated a year later the police investigated more thoroughly and concluded again that there was no substance to the charge. This view was strengthened by an unsolicited report on the situation from P.J. Nolan, the most widely respected criminal lawyer in Alberta at the time, who had been in Red Deer when the complaints were made. Nolan assured the commissioner that the Gaetz family resented the police because the police insisted upon treating them exactly as they did everyone else in the community.[9] Inspector A.E. Snyder, who had carried out the investigation for the police, reached the same conclusion and commented, 'Sergeant Dunning has done his duty in a most impartial manner and I very much doubt if it would be possible to send a man there who would please the *whole* community, and certainly not if he acts and does his duty as we wish him to do.'[10]

The police influenced local politics indirectly by being above the local situation and by providing an alternative to those who wished to turn a town into their personal fiefdom. Public recognition of the usefulness of a police force divorced from the local power structure found expression in the dozens of requests that came in every year for Mounted Police detachments. These sentiments were summed up vigorously, if not grammatically, by a senator from the North-West Territories, W.D. Perley, who wrote in support of a request for a detachment in the town of Wolseley, 'Any policeman appointed [sic] for Casual duty by a magistrate or the Town Corporation, will not be a good policeman like your policemen are, who knows [sic] no one and, beyond civility, cares for no one. Such officers are efficient and do good service.'[11]

The police were even less involved in territorial than in municipal politics. With the exception of the liquor law there was little ambiguity in the legislation of the North-West Territories. In the early years the lieutenant-governor exercised all executive functions and a tradition arose of close informal consultation between the lieutenant-governor and the commissioner. When the elected members of the Legislative Assembly later began to challenge the executive authority of the lieutenant-governor they carefully avoided any mention of the police because they knew they would have to pay heavily for the privilege of controlling law enforcement. The Assembly rarely mentioned the Mounted Police and when it did it took the form of politely worded resolutions urging the federal government to increase the size of the police.[12] Territorial politicians who never mentioned the police as members of the Legislative Assembly developed a sudden and vocal interest in the force as soon as they graduated successfully to federal politics. Senator Perley and Frank Oliver were two of these.

Ottawa was the source of funds, appointments, and promotions for the police and it was within the federal political system that they operated. Requests for patronage, employment in the force, and services of all kinds were channelled through the office of the cabinet minister responsible for the police. The most frequent contacts by far between police and politics were via patronage. Patronage was an inescapable part of the Canadian political scene in the nineteenth century, frequently deplored by public men when their party was in opposition but practised with great thoroughness when they were in office. The police could hardly escape involvement in a system which was generally considered to be an inevitable, if not particularly desirable, part of democratic politics. The smallest details of purchasing and personnel were subject to the dictates of political influence although the police escaped most of the extravagant waste and corruption that marred the performance of other government departments such as Public Works. Patronage operated within certain unwritten but well-defined limits and was rarely a serious handicap to the force.

It is quite safe to say that no officer in the Mounted Police to 1905 received his commission and very few received promotions without the exercise of political influence. Superintendent Deane's entry into the force was typical and is described in some detail in his autobiography. Deane had come to Canada after serving as a captain in the Royal Marines until reductions in that body eliminated all chances of promotion. Deane worked for a time as a clerk in the governor-general's office in Ottawa but the idea of serving with the Mounted Police attracted him more. He applied for a commission and even managed to make his request to Sir John A. Macdonald in person but without success. Deane then had a word with his cousin, T.C. Patteson, who was a power in the Conservative party and editor of the leading Conservative newspaper of the day, the Toronto *Mail.* Patteson wrote a brief note to the prime minister and within a week Deane had his commission.[13] The Macdonald Papers contain many other letters from grateful recipients of commissions in the force which leave no doubt that this was the normal method of gaining entrance to the police as an officer.[14]

Patronage requirements had to be met in the case of promotion from the ranks as well as officers appointed directly to commissions from outside the force. The Conservative prime ministers who led the government after Sir John A. Macdonald's death were mainly concerned with reducing the strength of the police but this did not prevent them from making what few apointments there were in the traditional manner. Sir John Thompson delegated patronage matters to W.B. Ives, President of the Privy Council, while Sir Mackenzie Bowell preferred to handle them himself.[15] The Liberal party more frequently than their opponents professed to be opposed to patronage but in office they used it in the same manner as the Conservatives. Commissions were handed out during Sir Alexander Mackenzie's term of office by Edward Blake, the Minister of Justice.[16] When the Liberals again came to office under Sir Wilfrid Laurier in 1896 patronage reached a new level of thoroughness and efficiency under the control of Clifford Sifton.

Laurier's frequent public pronouncements on the evils of patronage had led comptroller White to believe that under the Liberals politics could be eliminated from the force. He brought the subject up after the 1896 election during his first interview with the new prime minister. Laurier agreed, or appeared to agree, with everything White said and the comptroller had hopes that a new era had dawned for the Mounted Police.[17] He was soon disappointed. The first appointees to the force under the new government were unmistakably party men and they were given their commissions without even the formality of consulting the leadership of the police.[18] Laurier's distaste for the details of patronage simply meant that he delegated them to subordinates, in this case his minister of the interior and chief organizer, Clifford Sifton. Sifton continued to control all patronage matters in connection with the force until 1905 when he left the cabinet, but he seems to have started to lose interest in this sort of detail about 1903.[19]

In cases of promotions from inspector to superintendent the commissioner and comptroller had rather more control than in appointments to commissions. But patronage made its appearance in almost every case. If a vacancy occurred in the superintendent grade the commissioner would usually recommend three or four inspectors whom he considered fit for promotion. This list would then be placed in the hands of the cabinet minister concerned who would make the final choice on the basis of the political influence the respective candidates could command. There were no cases in which the commissioner was ordered to promote an individual he considered unfit. This is not to say that orders for the promotions of individual officers never came from above. Sifton, especially in his first few years as minister of the interior, issued such instructions several times without consulting either the commissioner or the comptroller. As it happened the officers in question proved to be well qualified.[20]

At the other extreme it was very difficult for the commissioner to obtain a promotion for a man who lacked influence. Perry discovered this elementary fact of life a year or so after he became commissioner. At this time he recommended a rather junior inspector for promotion to superintendent. White objected to the promotion, not so much on the grounds of seniority, but because two others had greater political influence. Perry was asked to reconsider and did so. Fortunately for the police there were few incompetents among the officers. The waiting list for commissions in the force was always so long that the formula for acceptance was competence plus influence and not influence alone. There are many examples in the history of the force which demonstrate this fact. One will suffice here. When a new assistant commissioner had to be chosen in 1892 it was possible to choose from several well-qualified men. The appointee, Superintendent J.H. McIlree, possessed strong political support as well as a Sandhurst education and the distinction of having been the first Mounted Police officer promoted from the ranks.[21]

Patronage was applied almost as thoroughly to the recruitment and promotion of constables and non-commissioned officers. The force could sometimes avoid patronage requirements by recruiting in the North-West Territories and tried to do so as much as possible, but there were times when not enough men appeared at Regina to fill the vacancies in the force. When this happened recruiting would be carried out in Winnipeg. This meant the appointment of an agent who had to be politically acceptable, but at least this did not affect the force directly. The police recruiting agent in Winnipeg until 1890 was W.C.B. Grahame and after that date the post was held by Alex Calder. Both were manpower contractors for the CPR. When the police first hired Calder to replace Grahame he was cleared by both Sir John A. Macdonald and the local Conservative MP, W.B. Scarth, who wrote: 'Re. appointment of Calder as Recruiting officer permanently. Although I understand that he was formerly a rabid Grit I learned that at the last election he voted and worked for me. I have therefore no objection to recommending him as permanent officer.'[22] Calder must have had an exquisite sense of political timing because he was later given Sifton's seal of approval as well and remained police recruiting agent in Winnipeg for many years.[23] He received two dollars for every recruit he found who was acceptable to the force.

Patronage was not entirely eliminated by recruiting in the West. It was still possible for a Member of Parliament to send a potential recruit out from the eastern provinces with political support that the police could not ignore. Comptroller White was enough of a realist to know that co-operation was essential in such cases. On one occasion he defended his record to Laurier. 'With regard to my own partizanship, I think I can safely say that since the change of Government in 1896 I have not asked Commissioner Herchmer to engage any man on a recommendation of a Conservative Member of Parliament. On the other hand, I have written dozens of letters asking him to strain a point on behalf of applicants recommended by supporters of the Government.'[24] White knew that the alternative to limited patronage in the West was full-scale patronage in eastern Canada. If it became necessary to recruit east of Manitoba every detail of the operation would be decided on political grounds. This included not only the recruits themselves but the newspapers in which advertisements were placed, the hotels at which recruiting was carried out, and the choice of physicians to perform medical examinations. The latter requirement was particularly troublesome for the police. Government-appointed doctors regarded the examination of recruits as a chance to pick up some quick and easy money. Recruits would quite often appear at Regina with physical shortcomings which only a blind man could have missed; with only one eye or five to six inches under the minimum height requirement.

From 1885 to 1900 the police usually managed to get the men they needed without resorting to recruiting drives in the East. Around the turn of the century the South African War and the booming agricultural economy of the North-West dried up the usual sources of manpower and by 1902 the force was faced with the prospect of recruiting in eastern Canada again. White suggested that the commissioner handle it personally.

I think the better plan would be for you to take the matter in hand yourself, bringing Dr Bell with you. There will be more or less kicking on the part of the Doctors who have been in the habit of examining recruits, but that is not the real difficulty we have to contend with; it is the pressure to accept men who are not fully up to the standard and having to divide the number of recruits not only between the different provinces, but between the different sections of each province.[25]

This plan did not materialize and the police had to fall back on the old method of selecting men from those recommended by friends of the government.[26]

Political consideration did not play an important part in promotions to non-commissioned ranks. There were occasional requests for the promotion of individuals in this category but the commissioner could usually get away with promising to give the man in question an opportunity to qualify for promotion.[27] It was more common for political influence to be used to arrange or prevent the transfer of constables and non-commissioned officers. If a popular man was to be transferred a Member of Parliament might request that he remain where he was to keep his constituents happy.[28] If, on the other hand, a member of the force chanced to offend the party in power in some way, he was likely to find himself in an undesirable location. Sifton issued the following instruction in 1903: 'See Fred White and have a Sergeant in the Mounted Police named Carson lately brought to Regina from Battleford moved to an outlying point – a long distance north would be the best place to put him.'[29]

The Mounted Police purchased substantial quantities of goods and services throughout the North-West Territories. Like that of any other branch of the civil service, police purchasing followed the accepted rules of patronage. For the most part this aspect of patronage was entirely routine. The lists of politically acceptable hardware merchants, lumber dealers, and so forth were consulted and there were no difficulties. Disputes arose only in the case of billetting detachments. The police lived in barracks at all the larger posts and also at some of the smaller ones. At other small centres the detachment would be billetted at one of the hotels with their horses at the livery stable. Hotel owners were valuable political allies since the hotels usually had the only bars in town. Political managers were therefore careful to keep on the good side of these people. The police were instructed as to which hostelries their men were to patronize.[30] The police went along with these arrangements willingly enough as long as the accommodations offered were reasonable. On at least one occasion, however, the commissioner refused to billet a detachment at a hotel owned by a senator unless he received a direct order to do so. He gave the reasons for his stand to White: 'The house owned by Senator Perley, at any rate up to the last enquiry was a dog hole, and our men could not stay there, cold and dirty and poor grub.'[31] The commissioner, at White's request, interviewed the senator personally and got him to admit as much. The detachment was sent elsewhere.[32]

The limits of patronage, at least as far as the Mounted Police were concerned, were quite clearly defined and generally accepted. It was taken for granted that commissions would be dispensed on political grounds. The government that appointed an officer from outside the country, however, was risking an outburst of criticism. Patronage could get a man into the force but it would not serve to protect incompetents indefinitely. In 1891 Sir John A. Macdonald received the following request from a Conservative Member of Parliament:

One Antribus [sic] engaged in the Mounted Police has been suspended for being drunk. I think it is second offence. No doubt it is a very serious offence for any man to get drunk, this is a point upon which we will both agree, but for a man to lose his position because he did get drunk only makes it a greater calamity for the unfortunate who gives way to one of the weaknesses of Mother Civilization. I want this man reinstated and kept there for two years drunk or sober. At the expiration of that time he will be entitled to pension. Then they can sack the bugger as soon as they like.[33]

In this case an endorsement from a friend and political ally of the prime minister was not enough. The officer in question, Inspector W.D. Antrobus, resigned a short time later.

Political pressure for the transfer of members of the force could not be applied too blatantly. A western Liberal wrote Sifton a letter soon after the 1896 election expressing satisfaction that two strongly Conservative policemen had been transferred elsewhere, but he added a note of caution. 'What we will require to guard against is that if the changes made should be too numerous it may create sympathy for the other party and react unfavourably to us.'[34] Sifton himself would have very much liked to transfer Superintendent Deane, who made no secret of his Conservatism, from Lethbridge to a less desirable post. He issued instructions to that effect on several occasions but each time public pressure from Lethbridge forced him to cancel the order.[35] The necessity to maintain discipline in the force also overrode political considerations on occasion. In 1904 the Liberal Member of Parliament for Edmonton, Frank Oliver, asked Sifton to instruct the commissioner not to transfer Inspector R. Belcher away from that city. The request was refused and instead Oliver received a lecture from Sifton.

I do not think it would be wise to interfere in giving instructions to retain Major Belcher at Edmonton. Where a Commanding Officer, after full consideration, decides that the efficiency of his force requires a change to be made, it is much more serious than it appears from the outside to deliberately overrule him. It not only affects the particular case in question but it affects his treatment of the whole force. It makes him afraid to make recommendations and creates in his mind the impression that he is not going to be backed up in what he does. I have never overruled Major Perry since he took charge of the Force in any matter affecting discipline and I dislike to do it now.[36]

Because there were definite limits to the patronage system its effects were not entirely negative. Patronage provided a measure of stability at critical periods in the history of the Mounted Police. When the government began to reduce the numbers of the force in the 1890s, letters from Members of Parliament and other influential individuals urging that this officer or that one not be forced out in the reduction of the force poured in.[37] This exercise of political influence acted as an effective brake on the reduction of the force. Patronage appointments were distributed on a regional basis and any drastic reductions would have upset the delicate balance between different parts of the country. A cabinet minister from New Brunswick pointed this out to the prime minister when the plans for reducing the force were coming into effect.

In case you should find it necessary to make such a reduction I wish to call your attention to the fact that of the fifty-two officers, only two were appointed from New Brunswick. One of them, Mr. W.S. Morris, was appointed on my recommendation and I believe he has given complete satisfaction in the discharge of his duties. I trust that in any change made his interest may not be prejudicially affected.[38]

A party newly in office, as the Liberals were in 1896, might have been in a better position to carry out the reductions; but the temptation to share in the spoils after so long in the wilderness proved stronger than the desire to cut back.

The chief drawback of the patronage system was that it created a certain amount of bitterness within the force. When an individual was promoted, those who were passed over were convinced that the promotion was entirely the result of political influence. Superintendent Deane, who was a very ambitious man, makes this accusation about almost every promotion that took place during his years in the police. Deane's accusations were not without substance but he conveniently forgot the fact that his own commission and promotion came about in exactly the same manner. The only appointment which caused serious and widespread irritation in the force was that of L.W. Herchmer as commissioner. With a little tact Herchmer might have overcome this initial disability, but tact was never one of his strong points.

Patronage was a more or less minor administrative burden for the Mounted Police. Direct contact with party politics at election time was a much more serious threat. What was at stake here was the credibility of the force in the eyes of the public and the police fought hard to keep their involvement to a minimum. The Police Act imposed some restrictions on political activity. Members of the force could not legally belong to a party organization and were forbidden to wear anything that could be construed as a party emblem. These regulations were enforced. In 1902 an inspector was elected to the executive of the Regina Liberal Association. Although the Liberals were in power at the time he was ordered to resign at once and did so.[39] The rule was extended to cover such organizations as the Orange Lodge which were not political in the strict sense but had strong informal political connections.[40]

Some police activities at election time were quite legitimate. The force stationed men at every poll on election days and thus prevented in the North-West Territories the kind of violence which was a common feature of elections in eastern Canada.[41] There can be no doubt, on the other hand, that members of the force were expected to vote for the party in power at election time. Constituencies in the North-West Territories were large but the number of voters in each one was relatively small. In close contests the police vote, especially in the Regina and Ft Macleod-Lethbridge areas where there were large concentrations of men, could well be decisive. On two occasions at least the candidates believed this to be the case. In the 1891 federal election in the constituency of Assiniboia West an unusual situation occurred. The contest was between two Conservatives, the official party candidate and incumbent, Nicholas Flood Davin, and an independent Conservative challenger by the name of Thomas Tweed.[42] Davin was convinced that Commissioner Herchmer was instructing members of the force to vote against him and complained to Sir John A. Macdonald. Herchmer denied the charge in a letter to White and said that Davin had been telling some members of the force that Herchmer intended to vote for him. 'I could not permit such a monstrous assertion to go unchallenged, seeing that both candidates were Conservatives; and I accordingly contradicted the statement.'[43] To prove his point Herchmer noted that the police vote at Regina was evenly split between the two candidates.

The other case involved the federal election of 1904 in the constituency of Mackenzie. Shortly after the election criticism of the police began to appear in the Yorkton *Enterprise*. The inspector in charge of the district reported that the owner of the paper had been an unsuccessful candidate in the election and attributed his defeat to the police vote.[44]

The leadership of the police generally deplored their involvement in elections. It made the whole force suspect in the eyes of whichever party was out of power. As a solution to the problem White advocated complete disenfranchisement of all members of the force. This proposal did not interest Sir John A. Macdonald in the least but White thought that Sir Wilfrid Laurier might be more receptive. He put the idea to the new prime minister a few months after he took office.[45] Laurier agreed to consider the matter but the response from others in the Liberal party was unfavourable. A prominent western Liberal, Walter Scott, wrote: 'As I said to you on Thursday, I agree that the proposed disenfranchisement would be proper but the fact certainly remains that any political effects such measure would have would be detrimental to the Liberals at this time.'[46] White heard nothing further from Laurier on the subject.

Some opposition newspapers would occasionally try to use the police as a stick to beat the government but these attacks usually involved individual policemen rather than the force as an institution. When the safe at the Calgary barracks was robbed in 1896 (chapter 10), the Conservative Calgary *Herald* tried to portray the punishments handed out as examples of Liberal partisanship.[47] The Ft Macleod *Gazette* scolded the *Herald* for these allegations on the grounds that they would be made the basis of attempts by eastern newspapers to have the force cut back.[48] The Edmonton *Bulletin,* Frank Oliver's newspaper, confused the issue further by claiming that the punishments were awarded not because the men in question were Conservatives but because they were Liberals.[49] After this the whole incident was forgotten but it was attacks like this which made those in charge of the police cringe at the thought of another election.

There were of course contacts between the police and politicians which were entirely legitimate and necessary. A citizen who felt wronged by some action of the police could and usually did complain to his Member of Parliament. Perhaps the most common of all requests the police received from elected representatives at all levels were those asking for the establishment of detachments in newly settled areas. Generally speaking the police tried to comply with these requests if men were available. Public demand, subject to the overall responsibilities of the force, was as good as any other method of distributing the police.

Considering how deeply the police were involved in the seamier side of Canadian political life, it had surprisingly little effect on either their reputation or their performance as a law enforcement agency. The Mounted Police were neither oppressive nor corrupt in the sense that political pressure induced them to over-look violations of the law. In even the most rabidly partisan newspapers of the day corruption of this kind on the part of the police was never the subject of so much as a rumour. The limits of political influence were clearly recognized and respected by all parties. The police may have sinned against the stricter tenets of political morality but their sins were always involuntary and never mortal.

8
The military tradition in the NWMP

One of the most persistent characteristics of the Mounted Police has been the survival of its original semi-military attributes. To this day the training of police recruits maintains a strongly military flavour and the force performs ceremonial duties which are the prerogative of the military in most other countries. The police took a large, if indirect, part in every Canadian military involvement between 1885 and 1945. These military activities and traditions seem to have no relationship to the day-to-day activites of the police and there is a strong temptation for the student of the history of the force to dismiss them as mere anachronisms which have no relevance to an analysis of the operations of the police. The military form, if anything, would seem to be in conflict with the civilian function.

There is some evidence to support such an interpretation. Although members of the force persistently thought of it as a rather specialized cavalry regiment, it was never in a position after the 1874 march westward to act as a military body. Only during the 1885 rebellion did the North-West Mounted Police, as such, engage in military operations and these were of a relatively minor nature. After 1885 the police were fully occupied with non-military duties. On the face of it, the military tradition should have begun to disappear from the Mounted Police after 1885 but did not. The stubborn persistence of military values and ideas in the Mounted Police must be accepted as an integral and important part of the force and studied as such.

When the rebellion broke out in 1885 the police were not entirely unprepared in a military sense. They had been keeping Louis Riel and his chief lieutenant, Gabriel Dumont, under surveillance for some years prior to the outbreak. The extent and nature of this intelligence work is unknown, the only surviving reference to it in the police records being a claim for payment for watching Dumont's activities in Montana in the early spring of 1883. This was submitted by a Métis scout named Oliver Pichette in 1888.[1] In the six months immediately before the rebellion began the police had predicted a rising in the spring unless the government took some action. The government declined to make any concessions to the Métis but police intelligence was sufficiently convincing to move the government to begin increasing the size of the force in the fall of 1884.[2] The increase was too gradual, however, to have much effect on the fighting efficiency of the force by the following spring. When the fighting started the force totalled five hundred and sixty-two all ranks, only a few more than the normal peacetime strength.[3] Approximately half this number could be withdrawn from detachment duty and made available for active service. The bulk of these men, a force of two hundred under the command of Commissioner Irvine, were concentrated at Prince Albert in October 1884 and sat out the rebellion guarding the town.[4] Aside from the fifty men who had been involved in the opening skirmish at Duck Lake and who were later withdrawn to Prince Albert, none of the garrison saw a shot fired in anger.

Riel and his followers had opened the rebellion by seizing control of the North Saskatchewan River valley from a point just west of the present Alberta-Saskatchewan border to as far east as the town of Prince Albert. The police posts in this area, with the exception of Battleford, were abandoned as indefensible. Battleford was surrounded and under seige until relief arrived from eastern Canada. Prince Albert, although on the edge of rebel territory, was also effectively cut off since the Métis controlled the established trails into the town. Commissioner Irvine decided to keep his small force of police in Prince Albert and to defend the town with the help of volunteers. To make Prince Albert a sanctuary for settlers from the whole district seemed a less risky undertaking than either attempting to withdraw them all through enemy territory or abandoning them while the police were used for purely strategic objectives. Irvine was later criticized by Major-General Frederick Middleton, commander of the small army which defeated the rebels, for not using his men in one or other of these two ways. Irvine's judgement seems in retrospect to have been sounder since the advantages which might have been gained from adding two hundred men to a force of five thousand did not outweigh the necessity to protect the civilian population. The military situation was far from desperate for the government forces and Middleton's criticisms were intended to direct attention away from his own indecision at the Battle of Batoche, where he failed to use his greatly superior numbers to best advantage.

As soon as the government at Ottawa heard of the outbreak on the Saskatchewan it rushed thirty-three hundred Militia and A and B batteries of the permanent artillery force to the North-West over the partially completed Candian Pacific Railway. Three columns of troops were sent northward from points along the railway to seal off the scene of the trouble and deal with the rebels. The largest contingent of about twelve hundred men, under General Middleton, moved northward from Qu'Appelle by the most direct route to the centre of the rebel activity in the Ft Carlton-Batoche area. A second column under Lieutenant-Colonel W.D. Otter moved north from Swift Current with the objectives of relieving the beleaguered town of Battleford and of neutralizing the Cree Indians in the area, especially the bands of chiefs Big Bear and Poundmaker who were believed to be ready to join the rebellion. Otter had just over three hundred men including seventy-four Mounted Police and fifty civilian volunteers. His force also boasted two seven-pounder field guns and a Gatling gun. The third column, the Alberta Field Force under Major-General Thomas B. Strange, was intended to prevent the rebellion from spreading to the warlike Plains Indian tribes in the Alberta District. To carry out this assignment Strange was given seven hundred men, including a small contingent of twenty police, and a nine-pounder field gun belonging to the force. The Alberta Field Force moved north from Calgary to Edmonton and then down the banks of the North Saskatchewan toward rebel territory.

As it happened the Mounted Police took part in only one of the three engagements which took place between the rebels and the government forces. Colonel Otter's column was the first to make contact. The small force reached Battleford without incident or opposition. It seems likely that the situation there would have remained quiet had not Otter decided to overawe the Indians with a display of force. On 1 May 1885, after several days in the town, Otter's contingent moved south from Battleford toward the Cree encampment known to exist at Cut Knife Creek on the strength of some vague rumours that Poundmaker was holding some Métis families prisoner. When the government force reached Cut Knife Creek, an inconclusive skirmish followed in which the Indians had no difficulty in defending their encampment. According to all accounts of the battle Otter's men were lucky to escape as lightly as they did. Poundmaker was content to defend his position and allow the attackers to withdraw unmolested when it became apparent that the assault on the Indian position was a failure. Otter's rather foolish adventure might easily have ended in disaster for his own force and marked the beginning of the general Indian uprising that the government feared the rebellion would set off. The police contingent in Otter's force had been acting as advance guard when the fighting began and took the brunt of the battle for the government force. Four policemen died in the action and two were wounded.

A week after Cut Knife Creek Middleton's column attacked the main body of rebels at Batoche, about thirty-five miles south of Prince Albert. After three days of fighting the outnumbered rebel force was defeated and dispersed. The Mounted Police took no part in this battle. Before Middleton began his attack he had sent Irvine a dispatch requesting him to co-operate by using his men to take the rebel positions in the rear. Irvine received the message but his men remained in Prince Albert throughout the battle, a fact which was the subject of a good deal of criticism from Middleton and the press. Irvine's apologists claim that he did not act because Middleton's dispatch was vague as to the date of the attack.[5] This combined with Irvine's other preoccupations is enough to explain his inaction on the first day of the battle at Batoche. But the scene of the battle was so close to Prince Albert that Irvine's failure to move on the subsequent days on which the battle continued can only be explained by excessive caution on his part or by his ignorance of what was happening on his doorstep. Irvine's action or lack of action made not the slightest difference to the outcome but the military reputation of the Mounted Police was not enhanced. Irvine's replacement by Herchmer shortly after the rebellion was a direct consequence of his apparent lack of military instinct in this situation. Had the police marched out and taken part in the Batoche engagement Irvine would have been difficult to remove.

The Mounted Police played only a very small part in the military operations to suppress the rising of 1885. Eight members of the force were killed in action or died of wounds; eleven others were wounded. It was clear that even had the police been at their maximum strength of a thousand men when the rebellion broke out they would have been unable to contain it by themselves. It was equally clear, however, that the holding action carried out by the police in the early stages of the rebellion had definite military value. Furthermore, the general relationship of goodwill and mutual respect between the police and the Indians had proved to be most valuable. Among the bands involved in the actual fighting, Indian participation in the rising was half-hearted at best as Poundmaker's actions demonstrated. As far as the government was concerned the police had proved their value. The prescription for preventing future outbreaks did not include any change one way or the other in the semi-military character of the force. What was required was more of the same with new leadership.

With the rebellion over the Mounted Police went quickly back to their normal peacetime routine. No wars or rumours of war disturbed the tranquillity of the North-West for a decade. Then events in Africa showed that the military tradition in the force, if dormant, was not far beneath the surface. In 1896 the British government took over the administration of the Sudan from Egypt and began to move in, a process which provoked resistance from the Sudanese and culminated in the battle of Omdurman two years later. The Mounted Police half a world away smelled gunpowder and heard the sounds of battle. The commissioner reported: 'There is a good deal of enthusiasm in the Force over this Soudan business and quite a number of officers and men would like to volunteer. I do not expect they would be accepted or even allowed by the Department to volunteer but how would it do to offer the services of say 350 picked men and horses.'[6] Herchmer's suggestion was received with a notable lack of enthusiasm by Prime Minister Laurier and was quickly forgotten. What is interesting about this bit of wishful thinking on the part of the police is the accuracy with which it foreshadowed their participation in the South African War four years later.

The rising tide of pro-imperial sentiment in Canada ensured that Canada would offer the British government aid against the Boers when the war began. The unexpected length and difficulty of the war ensured that the offer was accepted. Enthusiasm for the war, at least in English-speaking Canada, was so great that the only real question was who would be allowed to go. The first North-West Mounted Police officer volunteered for South Africa in October 1899, when the fighting was barely under way.[7] Within two months most of the officers in the force young enough to qualify, and many of the older ones as well, had volunteered.[8] Enthusiasm was equally great in the non-commissioned ranks. At Ft Saskatchewan the entire division with the exception of a few married men offered their services.[9] At first it seemed that all this zeal would be wasted and that only a token Canadian force would go to South Africa. To satisfy political commitments the government had to draw the first contingent entirely from the Militia in eastern Canada. Police volunteers were warned at first that there was no chance they would be allowed to go.[10] This gloomy prospect for the hawks in the Mounted Police was lifted by the series of disasters suffered by the British Army during 'Black Week' (9-15 December 1899). The British government, now aware that the war was much more serious than they had at first believed, welcomed participation by the Dominions from military necessity and no longer merely as a gesture toward Empire solidarity. More important, as far as the Mounted Police were concerned, the first months of the war in South Africa had shown that mounted troops were urgently necessary. The Canadian Militia was largely infantry and the Mounted Police were the largest body of experienced mounted troops in the country. It was almost inevitable that they should form the nucleus of further Canadian contributions to the war.

By 19 December 1899 it had been decided that a second Canadian contingent of two battalions would go to South Africa. The first battalion was to be recruited in eastern Canada and Manitoba. The second would come from the North-West Territories and British Columbia and would be drawn largely from the Mounted Police.[11] As many police as could be spared would be recruited and the remaining vacancies would be filled with civilians chosen by the force.[12] Slightly less than half the strength of the battalion, one hundred and thirty-seven men, were police; and almost all the officers were from the force.[13] Many of the civilian recruits turned out to be ex-policemen. There was no lack of civilian volunteers and in fact it became necessary to establish quotas to regulate the maximum number recruited by each division.[14] The free hand given the police to organize this battalion appears to have been partly the result of pressure exerted on the government by the governor-general, the Earl of Minto. Some years earlier Sir John A. Macdonald had offered the command of the Mounted Police to Minto and he had seriously considered the offer (chapter 4). He eventually turned it down but he remained a great admirer of the Mounted Police. The governor-general was a personal friend of Lord Roberts, the British commander-in-chief in South Africa, and he wrote to tell him that the second Canadian contingent would be much more useful than the first because of the presence of the police.[15]

It seems curious considering the composition of the First Battalion, Canadian Mounted Rifles, that the unit had not been allowed to retain its name and identity as Mounted Police. Perhaps the government did not wish to offend the Canadian military establishment, which was always slightly jealous of the reputation of the Mounted Police.[16] Perhaps also they wished to avoid giving the Imperial government the impression that the police were available as a unit for service in future entanglements elsewhere in the Empire. There was one other factor. Recruiting large numbers of civilians into the police for service in South Africa would have meant expanding the force at a time when the government was still trying to reduce its size. If the Mounted Police were to be phased out completely with the coming of provincial autonomy, there would be that many fewer to discharge when the time came.

The First Battalion, Canadian Mounted Rifles, was just leaving for its year of service in South Africa in January 1900 when recruiting began in the North-West for another unit with close ties to the Mounted Police. Lord Strathcona, who as Donald Smith had amassed an immense fortune through the Hudson's Bay Company and the Canadian Pacific Railway, offered the British government a mounted battalion for South Africa, raised and equipped at his own expense in Canada but part of the British Army. The offer was accepted and Strathcona, another admirer of the Mounted Police, chose Superintendent Sam Steele to recruit and command the unit which became known as Lord Strathcona's Horse.[17] Steele was hastily withdrawn from his post as second-in-command of First Battalion CMR just before it left for Capetown and began recruiting in the North-West in February 1900. He drew most of the senior officers of the battalion from the Mounted Police.[18] Steele was also allowed to recruit a few constables and non-commissioned officers from the police. These men could volunteer for Strathcona's Horse on the same terms as those who had left with the CMR; that is, they were granted leave from the police while on active service in South Africa and could return to their former duties when it was over.[19] A total of twenty-six men from the force served with Strathcona's Horse.[20]

The major contribution of the Mounted Police to the South African War was by these two units, but a few officers and men served in each of the other Canadian contingents and in the South African Constabulary organized in the later stages of the war by Baden-Powell. Five Mounted Policemen died in action in South Africa and the force collected its share of honours. Sergeant A.H.L. Richardson received the Victoria Cross while serving with Strathcona's Horse.[21] Sam Steele became Sam Steele, CB, KCMG; two officers were awarded CMGs and three others DSOs. Two non-commissioned officers and a private received the DCM.[22] The force as a whole received the right to use the prefix 'Royal' in 1904 in recognition of its services during the South African War. The experience had strengthened the military tradition in the Mounted Police and had created a precedent for police participation in later Canadian military operations outside the country. During the World War which followed a dozen years later, the Royal North-West Mounted were all but swallowed whole by the military and had to withdraw from police duties in the provinces altogether due to a shortage of men.

The South African War did not require such drastic measures. The police who served with the First Battalion CMR were away almost exactly a year, from 27 January 1900 to 9 January 1901.[23] For this relatively short period of time it was possible to make temporary arrangements for continuing regular police duties in the North-West and Yukon. Special constables were hired to carry out routine duties such as guarding prisoners.[24] A few detachments had to be closed down in almost every division. Constables had to take over some duties formerly carried out by non-commissioned officers since experienced nco's were very much in demand for South Africa. All members of the force who stayed in Canada put in longer hours. No serious problems were encountered as a result of the temporary shortage of men even when the problem was aggravated by the departure of the volunteers for Strathcona's Horse. This latter exodus was a little more than the force had bargained for. White was apprehensive about the shortage of officers in particular.[25] Fortunately for the police, the year 1900 turned out to be very quiet in the North-West Territories. Crops were good, everyone was moderately prosperous, and crime was infrequent. Even epidemic diseases and prairie fires, which usually created a heavy demand for the services of the police, occurred less frequently than normal. The months of manpower shortage passed quickly and when one hundred and twenty-three men of the First Battalion, CMR, returned to duty in January 1901 the crisis was definitely over.

The police continued to be involved with the war in a minor way until it came to an end in 1902. There were small recruiting quotas assigned to the North-West Territories for each of the succeeding Canadian contingents and the Mounted Police continued to handle all recruiting in their part of the country. A portion of each North-West Territories quota was set aside for members of the force.[26] Replacing these later handfuls of volunteers was no problem.

Even though the possibility of the Mounted Police fighting as a unit was normally remote, the force always spent a fairly large proportion of its time preparing for such an eventuality. At all posts except the small one- or two-man detachments, drill and other military training were part of the daily routine. This emphasis on military training was not part of government policy but came from the officers in command of the force. The government repeatedly refused requests by the commissioner in the early years for the establishment of a training depot where recruits could be taught the military arts. Commissioner French was informed in 1876 that, as long as a recruit could read, write, and ride a horse, little further training was necessary.[27] The commissioner in this instance was not acting from a desire to impose empty military forms on a reluctant body of men. Pressure for military training came from the ranks. French had been receiving reports and complaints about this from his officers for a year or so before he made his request in 1876. They reported that the men were on the verge of mutiny because the other demands on their time left no opportunity for learning the military skills which they felt they ought to have.[28] The officers of the force were better psychologists than the minister of justice in this case. They recognized the importance of discipline and tradition in maintaining *esprit de corps*. This pride in the force was particularly important, the commissioner knew, because of the scattered disposition of the police.[29]

Official discouragement did not prevent Commissioner French from carrying out what he took to be his duty. Once the initial difficulties of establishing the police in the North-West had been surmounted and their basic needs taken care of, he exhorted the members of the force not to neglect their military duties.

It must be obvious to any members of the Force who have had any experience of Mounted Corps that except in moral character and in physique the N.W.M.P. have but little comparison with ordinary Mounted Corps in the British Service. There is now no reason why this should exist any longer and the Commissioner calls on all Officers, Constables and Sub-Constables to put their shoulders to the wheel, and by making use of every opportunity for drill and riding to perfect themselves in their respective stations.[30]

French's dissatisfaction with the reluctance of the government to go along with his ideas about the necessity for military instruction played a large part in his resignation in 1876. The attitude of French's successors in the office of commissioner remained the same in spite of official disinterest. They continued his efforts to incorporate as much military training and discipline as possible into the daily routine of the police.[31]

Macleod and Irvine were no more successful than French had been in convincing the government that recruits needed a training depot in Regina. They had to be content with such drill and instructions as could be managed at the large divisional posts. To this end Irvine managed to arrange for the recruitment of a few non-commissioned officers from the British Cavalry and the Royal Marines as instructors.[32] The Mounted Police continued to draw its drill instructors from these sources for the next twenty years.[33] Other efforts were made as well. When Inspector R. Burton Deane joined the Mounted Police in 1883, he was fresh from a captaincy in the Royal Marines. The police could make good use of a man who was up to date on the latest developments in drill and training and Deane spent his first few months in the force organizing a system of drill instruction and reorganizing the regulations of the force.[34]

One of the results of the 1885 rebellion and the change in leadership it produced was a general tightening up of military discipline. This was made possible by the increased size of the force, which enabled recruits to be retained for several months at police headquarters at Regina before being sent out into the field. Until 1886 the police had made use of the British Cavalry drill regulations. One of Commissioner Herchmer's first acts after taking command of the police was to replace these with Mounted Infantry regulations.[35] The police liked to keep their training as close as possible to that of the British Army. Superintendent Perry spent two weeks observing cavalry training at Salisbury Plain for this purpose in 1897.[36] Officers who had served in South Africa were regarded as particularly well suited for the training of police recruits.[37]

When the British Cavalry adopted a new drill book in 1904 as a result of the South African experience, the Mounted Police went along. The police in following the lead of the Imperial forces were also ensuring that they remained in step with the Canadian armed forces, who did the same thing. Commissioner Perry in recommending the 1904 Cavalry drill book wrote: 'To my mind it is almost imperative that we should follow the lead of the Militia in the question of drill.'[38] During the years after 1897 when the numbers of the force were being reduced, it was the prospect of having to abandon the semi-military routine and training that bothered the officers most.[39] Their professional pride was at stake.

In the matter of weapons and equipment the police also preferred to take the military as their model. The field guns used by the Mounted Police were the same seven- and nine-pounder types used by the Canadian Artillery. Although some of the ammunition for these pieces was as much as fifty years old, the police practised with them regularly.[40] The police were never equipped with Gatling guns but did receive some Maxim machine guns in 1896.[41] The desire for standardization of weapons also resulted in a brief and unhappy experiment in which the police adopted for a time the Ross rifle, notorious in Canadian military history. When the Canadian government placed orders for the Ross rifle in 1902 the police decided that the time was ripe to replace their aging and obsolescent Winchester carbines with the new weapon.[42] Because the police arms were in daily use the force had first priority and received the first consignment of the new rifles before any were issued to the Militia. These short-barrelled versions of the Ross rifle arrived in 1906 after many postponements and delays and were at once tested by the police. They were found to be not only unserviceable, prone to jam and to fall apart under normal conditions of service, but actually unsafe for the user. The police were well aware that the government was heavily and almost irrevocably committed to the Ross rifle but, in spite of the political implications, the rifles were withdrawn immediately from service and the old Winchesters re-issued.[43] The Militia Department would have done well to cut its losses and follow the example of the police in this case.

The strength of the military tradition in the Mounted Police should be evident from the foregoing discussion. There were also occasional outside pressures for the government to incorporate the force completely into the Canadian military system. Such suggestions usually emanated from individuals associated with the Militia. Shortly after the 1885 rebellion a former minister of militia and defence, Senator L.F.R. Masson, wrote to Sir John A. Macdonald to suggest that the Mounted Police should be placed under the control of the Militia Department on the model of the French gendarmerie.[44] The governor-general at the time, Lord Lansdowne, agreed with Masson's view that the rebellion had made necessary a change in the role of the police. He suggested a combined force of Mounted Police and Militia to overawe the Indians.[45] Five years later another participant in the rebellion, Major C.A. Boulton, raised the question of integrating police and Militia in the House of Commons.[46]

The government as consistently resisted these pressures from outside as they did those from within the force to increase the military character of the police. The civil authorities knew that the dual civil-military character of the Mounted Police created certain difficulties and tensions. They also saw what many critics of the police, both inside and outside the force, failed to see – that these tensions were creative and that the force owed much of its usefulness to its dual character. Thus in the early days of the police, officers were instructed to avoid the use of military titles.[47] When the force was being taken from the Department of Justice in 1876, there was some pressure to place it under the Militia Department. The deputy minister of justice who had been in charge of the police to that point argued successfully that it should go to the secretary of state's department instead. 'The original design in charging the Department of Justice with its organization and control was to avoid anything of a military character, and to preserve that of a police force, as administered in Ireland and the various colonies. ... I think that to put the force under the military authorities would be very detrimental to their police character, and to successful performance of the duties now imposed upon them.'[48]

Other perceptive individuals agreed with this assessment. General Selby-Smyth's report on the force in 1875 was very definite on this point. Smyth admitted that the police were too scattered to be very useful from a military point of view but went on to say: 'Militia are not available in the North West Territory, nor do I consider a mixture of the military and civil element at all desirable. There is sufficient of the military character about the police and they have the advantage that every man is a limb of the law, whereas military cannot act without a magistrate or constable.'[49] Efforts in later years to form a semi-military reserve body of ex-policemen living in the North-West Territories also came to nothing because of official discouragement.[50]

The training of a military organization is always carried out with some particular goal in mind. The officers responsible train their men to meet some specific set of circumstances which they think is likely to arise at some point in the future. Like most other military organizations the Mounted Police tended to spend their time preparing 'to fight the last war.' From 1885 to 1899 the police made ready to deal with another Métis-Indian uprising. After the South African War the emphasis changed to possible co-operation with Canadian and Imperial forces in a larger conflict.

The police performed in the North-West Territories those symbolic and ceremonial duties normally carried out by the military. They provided escorts and guards of honour for all dignitaries who visited the North-West, a tradition which has persisted to the present day although most of the other military functions of the police have disappeared.[51] Displays of horsemanship and cavalry exercises performed for the public, the beginnings of the famous musical ride, also date from this period. By the turn of the century the police were much in demand for performances at fairs and exhibitions not only in the North-West but across the country. Requests from outside the Territories were generally discouraged because of resentment on the part of the Militia.[52]

The ceremonial functions carried out by the police were in one sense the most useful element of the military tradition. They symbolized the social status attached to military activities and reinforced the prestige of the Mounted Police. Social standing and prestige were intimately connected with the ability of the police to command public support and co-operation in law enforcement. Without such support the police could not have successfully carried out their duties in the North-West Territories. This point is illustrated by an incident recorded in the autobiography of Superintendent Sam Steele. His predecessor in command of a post in the District of Assiniboia had been on bad terms with the magistrate for that area, H. Richardson. Judge Richardson decided to show his independence of the police by swearing in a special constable to serve a warrant for a minor offence on two British settlers. When the special constable arrived at the homestead of the two men and stated his business, they at first refused to believe him. He finally managed to convince them that he was in earnest and at that point they took down their rifles and ran him off the property with a few shots over his head. Judge Richardson was forced to relent and a Mounted Police constable was sent to make the arrest. The settlers offered no resistance to this member of the force and returned with him without even a mild protest.[53] The military tradition was important to the Mounted Police not so much because they might have been called upon to fight but because it reinforced the prestige which gave them so much of their effectiveness.

9

Crime and criminals in the North-West Territories

1873–1905

Crime, like beauty, is in the eye of the beholder. Every society in every age works out its own definition of anti-social and therefore proscribed behaviour. In the last century and a half, however, this truism has acquired new complexities which have made the relationship between legislation and the maintenance of social order much less straightforward than before. The idea of a graduated system of punishments tailored to the seriousness of the offence is one of the most important of these new developments. In theory the police are merely the agents of society in identifying and apprehending offenders to whom the courts then apply the appropriate punishment. In fact the police play a mediating role in determining which offences will be taken most seriously. There are many areas of ambiguity in the law which leave enforcement open to interpretation. An almost infinite variety of situations arise which come under the heading of extenuating circumstances. Legislators have a habit of trying from time to time to outlaw basic human appetites which all may agree should be curbed but which few really wish to see effectively diminished. All these factors help ensure that the police play a dominant part in determining the quality of life in any society.

This kind of selective perception and enforcement of the law is apparent in the history of the North-West Mounted Police. The police had very definite ideas about which crimes were more dangerous than others. Sometimes this ranking corresponded with the degree of seriousness implied in the penalty provided by law, but this was not always the case. The police operated on the assumption that their first duty at all times was the maintenance of peace and order. This meant that crimes of violence were always accorded top priority. Illegally carrying a firearm, for example, carried no greater penalty than some contraventions of the liquor laws, but the police enforced gun laws rigidly although this was not always true of the liquor laws. Crimes against property occupied second place in the hierarchy. Many of these were considered of minor importance but some offences against property could threaten the orderly conduct of life and were dealt with accordingly. Moral offences such as gambling, prostitution, and the like received much more sporadic and superficial attention. One category of moral offence, violation of the liquor laws, was an exception to this rule and is discussed separately in a later chapter.

The least serious offence involving violence to concern the police was assault. In some respects the North-West Territories may have been peaceful but they were not without their share of this kind of violence. The police records are crammed with assault cases of varying degrees of severity. Even the smaller divisions reported at least two or three cases a month. Punishments awarded ranged all the way from a fine of fifty cents to two months in jail.[1] The great majority of assault cases resulted in small fines of between one and ten dollars. Such minor cases were seldom reported in detail and it is difficult to know exactly who was involved and what was the nature of the offence. The small size of the fines and the fact that very many cases were dismissed or given suspended sentences seems to indicate that in most cases minor community quarrels were involved. The police accepted such small incidents as inevitable and tried whenever possible to act as arbiters. This interpretation is supported by a statement of Inspector Joseph Howe in 1897 who complained about 'The immense amount of work entailed upon the Police in connection with the most trivial cases (the outcome most often of mere spite and jealousy)...'[2] In another case Superintendent Deane described such an incident. 'The afternoon of the 24th was somewhat uselessly consumed in hearing a charge of assault preferred by Mrs. Davis, a livery stable keeper's wife, against Mrs. Keys, a blacksmith's wife, and the expressions of endearment etc., used by the respective ladies led to Mrs. Keys heaving clods of earth over the garden fence at her neighbour.'[3]

If a cowboy got drunk and started a fight in a bar he could expect fast action and a light penalty from the police. If he chose to make an issue of it he could expect to spend some time behind bars. One J. Donohue assaulted a Mounted Police constable in Calgary in 1902 and received a month in jail. The judge who awarded the sentence, Chief Justice McGuire, said that the prisoner had got off lightly only because of his ill health. 'He further impressed upon all present that as the N.W.M. Police was very small in comparison with the population in and about Calgary he intended to back up all members of the force as long as they in no way exceeded their authority.'[4] Violence which had the effect of leading to further violence or which undermined respect for the law was not taken lightly. The police recognized that to prevent all fights and quarrels was not humanly possible; their concern was to prevent the public from accepting violence as a normal way of life.

The police knew that if tempers were lost in a fight it could end in injury or death. The loser of a barroom fight in 1902 ended it by drawing a revolver and killing his opponent.[5] The second line of defence against such occurrences was to try to limit the availability of deadly weapons. The police accordingly enforced laws against the carrying of firearms as strictly as possible. (It should be noted that the shooting just referred to occurred in Calgary, which had its own municipal police. The Mounted Police were not called into the case until some hours after it happened.) Stiff punishments were imposed when the police felt that public order was threatened. Fines of a hundred dollars and jail sentences of up to twenty-one days are recorded.[6] In other cases the police recognized that no serious danger was involved and penalties were light, as when Inspector Joseph Howe remarked: 'The dime novel reader was to the fore in the cases of two lads carrying concealed revolvers.'[7] In another case a dude travelling west on the CPR announced his arrival by stepping off the train at a small stop in Saskatchewan and firing his gun into the night air. A Mounted Police inspector who happened to be on the train took his revolver away and ordered him back on the train. The would-be desperado went meekly.[8]

In one instance at least the police sympathized with the offender in a firearms case. Superintendent Deane reported sending Inspector W.H. Irwin to Cardston to try a case:

A man named Donaldson living there had made some filthy remark in connection with the name of a Miss Mary Macleod, sister of the ex-editor of Cardston *Record.* The young lady compelled Mr. Donaldson at the muzzle of her revolver to make her an abject public apology which I understand he did in haste.[9]

A small fine was imposed for this display of righteous indignation. By limiting the immediate availability of deadly weapons the police prevented most of the random and casual violence which tended to occur when tempers were lost, as in the case of the Regina man in 1896 who shot an acquaintance for refusing to drink with him.[10] The police were both fascinated and repelled by the number of shooting incidents in United States border towns. Their attitude towards the practice of carrying guns was based to a large extent on a determination not to let the same sort of thing happen on their side of the border.

Murder, the ultimate crime of violence, was treated by the police with all the seriousness that it deserved. Except for a handful of cases murderers caused the police little trouble and were apprehended with surprising ease. Most murders were unpremeditated crimes of passion, committed on the spur of the moment.

The murderer was usually too stunned by what had happened even to think about getting away. In one case the police were notified of a murder at 8:30 AM and the prisoner was arrested and awaiting trial before noon.[11] Murderers who did have the presence of mind to escape rarely remained at large for periods of more than a few days, even if they managed to get out of the North-West Territories. For example, the perpetrator of the barroom shooting at Calgary in 1902, mentioned earlier, got away but was captured within three days.[12] The police communications network was simply too well organized for the average man to escape.

In most murder cases, assembling the evidence, guarding the prisoner, and attending the trial absorbed far more of the energies of the police than the actual capture of the suspect. One fairly typical murder case occupied 'B' Division at Regina from 22 June 1893 to 10 February 1894. It began with the discovery by some CPR section men of a body under a pile of railway ties near Grenfell on the main line of the railway. The body was decomposed beyond recognition but it was possible to see that the back of the skull had been crushed by a heavy blow or blows. Questioning the CPR employees who had been working along the section of line where the body was found, the police discovered the dead man had been seen in the company of two others near where the section men had found him. This had been on 10 June, twelve days earlier. Further investigation revealed that the dead man was an itinerant Italian scissors grinder by the name of Giovanni Petterali.

Petterali had been seen in the company of the other two, also Italians, before 10 June but after that date his companions were only seen by themselves. Descriptions of the two men were sent out and they were arrested by the Winnipeg police on 26 June. Inspector Charles Constantine and Sergeant C. Brown spent a week investigating the case, and by the time of the preliminary hearing, 3 July, had ample evidence to send the two suspects, Antonio D'Edigio and Antonio Luciano, to trial. The trial did not take place until the following January (1894) in order that the defence could have time to obtain character references for the accused from Italy. When the trial began it occupied eighteen days during which, in addition to those men testifying, the police had a sergeant and seven constables assigned to guarding the prisoners and looking after the jury. The prisoners were found guilty although they were defended very ably by a lawyer described by Superintendent Perry as having the largest criminal practice in western Canada.[13]

Two other individual murder cases deserve mention here, not because they were typical, but for the opposite reason. They were unusual and provoked a very strong reaction from the police because they represented the two developments the force most wished to avoid. One was the case of the Cree murderer

Almighty Voice (1895-7). In October 1895 Almighty Voice, who had been jailed for cattle killing, escaped and then killed a police sergeant, C.C. Colebrook, who tried to recapture him. Almighty Voice managed to elude the police for a year and a half with the help of other members of his tribe, a fact which the police considered the most disturbing aspect of the case. The incident showed signs for a time of developing into a third western Canadian rebellion. Almighty Voice was finally discovered and cornered with two other Indians in May 1897. Two more policemen were wounded and three killed trying to capture him. Finally the police surrounded the patch of bush in which Almighty Voice was hiding and shelled it with two field guns, bringing an end to the whole tragedy.[14]

The only other case which caused as much concern and public excitement was that of Ernest Cashel in 1903 and 1904. Cashel's origins are uncertain. Before he came to Canada he was reputed to have been a member of Butch Cassidy's gang in Wyoming, but it is impossible to check this story. In any case Cashel was arrested by the Calgary police on a charge of forgery in October 1902. He escaped and took refuge with a settler east of Lacombe by the name of Isaac Rufus Felt whom he shortly murdered and dumped in the Red Deer River attached to a large rock. When the Mounted Police caught up with Cashel west of Calgary in January 1903 they suspected the murder but could not prove it without the body. Cashel was tried and sentenced on several charges of theft. A few months later a rancher discovered the body of the unfortunate Belt and it was easy for the police to prove that he had been killed with the revolver which Cashel had in his possession when he was arrested. Cashel was tried and convicted of the murder. He was awaiting execution at the police post at Calgary in December 1903 when his brother managed to smuggle a gun to the condemned man.

After escaping on 10 December Cashel remained at large for over a month. He was the subject of the most intense manhunt in the history of the police to that point. Every other division was denuded of men to help in the search. Public hysteria threatened in the Calgary area with dozens of false reports that the escaped killer had been sighted. The fugitive was finally discovered only a few miles from Calgary and was recaptured when the police burned down the shack in which he was hiding in order to flush him out. He was executed the following month.[15] What Cashel represented to the police and public alike was the kind of professional criminal who did not hesitate to kill anyone who got in his way. This sort of murderer was a new phenomenon in the North-West Territories and the police were determined to spare no effort to make an example of him.

Mob action was considered by the police to be the most potentially dangerous of all manifestations of violence. Reporting on one such incident, Superintendent Griesbach wrote:

You are no doubt aware that in this District during the last 14 years on three occasions mobs have assembled and on two of them, to my own knowledge, bearing arms. I consider that in a well-governed country such exhibitions of mob law should be strongly repressed, otherwise sooner or later serious consequences will ensue.[16]

The superintendent suited his actions to his words in this case. A dispute had arisen between two settlers over the ownership of some homestead land at St Albert near Edmonton. The case was being adjudicated by the Dominion Lands Commissioner but not fast enough to suit one of the claimants. This man, Octave Mogeon, collected a group of his friends and proceeded to destroy the buildings erected by the other claimant. The police rounded up no less than fifty-six men and had them tried on charges of creating a riot.[17]

The reaction of the police to anti-Chinese riots in Calgary in 1892 also illustrates their concern about any form of mob violence. By 1892 relations between the Mounted Police and the municipal authorities in Calgary had been strained for some time. The mayor of Calgary and the chief of police harboured an intense dislike for the Mounted Police. This situation was due largely to disputes over enforcement of the liquor laws. In any case it was police policy to stay out of municipal law enforcement if possible and the force was normally very reluctant to interfere in any way with events in Calgary. In July 1892, however, a serious outbreak of smallpox took place in the city. The disease made its appearance first in a Chinese laundry and when this fact became known a mob collected and began ransacking Chinese dwellings. The mayor happened to be away at the time and the Mounted Police moved in at the request of 'several respectable citizens...'[18] Most of the Chinese community took shelter at the Mounted Police barracks and the mob was easily dispersed. No further trouble occurred in spite of the arrival on the scene of an anti-Chinese agitator by the name of Locksley Lucas who, with the mayor acting as chairman, gave several speeches trying to stir up the populace against the Chinese.[19]

At this point the Calgary Police Committee requested that the municipal police be replaced by a town detachment of the Mounted Police. Inspector A.R. Cuthbert reported:

It is difficult to determine how the whole thing will end, the feeling is bitter between sections of the town, the respectable portion with a majority of the town council are for law and order, the remainder under the mayor are in favour of letting the mob have its way and no police protection. There is no doubt that at the present time should it become known that the Mounted Police would not interfere, life and property in Calgary would be at the mercy of a drunken mob.[20]

Herchmer favoured the establishment of a town detachment also but the proposal was eventually rejected although the Calgary authorities were given to understand that the force would intervene on similar occasions should they arise in future.[21] The significance of the affair lies not in the fact that a detachment for Calgary was refused. The significance of the police reaction is that no other crime or series of crimes could have made them attempt to reverse such a well-established policy. Disorders of this kind, the police believed, threatened the very basis of law enforcement and could not be allowed to occur.

Minor incidents of mob action, especially those in which public sympathy and that of the police was on the side of the offenders, were more difficult to handle than obvious riots. Such a case occurred in Lethbridge in 1895. One James Donaldson seduced the wife of a man at whose house he was boarding. The man became despondent for this and other reasons and committed suicide. Donaldson then had the effrontery to appear at the funeral as chief mourner. This was too much for the local citizenry, some of whom turned out that evening and applied what Superintendent Deane described as, 'a rather mild daub of tar and feathers...'[22] Donaldson at first refused to lay charges against his tormentors because public opinion was running so strongly against him. 'The entire population including ministers of religion are of the opinion that Donaldson was well served, and the only pity is that it was not kept out of the newspapers.'[23] Commissioner Herchmer was not pleased, reprimanded Deane for not preventing the affair in the first place, and insisted that charges be laid by the police. With some difficulty, since he had hurriedly left town, Donaldson was located and persuaded to give evidence. The members of the mob were subsequently acquitted although the trial was held at Ft Macleod in order to obtain a more impartial jury. At the trial it came out that Sergeant Hare of the Mounted Police had been a member, if not the leader of the tar and feather gang. He deserted immediately to the United States.[24]

The next time a similar situation showed signs of developing Deane handled it differently. This time a CPR brakeman came to Deane and complained that his wife intended to run off with Archibald McKay, a tailor and ex-Mounted Police constable.

I had heard of this liaison and some feeling in town was arising in consequence. Some 5 or 6 men, sympathizers with the husband, looked for A. McKay and would probably have handled him roughly if they had been able to find him. I suggested to the aggrieved husband that he should forbid the stage driver to carry his wife, and this he did, for later on in the morning she came to me. I referred her to her husband and instructed Constable Lewis to tell A. McKay that if he remained in town evil might befall him which I might be unable to prevent.

This MacKay is a tailor, working for Mr. E.J. Hill and the message brought up that gentleman and the Methodist Minister, apparently to convert me to the Doctrine that the mob law, which he thought meritorious in the case of James Donaldson and his tar and feathers, became quite reverse when brought in conflict with E.J. Hill's business interests. Mr. Hill asked if A. McKay could not have police protection, and I replied "certainly" but that I had not enough men to guarantee his not being tied up for instance to a telephone pole and given a sound flogging. I should probably not hear of the circumstances until after the occurrence and one had to look for a similar public sympathy in such a case as was accorded the tar and feather gang. Mr. Goard, the Parson, I think agreed with me. A. MacKay left town for British Columbia on the 28th instant, and the brakeman and his wife, who is still here, have concluded a sort of armed truce.[25]

There were no further attempts at private enforcement of public morality in Lethbridge. Superintendent Deane's actions in this case amounted to a recognition that legal proceedings would be futile where public opinion was unanimously in favour of those who broke the law. To handle the situation informally was the only effective approach.

Most crimes against property were regarded by the police as a routine part of their work. Small thefts and the occasional burglary were investigated and solved if possible. But since such cases were difficult to prove and impossible to anticipate they caused the police few sleepless nights. The police paid special attention to theft and burglary only if they showed signs of being the work of organized professionals, which was rare, or if they involved violence or large amounts of money, which was rarer still. Until about the turn of the century a year could pass in any given division with only a few minor thefts or even none at all. When two cases of theft occurred in the town of Boucher, Saskatchewan, in two years it looked like a crime wave to the inhabitants. They applied for a permanent police detachment but were refused, the police pointing out that in both cases the offenders had been arrested and convicted.[26] After 1900 thefts increased considerably and a special Detective Branch came into being to help deal with the problem.

Curiously enough two of the larger robberies which occurred in this period were thefts from Mounted Police posts. In 1890 about $1700.00 was stolen from the safe in the orderly room of the police post at Ft Macleod. The thieves, a constable and an ex-constable of the force, were caught but only a small portion of the money was recovered.[27] Six years later at Calgary some $600.00 disappeared from the police safe. The mystery in this case was never solved. Some of the evidence seemed to indicate that the commanding officer at Calgary, Superintendent Joseph Howe, had taken the money home rather than leave it in the safe over the weekend but nothing conclusive was ever established.[28]

It would appear that the police went to considerable lengths to deal with cases of fraud and embezzlement but there were so few of these that it is impossible to draw any general conclusions. Most of the cases which fall into this category involved the Post Office.[29] If the offender was successful he usually fled the country. The police would go to some lengths to get such people back. In 1893 the postmaster of Whitewood, Assiniboia, took his fellow townsmen for about $2500.00 and escaped to the United States. Inspector Charles Constantine spent a month looking for him in Chicago and Pittsburgh. Constantine was unsuccessful but made arrangements to have the man arrested if he came to the attention of the police in those cities. The Chicago police picked him up a few months later.[30]

A more enterprising group of confidence men a few years later sold the manager of Molson's Bank at Calgary over $11,000.00 worth of phony gold bricks, alleged to have come from the gold diggings of the Yukon. The bricks turned out to be copper but the fraud was not discovered for several days, by which time the swindlers had long since departed. The Mounted Police traced them as far as Seattle but there the trail disappeared.[31]

Some mention has already been made of the problems created for the police by stock theft around the turn of the century. If there were enough policemen to make the patrol system operate properly stock theft could be kept under control. This ceased to be the case after 1897 and the difficulties inherent in this type of criminal activity began to assert themselves. Horse and cattle stealing was hard to detect and harder to prove because of the numbers of animals and the problem of identifying individual beasts. The police compiled files running to hundreds of pages on cases which involved a few head of livestock. In many such cases it was almost impossible to prove either original ownership or intent to commit theft. The usual argument was that the cattle or horses in question had strayed in amongst another herd and had not been recognized. Some of the difficulties were removed in 1897 when the Criminal Code was amended to make brands *prima facie* evidence of ownership.[32] Many small farmers did not bother with brands, however, or failed to register them. Many cases therefore depended upon the ability to prove the age of a given animal. Each side would produce expert witnesses who would give lengthy and diametrically opposite testimony. The result was usually acquittal for the accused.[33]

Stock theft was more serious than an equivalent amount of ordinary theft because it tended to exacerbate an element of class conflict already present. In areas where the homesteaders were beginning to encroach upon the large ranches there was hostility between farmers and ranchers. In this situation one of the easiest ways to get back at a neighbour for offences real or imagined was to make off with a few of his cattle when the opportunity presented itself. Superintendent

Deane described the situation in 1901 with his usual insight. 'The little men "smuggle" a calf when and how they conveniently can. The big men (or some of them) want to have the entire range to themselves and be free to do as they like.'[34] Both parties complained frequently to the police but their complaints were always general. Whenever the police investigated specific incidents no one could be found who was willing to give evidence. In a summary of many reports from the field, Commissioner Perry wrote:

The large ranchers in the West are very jealous of the settlers who are crowding them out. They believe that these settlers are fattening at their expense. Around Calgary there is a great reluctance on the part of the ranchers to have their names mixed up with any complaint. Why I do not know. Some of them doubt even the men in their own employ and almost expect the police to protect them from their employees.[35]

The reluctance of both ranchers and farmers to become involved is understandable. It is one thing to report a theft or burglary committed by persons unknown to the police and quite another to accuse a neighbour who is in all other respects a reputable citizen. The social penalties for such an accusation if it is not substantiated were too great to make it worth the risk.

The result of this situation was general frustration and some dark mutterings about vigilantes and lynch law. The Calgary *Herald* complained in an editorial that the Mounted Police had been reduced so much that cattle stealing was now commonplace. So far, the editor continued, the North-West Territories had been free of vigilante justice, 'but the stockmen are becoming so incensed at the repeated depredations of the cattle "rustlers" that one of these fine days we will wake up and find that Judge Lynch has set up his court here.'[36] The police dismissed such predictions as idle talk.[37] Nevertheless some action seemed imperative and the police responded by hiring special stock detectives to work exclusively on such cases. The Western Stock Grower's Association also employed one and after 1901 the problem became less serious.[38]

Professional criminals who operated on a large scale were not common in the North-West Territories in the period to 1905 although the police occasionally professed to believe otherwise. Inspector Charles Constantine in 1887 advanced the rather peculiar theory that the Territories were the repository of all the more expert criminals driven out of other parts of Canada and the United States.[39] There is no evidence in the police records or anywhere else to support this idea. In fact the reverse seems to have been the case. The North-West was too thoroughly policed to present an attractive prospect for criminals and until about the turn of the century there was neither enough wealth in the area to support a professional criminal nor a sufficient density of population to provide the necessary cover. Before 1900 there were occasional rumours of gangs being organized to rob trains or systematically rustle cattle but when investigated they always failed to materialize.[40] When the professional criminal did begin to make his appearance in the first few years of the century the indications were much less dramatic; a general increase in the number and size of thefts and the occasional safe expertly blown.[41] The police responded with their own experts, the men of the Detective Branch, and Commissioner Perry's reorganization of the reporting system. With only a few exceptions the criminals encountered by the North-West Mounted Police in their first thirty years were amateurs, part-time offenders who spent most of their time in more or less honest pursuits.

The duty which aroused the least enthusiasm in the breast of the average Mounted Policemen was the enforcement of those laws designed to protect the moral well being of the inhabitants of the North-West Territories. The police were very much aware that vigorous efforts to eliminate such things as gambling and prostitution were futile. They would inevitably fail, for one thing, and for another, no matter how much energy was expended, no one would be completely satisfied. Those who happened to enjoy these pursuits would feel persecuted, while the puritanically-minded would never be satisfied that enforcement was strict enough. The response of the police was therefore to enforce these laws as infrequently as they could. If offenders were too blatant in their operations or if public pressure was exerted, the police acted. The same was true if moral offences seemed to be connected with more serious crimes. On the whole, however, the police preferred to control rather than eradicate. A vice which took place at a known location and within unwritten but strict limitations was much to be preferred to one driven underground and therefore out of reach.

Gambling and violations of the laws relating to amusements on the Sabbath were almost entirely ignored by the police. There is no single case in the police records to 1905 in which the police moved to enforce Sunday observance except as the result of a complaint. Such complaints were infrequent, occurring perhaps once or twice a year in the whole of the North-West Territories. Gambling offences appear even less frequently in the police files. In 1888 the managers of the Fall Race Meeting at Calgary requested that the police allow games of chance to be held. White replied that it would not be possible to alter police duties imposed by statute.[42] The tone of the letter made it clear that, in spite of the refusal, White did not regard gambling as a very serious offence. On one other occasion Commissioner Herchmer reported that he had been obliged to place a detachment in Calgary because gambling, along with the illegal sale of liquor, had 'reached a stage which necessitates active steps to suppress it.'[43] Beyond these few instances the Mounted Police were content to let the individual do battle on his own with the gods of chance.

Traffic in narcotics, mainly opium, took place on a surprisingly large scale over the international boundary in the late nineteenth century. There are frequent references to it in the police records. From the point of view of the present the attitude of the police toward drug trafficking and addiction seems astonishingly casual. Narcotics cases were treated as rather less serious matters than liquor law violations. In 1896 an opium addict at the urging of his friends asked the police to lock him up for a few months so that he could kick the habit. But when the time came to actually go into the cell he changed his mind. The police awarded him a suspended sentence on a charge of intoxication and let him go.[44] When a prostitute at Calgary was found dead of an overdose of morphine a few years later, the discovery provoked neither surprise nor any particular interest on the part of the police.[45] Drugs were simply not a social problem of any importance since the numbers of people affected were so few.

The police did, of course, confiscate drugs which came to their attention. A shipment of one hundred and forty-one pounds of opium was seized at Swift Current in 1891.[46] The traffic in drugs appears to have been largely one way, from Canada to the United States. Most drugs were smuggled in by employees of the CPR who worked on the company's steamers which travelled to Asian ports. The police made some effort to keep the traffic under surveillance, as the following report indicates:

I have the honour to state that Donald McLean, better known as "Little Danny" or "Opium Dan" is not occupying lands in Township 23, Range 2, west of the 3rd Meridian. McLean rented these lands to one Naismith who left this Fall for Maple Creek. McLean is working on a Pacific Steamer, as cook or steward, but I suspect he is doing this to work his trade in opium. McLean is worth at least $15,000.00 in cash.[47]

On one occasion a saloon in Sweet Grass, Montana, known to be a depot for smuggled opium, was closed down by the American authorities after Mounted Police reports were forwarded to them through diplomatic channels.[48] It should be noted that in this case it was not primarily the opium which bothered the police. They considered the saloon to be a haven for both Canadian and American horse thieves and other undesirables and generally a centre of disorder which spilled over onto Canadian jurisdiction.

Next to liquor law violations, the most widespread moral offence by far was prostitution. It was illegal both to be a prostitute and to patronize one but these two laws were evaded more often than any others in the Criminal Code. The police attitude toward prostitution was generally the same as for other manifestations of public immorality as defined by law; they preferred to have it more or less in the open where they could keep an eye on it. An occasional prosecution was all that was necessary to demonstrate that the police retained the upper hand. Thus when a sentence handed out by Superintendent Deane for frequenting a house of ill fame was appealed, he asked leave to argue the case before the higher court, explaining his reasoning as follows:

As Police Officer in charge of the District and responsible for order therein, I am very much interested in the eventual decision, because there are a few persons in town, pimps, etc., who are at the bottom of most of the rows that take place and I am bent on making them understand that when they get a Police hint to behave themselves or leave town they must comply forthwith.[49]

Significantly what Deane asked for and got from the higher court was a suspended sentence on the charge.

Normally the police attitude toward prostitution was even more favourable than the case described above would indicate. In 1894 Deane reported that he was being pressured by the town's clergymen to stamp out prostitution completely in Lethbridge. The request annoyed the superintendent.

If they would turn their attention to the juvenile depravity and promiscuous fornication that is going on under their own eyes and in their own congregations, they would be kept so busy that they would have no time to think of the professional ladies, who at all events are orderly, clean, and on the whole not bad looking.

Not long ago the two ministers above mentioned formed themselves into a delegation and interviewed the Town Council in public session convened and talked about the "soiled doves" etc. The whole town was there to see and hear. The "doves" had a lawyer present to watch the case for them and I was told that the whole business was great fun. The Reverend gentlemen got no satisfaction from the Council and retired covered with ridicule.[50]

Deane's attitude was not a personal idiosyncracy. A few years after the incident mentioned above, the Lethbridge Town Council fell temporarily under the sway of respectability and passed a resolution asking the Mounted Police to close up all houses of prostitution in the municipality. As it happened, Superintendent Deane was on leave at the time and the division was under the command of Inspector A.R. Cuthbert, who recorded his reaction to the request:

I informed the Town Council for obvious reasons, that should houses of ill fame be removed from the municipality, they would not be allowed to exist in the District and outside the Municipality; whereupon a Council meeting was held, their previous actions reconsidered and the latter left to the discretion of the Police. It is needless to add that the best course is to leave them within the Municipality where they can be under a certain amount of control without more than the usual Police supervision.[51]

The same attitude prevailed in other areas and approaches differed only slightly. Some police officers preferred to stage an occasional raid to satisfy that part of the public which felt something should be done.[52] This approach was not without its pitfalls either since one raid turned up two members of the force among the clientele. These two worthies claimed to be investigating on their own time but the commissioner, unimpressed by their zeal, felt compelled to bring charges against them under the Police Act.[53]

Crime, like other human activities, tends to reflect the predominant social ideas of the era in which it occurs. In the case of the nineteenth-century Canadian West, crime was very closely tied to class and to popular concepts of class. Respectability was the dominant virtue of the middle and upper classes, which meant that criminal activites were associated in the public mind with lower classes. A middle class individual who was discovered in some serious violation of the law became almost automatically a social outcaste. Everyone expected that the lower orders would break the law. It was one measure of their inferiority. Many of these attitudes prevail still but in a much diluted form. They were a good deal more pronounced a century ago.

This fact helps explain a number of more or less puzzling aspects of both criminal activity and police attitudes to that activity. The reluctance of rustling victims to become involved in aiding the police is one example. The police explained this phenomenon by the theory that such people feared retaliation. This does not seem a very plausible explanation. The victims had already suffered losses and they would continue to do so. The large ranchers certainly did not fear violent retaliation from the small farmers. What they did fear was the social pressure which would have been exerted on a man who accused someone of his own class or social level. Few were willing to run the risk of falsely accusing a respectable citizen, especially since stock theft was so difficult to prove. In 1905, to give one example of the hazards involved, the police arrested a prominent citizen of Calgary on a charge of horse stealing which they were subsequently unable to prove. The force was censured in an editorial in the Calgary *Herald* and Inspector D.M. Howard, who had been in charge of the case, was immediately ordered to duty in the far North.[54]

Much the same set of attitudes explains the reluctance of the police to strictly enforce the laws governing such moral offences as prostitution. The public liked to believe that the offence of frequenting houses of ill fame was almost the sole prerogative of the lower classes. So long as houses of prostitution remained quiet and did not impinge upon the sphere of the respectable class they were not molested. If the laws were strictly enforced there was always a good chance that raids would turn up a respectable citizen or two. This would have meant only trouble for the enforcers and town authorities were thus anxious to transfer this unpopular duty to the Mounted Police whereas the police were equally anxious to avoid it.[55] Styles in criminal activity change and so does the relationship between evader and enforcer of the law. So-called 'white collar' crime is a characteristic of our own day as lower class crime was of the nineteenth century. The successful criminal no longer has an identifiable life style of his own as he did a century ago.

The attitudes of the police toward the relationship between class and crime is nowhere more clearly illustrated than in their approach to the problem of vagrancy. Every summer the North-West Territories was inundated by a flood of transients. Some of these were genuine tramps; dropouts from society who lived the life of the hobo by choice. Most of them, however, were young men in search of work. They represented an unacknowledged social problem of the day, unemployment, for which there were no conventional solutions. The employed labourer had his place in the social scheme, the man without a job did not. He was at the mercy of the construction companies and farmers who might give him work for a few months or weeks from time to time. As soon as the job ended he became, in the eyes of the police and public alike, a crime looking for a place to happen. The police term for this group was 'the floating population,' a phrase which was invariably used in the context of a threat to the social order.

The penalties imposed for vagrancy were severe. The law provided a very wide range of sentences for vagrancy; from small fines to six months in jail. Substantial jail sentences were awarded much more frequently than the lesser penalties.[56] Many vagrants were simply ordered to move on within twenty-four or forty-eight hours.[57] Others were given suspended sentences to let them know that the police were watching them and would tolerate no misbehaviour.[58] If jobs could be found for vagrants enjoying the hospitality of the police guardrooms, they were sometimes released before their sentences had expired.[59] On the whole, however, the system bore harshly on transients. The police treated them as a problem to be dealt with by whatever means were available rather than as citizens temporarily down on their luck. There is little evidence in the police records to indicate that transients were any more prone to break the law than that part of the population which was more or less permanently employed. The source of the police attitude was rather an uneasy feeling that those without roots in a particular community had less to lose than permanent residents and would therefore be more likely to break the law.

One of the most widely held public assumptions, then as now, is that the crime rate is directly related to the state of the economy. The proposition is that since poverty presumably breeds crime the crime rate will be higher in bad times, lower when there is general prosperity. The experience of the Mounted Police indicates that no simple, direct relationship exists. If anything, in the period under study, the crime rate tended to be higher when the economy of the North-West Territories was booming and lower when it was depressed. Usually in the police papers complaints of increases in crime accompanied reports of good crops, full employment, and general prosperity.[60] Reports of destitution, the distribution of relief, and hard times tend to be found alongside comments about the absence of criminal activity.[61] The police were filled with apprehension at the prospect of large numbers of seasonal workers being idle in the winter but their predictions were seldom borne out by actual increases in crime.[62]

Some of the more perceptive individuals of the force noted this discrepancy between expectations and events and commented. During a bad winter at Regina, Superintendent Perry wrote: 'I anticipated that, owing to the straitened circumstance of many people, thieving could be prevalent but such has not been the case. Fewer cases have been reported than for many previous months.'[63] The obvious explanation in this case was that there was little of value around to attract the thief. Superintendent Deane in 1889 observed: 'This district has generally been very quiet - business is dull - the mines work only half time - money is scarce, and whiskey much the same.'[64] But such a theory does not help account for the fact that all types of crime, including assaults and other crimes of violence, tended to increase when times were good economically. So many possible causes exist for fluctuations in the crime rate that any attempt to establish a relationship on the basis of this single situation would be unproductive. What the evidence does seem to indicate is that the rapid changes engendered by periods of fast economic growth had a general unsettling effect on the population which found expression in crimes of violence as well as crimes against property.

It will be evident from this brief survey of criminal activity in the North-West Territories that the Mounted Police were generally successful in enforcing the law. They kept a firm hand on those areas of delinquency which they considered to be important. The police view of what was important usually coincided with that of the public; an important element in maintaining their reputation. Enforcement of the law also emerges as a factor of the utmost importance in the maintenance of social stability. Without an enlightened and humane approach to its application, the best legal code imaginable would be useless. A good police force, on the other hand, can do much to moderate the bad influence of harsh and unjust laws.

The attitudes toward crime discussed in this chapter also have an important bearing on the myth of the orderly character of Canadian society. Obviously there was a good deal of violence in the North-West Territories and equally obviously both police and public expected it to occur. The point is that they expected it to be confined to the lower classes and it generally was. The thing that shocked Canadian observers of life in the American West was not violence per se, but the fact that it sometimes occurred among social and economic groups which in Canada would have fallen into the category of the respectable middle class. What conditioned the Canadian view of the United States was not so much hypocrisy, although there was undoubtedly an element of that, as a different view of the relationship between crime and class.

10

The enforcement of the liquor laws:
The identity crisis of the NWMP

A STORY OF UTOPIA

During the early days of the land of Utopia, when only a certain portion of the land was settled, the gifted people who made the perfect laws were much exercised in their minds as to the exact set of laws that should be made and carried into effect in the heart of the land which, while rather far from the older and better settled portions, was attracting no small attention in over-populated countries, as a most desirable field for immigrants.

Amongst the people who are not legislators, but who were persuaded that they and only they were able to decide as to what other people should and should not do were a class of people who had, in their younger days, been too partial to the flesh of pork, and in consequence suffered from indigestion and ill temper, so they took upon themselves and held meetings where the direful effects of pork were enlarged on, and to get up petitions praying the government to prohibit the use of pork, as an article of diet, in that part of Utopia which immigrants were now pouring into. The Government of the day, either impressed by their arguments, or, what is more probable, being afraid of losing votes, accordingly passed a law, to the effect that no pork of any description should be brought into, sold in, or eaten in the new territory. This was very sweeping, but they managed to soften it down a little by allowing the Governor of the Territory to issue permits to responsible persons, allowing them to have in their possession for "domestic use" a few pounds of pork, for which magnificent privilege they had the honor of sending the Governor a small consideration, being about fifty cents for each permit, eight pounds. Directly the people of the New Terri-

tory found they were debarred from eating pork they began to want it for break-
fast, dinner and supper, and many were the applications sent to the Governor for
permits, and many a good meal was eaten when the pork arrived.

The illicit dealers in pork began to spring up in the various new towns and
they did a roaring trade, people would come into their stores and ask for some
beef or mutton and give a peculiar wink when the storekeeper would cautiously
slide a small rasher of bacon (and the vilest rattlesnake pork at that) over the
counter and in return receive twenty-five cents.

The government employed a large body of men whose duty was to maintain
order, but more particularly to see that no illicit trade was done in pork, and as
the larger proportion of these men themselves were rather partial to ham and
bacon it will be readily understood that they were very often afflicted with
blindness, some of them, the worst among them, would make it their business to
inform and get the dealer convicted, in which case the genial informer received
half the fine; the fine ascended from $50.00 for the first offence to $400.00 and
six months imprisonment for the fourth. Perhaps one of the funniest features of
the whole business showed itself on the occasion of any public banquet. When
an event of this kind occurred, a very large permit was usually granted, and the
alleged banquet resolved itself into a simple gorge of pork, and it has frequently
been the case that the Governor himself has been present at a banquet, and has
done his share towards reducing the succulent food. It would be impossible to
recount the many absurdities and wrongs that arose from this extraordinary
attempt at legislation, but at length the people of Utopia began to see that it was
possible for a man to eat pork without being a glutton, and that, because one
man could not restrain his appetite, it was not necessary to compel everyone to
abstain entirely, so they, after a great effort, had this pseudo prohibition law re-
pealed – in Utopia.[1]

The anonymous author of this allegorical account of the liquor legislation of
the North-West Territories put his finger directly on the dilemma which faced
the Mounted Police in the period from 1886 to 1892.[2] The police had initially
been sent to the North-West with the elimination of the liquor traffic with the
Indians as one of their primary objectives. They had been highly successful in
stamping out the trade and controlling the excessive consumption of liquor by
the tribes. The early reputation of the force was to a large extent founded upon
this success.

When settlers began to arrive in large numbers after 1885 the situation changed
rapidly and permanently. The new arrivals, or most of them, strongly resented
the total prohibition imposed by laws designed to keep liquor out of the hands
of the Indians. As usually happens in such cases, resentment was directed against

those responsible for enforcing the law. The police quickly became very unpopular as a result. This was something new for the police, who were more accustomed to the role of friend and protector of the settler and now found themselves cast as persecutors. The situation for the force was much more serious than the discomfort caused by unpopularity. The police knew that their success in controlling more serious crime was directly proportional to the amount of co-operation they received from the public. They could see, from the beginning of settlement, that a thirsty population was less disposed to be helpful than one that was allowed to indulge this minor vice. More serious still, the resentment caused by liquor law enforcement eventually threatened the actual survival of the Mounted Police. In the early 1890s when the federal government was attempting to turn over law enforcement to the Territorial Government, any indication of public dissatisfaction with the police would have served as an excuse to disband them.

There were arguments in favour of strict enforcement of the liquor laws which made the position of the police much more difficult than it might otherwise have been. The police had a great deal of emotional capital tied up in the issue of liquor law enforcement because of their early successes with it. There were also more practical problems. Alcoholism and ordinary drunkenness were unquestionably the most important perceived social problems of the day.[3] Drinking to excess brought misery and suffering to many thousands of people, especially the dependents of those men who could not resist an opportunity to drown their sorrows. Temperance groups proliferated in the North-West Territories as in the rest of the country. They were sufficiently numerous and well organized to be a major factor in any assessment of public opinion. Improperly used, liquor was also a threat to public order. A very high percentage of assault cases were directly attributable to drinking. The attitudes of the police towards the liquor laws were highly ambivalent because from their point of view they were forced to make a choice of evils. They had also in a real sense to choose their role in society. The choice was between co-operation and conflict, between the attempt to impose moral standards and laissez-faire. In the end the course of the police was determined by new Territorial liquor legislation in 1892 which brought an end to prohibition. This did not mean that the choice was a meaningless one for the police. Until 1892 day-to-day decisions had to be made about the extent of enforcement in the field. Although there was never the broad concensus within the force on the liquor question that existed with regard to other kinds of crime, the police came out strongly in favour of abolishing prohibition several years before it was actually accomplished. There can be no doubt that this stand had an influence on the legislators.

After their initial success in breaking up the established whisky trade from Montana in 1874-5, the police made every effort to seal off the borders of the

North-West Territories to all liquor imports. Never completely successful, they kept the traffic more or less under control. Every vehicle entering their jurisdiction was searched, often several times by different police patrols.[4] The possible routes by which illicit liquor could be imported were well known. These were patrolled regularly and on some occasions the police received tips in advance. One such police interception of a liquor shipment has been described in an earlier chapter from the account in the diary of Constable R.N. Wilson. The procedure involved was simplicity itself. Once the police knew where the liquor was coming from and the approximate time, a patrol was sent out to wait for the smugglers to cross the border and then arrest them. With their heavily loaded waggon the smugglers were captured easily and had no chance to flee. In the incident described by Wilson the smugglers included an ex-policeman who should have been familiar with the methods of the force, a fact which emphasizes the limited choice of routes available to the smuggler.[5]

Penalties for selling liquor to the Indians were severe and became even stiffer as the years passed. By the mid-1880s the maximum sentence for this offence was a fine of $300.00, six months in jail, and confiscation of teams and waggons used in the trade. In contrast to the change in attitudes which took place as far as the sale of liquor to white settlers was concerned, there was no change after 1885 in the police approach of denying liquor to the Indians. Individuals convicted of selling liquor to settlers were usually awarded a fine, frequently the minimum fine of fifty dollars, while convictions for selling liquor to the Indians almost invariably brought jail terms.[6] After prohibition ended in 1892 the efforts to prevent Indians from getting liquor were not relaxed. If anything they were stepped up because the police had the support of public opinion and the greater availability of liquor put them on their guard.[7] Even after the turn of the century when the police were shorthanded and faced with all the problems created by a massive immigration, prevention of liquor sales to the Indians maintained its priority. In 1904 a resident of the village of Mistawasis reported strangers peddling liquor to the Indians. The officer in charge of the district, Superintendent W.S. Morris, at first refused to station a man in the area because he was shorthanded. The commissioner overruled him and ordered a man to the village even if it meant reductions elsewhere.[8]

The difficulties experienced by the police in enforcing prohibition on the general public were paralleled to a great extent within the force itself. As the allegorist pointed out, the police were not immune to the same temptations that affected other men. The first contingent of one hundred and fifty men left Ottawa in October 1873 for the North-West. Before their train had reached Prescott, Ontario, a bare hundred miles from Ottawa, a man had been dismissed from the force for drunkenness.[9] This case soon proved to be no isolated incident. By the time the train reached Collingwood, Ontario, two days later, the commanding officer had found it necessary to issue a memorandum advising the men to be moderate in their drinking habits.[10] One of the first General Orders issued for the force prohibited policemen from buying liquor at the Hudson's Bay Company store at Ft Garry.[11] This order was quickly followed by another which established a standard penalty for drunkenness: a three dollar fine if found drunk off duty, double that if on duty.[12]

Once the police left the temptations of civilization behind and moved into the far reaches of the North-West Territories it was expected that the problem would solve itself. To a certain extent this expectation was fulfilled and the number of cases of intoxication declined noticeably on the empty prairie.[13] At no time, however, did they disappear completely. Members of the force exhibited a remarkable ingenuity in obtaining supplies of liquor. A sympathetic officer would sometimes share his supply.[14] The hospital stores were raided on one occasion after the police were established in the North-West.[15] Successive commissioners made repeated efforts to stamp out drunkenness in the Mounted Police. Punishments escalated steadily from the original three dollar fine of 1874 to one month's pay and reductions to the ranks in 1881.[16] Commanding officers constantly reminded members of the force that they had come to the North-West to prevent the liquor laws being broken, not to break the laws themselves. Judging from the number of times these exhortations were repeated they were none too successful.

The root of the problem lay in the fact that it was too easy for constables to sample the product they confiscated from smugglers. 'It is a very great temptation to our men when searching carts to be offered liquor...,' Commissioner French reported in 1875.[17] French was describing a practice which appears to have been quite widespread but this did not mean that the police could be bought off by smugglers with gifts of liquor. The confiscated spirits were simply considered by all parties to be the legitimate spoils of war. This is obvious from Constable Wilson's description of the fate of some of the liquor captured by his patrol in 1882. It apparently did not occur to the captured smugglers that the police were doing anything out of the ordinary in helping themselves to the captured alcohol. There were numerous others ways for a policeman to retain some of the liquid evidence for his own use. Superintendent Deane in his autobiography mentions that members of a successful anti-smuggling patrol would sometimes bring in only a part of the captured liquor. The rest would be buried and retrieved at leisure. Deane made this discovery by following a constable who was rather too anxious to return to the scene of the crime.[18]

It was quite all right, as far as the white population was concerned, for the police to sample in this manner liquor intended for the Indians. But the thought of the police enjoying illicit beverages intended for their own parched throats had quite a different effect upon the settler. By the late 1880s public resentment was so strong that a solution had to be found to the problem of drinking within the force. By 1890 beer canteens were established at divisional posts for constables and non-commissioned officers. This had the desired effect of moderating the problem and bringing it out in the open. Superintendent Deane commented: 'There is no doubt whatever that it is a convenience to the men, and has a tendency to keep them in Barracks, and out of saloons and bar-rooms in town.'[19] Almost everyone was satisfied except the saloon keepers, who regarded the canteens as unfair competition.[20]

Once the new liquor law came into effect in 1892 the situation eased still further. The police then no longer enjoyed a privilege, the right to drink without fear of prosecution, denied to the public. As far as the problem of drunkenness within the force was concerned the increased availability of liquor had no marked effect. Superintendent Deane reported an outbreak of intoxication when the new system came in. 'The introduction of the licence system has had a most disastrous effect upon the Division, the very opposite effect to that which is observable in the general public. The only explanation is, that a dollar will buy more whisky than under the old system.'[21] Within a month or two the novelty wore off and drinking within the force reverted to the status of a minor disciplinary problem.

This reasonable solution of the liquor problem within the force foreshadowed the settlement adopted two years later for the general population of the North-West Territories. Unfortunately it was not until a major crisis of confidence between the police and the public had developed that the laws were changed. In the years before 1885 the police had made no distinctions between the liquor laws as they applied to the native peoples and to the settlers. As long as the white population was small it was possible to do this with a reasonable degree of success. The key to enforcement of the law lay in the clause which permitted the lieutenant-governor of the Territories to issue permits to individuals allowing them to import specified kinds and quantities of liquor for their own use. Those people who had sufficient influence got their permits and were satisfied. In the early days it was easy to identify local opinion leaders and issue permits to the minimum number of members of the social hierarchy, as when in 1875 the police seized a quantity of spirits from the Hudson's Bay Company but released it when they learned that it was destined for the Anglican Bishop of Athabaska.[22] Dissent, if any, was confined to those without an effective voice. The situation was basically unhealthy since in effect it amounted to prohibition for the poor but not for the well-to-do and influential. Such a system could not survive the emergence of a larger, more diverse, and inevitably, more egalitarian, society.

Two manifestations of the rapidly changing character of western Canadian society in particular, the formation of towns and the appearance of newspapers, helped bring down the old system. The towns created new local élite groups or at least groups which aspired to leadership. These were distinct from the older élites of the fur trade in the northern prairies and the cattle ranchers in the south-west. It is significant that the first and most vigorous public protests against the liquor laws came from Prince Albert in the former area and Calgary in the latter. The newspapers created a public opinion on the question which had not previously existed and gave a voice to that part of the population which had hitherto not made itself heard. Pioneer newspapermen were rarely abstemious individuals and few newspapers supported the cause of temperance. Even before the completion of the railway in 1885 there were definite signs that the liquor situation was passing beyond the control of the police. In 1883 a Hudson's Bay Company factor at Prince Albert wrote to the lieutenant-governor to complain about the sale of liquor in that community. Until recently, he reported, the Mounted Police detachment had sympathized with the offenders. There had been a wholesale change of personnel to correct this situation and things had improved considerably but he asked for still more police since the local newspaper was strongly anti-prohibition and was inciting the citizens of Prince Albert to violate the law.[23]

The Hudson's Bay man undoubtedly exaggerated the seriousness of the situation at Prince Albert but reports from other parts of the North-West indicated that it was not unique and could be expected to get worse instead of better. A few months later Sir Hector Langevin, Minister of Public Works in Sir John A. Macdonald's cabinet, wrote to his chief: 'I have received a letter from the North West today, stating that in order to prevent the illegal use of whisky at Silver City, the cause of temperance would be served by having one or two licences granted there, in as much as the Mounted Police with all its activity and determination, is unable to stop the illegal sale.'[24]

Langevin's letter reveals that a change in the status of the liquor permit had taken place by 1884. The response of the government of the North-West Territories to the influx of settlement had been to issue permits more freely than before. The clear intention of the law was that the permits allowed only for personal consumption of the imported spirits but many of the newer permit holders used them or allowed them to be used by others to import liquor for resale to the public. The Mounted Police did not recognize the change, which was entirely *de facto*. The police instead of going along with the trend like other branches of government stepped up their campaign to enforce the law. This decision to enforce strictly an area of the law which was ambiguous to most of the public brought immediate cries of outrage. It looked to the average citizen of the Territories as if the government was giving him the right to drink with one hand and punishing him with the other. This view of the situation was not entirely without justice. In 1885 a meeting of three hundred citizens of Calgary sent a telegram to the prime minister asking that the Mounted Police be withdrawn from Calgary and all other incorporated towns, 'owing to the arbitrary, capricious and tyrannical manner in which they have administered the law...'[25] The Calgarians got small comfort from Macdonald, who replied blandly that the police were bound to enforce the law until it was changed. If they had been arbitrary in their approach, he continued, details should be sent and a full investigation would be made.[26] The angry citizens must have consulted a lawyer and discovered that the police were acting entirely within the law, because no details were forthcoming.

The protest meeting of 1885 in Calgary, although it cleared the air temporarily, did nothing to change the fundamentals of the problem. The illegal liquor trade continued to grow and so did the public conviction that the laws were being applied unfairly. Two years after the first meeting the citizens of Calgary tried a different approach. A spokesman, one Bleecker, asked the North-West Territories Council to change the liquor law so as to allow the sale of liquor under licence. To support the request he pointed out that in spite of the efforts of the police it was possible to buy a drink twenty-four hours a day in Calgary any day of the week. Fortunes were being made in spite of the law. One saloon keeper admitted losing $5000.00 in fines and seizures in the course of a single year but since his profit amounted to $20,000.00 he was still very much in business.[27] Bleecker hastened to assure the Mounted Police that he had no intention of denigrating their work, he merely wished to demonstrate that the law was unenforceable.[28] Superintendent W.M. Herchmer, in command of the division at Calgary, reported to the commissioner that conditions in the town were substantially as described to the North-West Territories Council. He also agreed with Bleecker that effective enforcement of the law was impossible because public opinion was strongly on the side of the saloon keepers.[29]

Resistance to the liquor laws took a different and more serious form in Prince Albert in the same year. Open conflict between the Mounted Police and the citizens of Prince Albert broke out on two occasions. In retrospect there is a comic opera air to these proceedings but that should not obscure the seriousness with which both parties regarded them at the time. A Mounted Police constable by the name of Leslie was sent to search for liquor at a dance held at a Prince Albert hotel in December 1887. While carrying out a search of the hotel's stables he was discovered by the town constable, charged with vagrancy, and subsequently convicted on the charge by two local justices of the peace. The force naturally appealed the conviction on behalf of the constable and it was set aside by Mr Justice McGuire of the Territorial Supreme Court, who called it a prostitution of the law and a travesty of justice.[30] The case was also referred by the minister of justice to the lieutenant-governor, who warned the justices of the peace involved that this kind of behaviour would not be tolerated. None of these measures could do anything to remove the public discontent of which the incident was only a symptom.

The second act of the Prince Albert farce, which occurred some months later, demonstrated that relations between police and public had not improved but deteriorated. This time Constable Leslie returned the favour and arrested the constable. Leslie had been attempting to break up a fight in a bar when the town policeman arrived on the scene and tried to assist him. In the heat of the moment, or so Leslie claimed, he did not recognize the town policeman and warned him to stay out of the way. The town constable replied that no son of a bitch was going to stop him, at which point Leslie arrested him and marched him off to the police guardroom. What happened to the original fight is not recorded in the report. The combatants probably adjourned to watch this more interesting confrontation. An angry mob of citizens tried without success to prevent the Mounted Policeman from taking his prisoner in and the town constable spent the night in jail. The following day the Town Council threatened the Mounted Police with civil action for false imprisonment while for a time the police considered prosecuting both the town constable and two members of the Town Council who had been among those attempting to prevent his arrest. However, tempers cooled quickly on both sides, the prisoner was released, and relations patched up.[31]

In the face of this kind of public hostility there was little the police could do about enforcing the liquor laws. Their task was made no easier by two judicial decisions handed down by Mr Justice Rouleau of the Territorial Supreme Court in 1888 and 1889. In the first of these the judge ruled that the police could not search saloons or bars without warrant.[32] In the second he provided legal support for the popular notion that the permit system could be stretched to cover the sale of liquor by holding that once liquor had been legally imported into the North-West Territories, anyone, and not merely the holder of the permit, might thereafter lawfully have that liquor in his possession.[33] The police hastily consulted the law officers of the government and the decisions were reversed before long. But the fact that these legal ambiguities were quickly removed could not change the fact that public feeling against the liquor laws had been strengthened by the support of so prestigious an individual as the judge. Superintendent McIlree, then in command of the Mounted Police at Calgary, felt the heaviest weight of public disapproval and complained: 'Neither a policeman nor a civilian will inform except in isolated cases, as owing to the general feeling against the liquor law, it means social ostracism to the informer.'[34]

McIlree was not exaggerating the problem in the least, nor was it confined to the two centres of Calgary and Prince Albert. The following editorial from a Medicine Hat newspaper indicates the state of public feeling elsewhere.

Considerable consternation was imminent in the city Monday over the rumour that a whiskey informer was at large. The rumour developed into a fact, and the majority of the citizens were expressive of their indignation. The action the citizens of Medicine Hat have ever adopted in a case of this kind should prove a valuable example to anyone nursing this intention. As it is considered by any man who is a man, so it is considered by the majority of the people in Medicine Hat to be a low, mean and infamous piece of business to inform on a fellow citizen under such arbitrary laws as control the liquor traffic of the Northwest. Any words of condemnation are inadequate to express the opinion of the people of such despicable, degrading and disingenuous conduct on the part of any man. The most vile oath would be far too sacred to apply to a man so wholly depraved, unworthily artful and devoid of all honour, as to inform on a man, or a number of men, who had at all times befriended him.[35]

All the police got in return for their increasingly unpopular efforts to uphold the law was the frustrating awareness that more illegal liquor was being sold every week within their jurisdiction.

It was becoming increasingly clear to the police that their usefulness as a law enforcement agency was seriously threatened by public resentment over the liquor question. The Calgary Monthly Reports for 1888 showed that the Mounted Police in that division were occupied with liquor cases almost to the exclusion of all other kinds. Faced with this realization the important question for the police became that of how they were to extricate themselves from their dilemma. Opinions on this question differed within the force. Comptroller White favoured a relaxation of efforts strictly to enforce the liquor law in the hope that the legislation would be changed before long.[36] The commissioner supported continued strict enforcement regardless of the consequences.[37] The man most directly affected, Superintendent McIlree at Calgary, seems to have realized better than either of his superiors that a different strategy was necessary to bring about a permanent solution. He announced that he intended to set up a town detachment in Calgary which would concentrate almost exclusively on liquor law enforcement, in spite of the judicial barriers erected by Mr Justice Rouleau.[38] It is clear from McIlree's comments in this and other reports that he had no illusions about the possibility of successfully enforcing the law. What he hoped to achieve instead was to create enough public pressure on the Legislative Assembly to bring about a change in the law.[39]

The position of a superintendent in the field in a case like this was a strong one. McIlree could scarcely be censured by his superiors for what amounted to the strict performance of his duty. The commissioner in any case supported McIlree's position, if from a different set of motives. The comptroller realized that he had been outmaneuvered and capitulated. In late 1890 the police began a stepped-up campaign against liquor violations. The lieutenant-governor promised to co-operate by restricting the number of permits issued.[40] Those individuals who were known to have allowed others to use their permits to cover the purchase of liquor for resale would be refused further privileges. A few months later all divisions were ordered to search saloons, bars, and hotels at irregular intervals to ensure surprise.[41] The strategy adopted by the police had its effect. It might not have been necessary in the first place had not the whole question of liquor legislation become embroiled in a constitutional controversy between the Legislative Assembly and the lieutenant-governor which held up almost all substantive legislation for several years.[42] Legislation allowing for the licencing of bars was passed by the Assembly in January 1892 and came into effect at the end of April that year.

The change in the liquor laws came none too soon. In addition to the public disaffection against the police a more direct political threat had emerged. Commissioner Herchmer believed that the inquiry into his conduct as head of the force instigated chiefly by Nicholas Flood Davin was largely a result of the unpopular position taken by the police in the liquor controversy.[43] In this Herchmer was probably correct. While Davin's actions were not directly motivated by the liquor situation, the public mood was. It was this mood that made the inquiry politically possible in the first place. The police were unpopular for perhaps the only time in their history. It is clear that Davin sought to take advantage of this swing in public opinion and equally clear that had it not existed the inquiry would never have got off the ground. By the time the full-scale judicial inquiry was held the laws had changed and the police were back in the good graces of the public. It is significant that after the inquiry cleared the commissioner, Davin made no effort to follow up his charges by making them into a political issue.

The new law did more than bring prohibition to an end. It removed altogether much of the burden of enforcement from the Mounted Police. By providing for the appointment of liquor licence inspectors in incorporated towns the law made possible a graceful withdrawal on the part of the force. The licence inspectors, usually the municipal police, had no more success in enforcing the new law than the Mounted Police had with the old one. Superintendent Deane commented rather sourly: 'I often wonder whether the Territorial Government are or are not proud of their inspectors and of the work they do in carrying out the law. I wonder whether they think they are worth the salaries they draw; I don't.'[44] Most officers in the force, however, felt that the new law was all to the good. The commissioner and comptroller were more than happy to be able to refuse requests from towns for assistance in enforcing the liquor laws on the grounds that this was now a purely municipal responsibility and no concern of the Mounted Police.[45]

The police were still very much concerned with cases of drunkenness, but the whole atmosphere was now different. In 1897 Superintendent Howe reported from Regina: 'Convictions were made in five or six cases of intoxication, the usual small fines being inflicted and cheerfully paid.'[46] The illegal sale of liquor remained a Mounted Police responsibility only in cases involving sale to the Indians and in one other special circumstance. If drunkenness became a serious problem in and around railway construction camps the government could proclaim a special piece of legislation called the Public Works Peace Preservation Act which among other things temporarily prohibited the sale of liquor for ten miles on either side of the right of way. This procedure was followed during the construction of all railways built in the North-West in this period.[47] These were special cases which did not affect the general public. From 1892 enforcement of the liquor laws ceased to be a source of conflict between police and public.

The peculiar circumstances, both political and psychological, which surrounded the liquor controversy go far to explain why in this one instance the police departed from their normal approach to moral offences. The eventual decision of the police to do what they could to bring about a change in the law was very much in character. What at first glance appears to be an exception to the general relationship between crime and class in the North-West Territories and the police view of that relationship, proves on closer examination to be a special case. As with other moral offences the police tried to avoid confrontations with otherwise respectable citizens.

It is an intriguing fact, given the importance of the liquor question to the police, that prohibition and temperance politics, which were a very important part of local and Territorial politics until 1892, did not enter into the police assessment of the situation and are mentioned only once in the police records.[48] The police realized that even if the prohibitionists were in political control, as they were in some areas, a substantial minority of the population would still be alienated by enforcement of the liquor laws. To be enforceable at all, laws regulating the morals of the public must have virtually unanimous support and such cases are rare. In the instance of the liquor laws as in others the police succeeded in emerging intact because they based their actions firmly upon the social realities of their time and place.

11
The NWMP and minority groups

One of the most important criteria for assessing the claims of a society to have established social justice is the way in which it treats its minorities. If there is justice for those who lack the power to demand it effectively there is justice for all. If some are oppressed by others the entire social fabric is weakened. Not all minorities are powerless, of course. The rich, as Sir John A. Macdonald pointed out during the Confederation debates, are also a minority. But the rich normally have little trouble protecting their own interests. Other minority groups vary widely in their ability to manipulate the institutions of society and government to their own advantage. In nineteenth-century Canada minority groups ranged all the way from the native peoples who were virtually defenceless to the settler from the United States who was almost indistinguishable from his Canadian counterpart.

The first question which arises in considering minority groups in the North-West Territories in the last third of the nineteenth century is, which groups fall into this category? Even settlers from eastern Canada were not a majority in numerical terms. On the other hand the Canadian element in the population thought of themselves as a majority and with good reason since the North-West, however isolated, was only part of a larger whole. The settler from the United Kingdom was much the same, acting always on the assumption that the Canadian North-West was his birthright, an assumption shared by the Canadian government, which regarded British settlers and those from eastern Canada as equally desirable. The American settler, although on the whole even better adapted to life in the Canadian West than the British immigrant, does not qualify as part of the majority. What made the Americans a minority group was their political outlook, or at least what Canadians generally assumed that outlook to be. In the view of the authorities American settlers needed to undergo a process of Canadianization before they were fully acceptable.

Immigrants from continental European countries were clearly minorities, readily identifiable as such by their language and customs. Like the Americans they were officially regarded as good settler material, able to take their place with the majority after a period of tutelage. Indians and Métis were a minority group after about 1885 and were even more easily identifiable than the Europeans but much less amenable to assimilation. The final important minority group in the North-West in this period was organized labour, obviously a different kind of group from the others but at least as foreign to the generality of the rural population and in many ways the least powerful segment of the population.

The police treated all these minorities differently from the rest of the population, indeed there was a different approach for every group. This did not mean that the ideal of equality before the law was abandoned, nor did it mean that the powerless suffered from official discrimination. Differential treatment was based in part on the recognition that some minorities had disabilities and was intended rather to protect them than oppress them. In part also differential treatment grew out of the primary preoccupation of the Mounted Police with the maintenance of order and compliance with the law. Not to have recognized that outsiders had different concepts of the citizen and his relationship with the state would not only have been unrealistic but would have operated to the disadvantage of most minorities. The police tried to ensure that in the long run social stability in the North-West would be the product of a concensus on Canadian ideas of law and order.

The native peoples of the North-West Territories, Indians and Métis, became a minority in the years following the completion of the Canadian Pacific Railway in 1885. Up to this point they had been the primary concern of the police. Once they ceased to be a major threat to the advance of settlement there was a subtle shift in the attitude of the police which gave rise to some changes in policy. The relationship after 1885 was no longer the old one of mutual respect as exemplified by Colonel Macleod and Chief Crowfoot. Now the relationship was paternal, with the Indians protected and pitied but not respected.[1] There was less emphasis on persuasion and co-operation and more on coercion. A sign of the times was a General Order issued in 1890 which instructed all detachments not to allow Indian prisoners out of the guardroom without ball and chain.[2] This precaution was reiterated in the 1895 edition of *General Orders for the North-West Mounted Police*, along with instructions to avoid feeding Indian prisoners at hotels and restaurants if at all possible.[3]

The police were also more willing to go along with the occasionally rather high-handed methods of the Indian agents. In 1888 Herchmer wrote to the commissioner of Indian affairs asking for stricter controls on Indians leaving reservations near Calgary. 'If the same stringent rules administered to the Northern Indians about leaving their Reservations were issued by your Department in the South, the NWMP are now in a position to rigidly enforce them without danger to the general peace of the country.'[4] In 1903 the agent on the Peigan reserve sentenced a recalcitrant brave to two months' imprisonment. This action was technically illegal since the agent only had the authority to commit for trial. The police continued to hold the prisoner at the request of the Indian Department while the agent altered the documents in the case.[5]

This changed approach represented a concession on the part of the police to popular prejudices against the Indians. There can be no doubt that most settlers, and indeed many members of the police, regarded Indians as inferior beings to be tolerated only as long as they stayed out of the way. A freighter by the name of William Wallace Clarke, snowbound in the Touchwood Hills in the winter of 1875, had the leisure to record his feelings about the Indians. 'There is horror and loathing in the very thought that the miserable, ragged, filthy, crawling wretch of an Indian papoose or even its parent should sit in the same heaven with us.'[6] In 1888 Constable Simons of the Mounted Police was accused of giving some iodine to an Indian woman who drank it and died from the effects. In his report on the case, Simons's commanding officer wrote: 'Simons has retained Mr Haultain for his defence, but I do not think any Western jury will convict him.'[7]

In another case Superintendent Deane dismissed charges of intoxication brought against a constable by an Indian scout. He explained his reasons for doing so to the commissioner. 'Ever since Mr F.W. Haultain told me of the true circumstances attending the conviction of John Bush here in 1884, I, in common with others, have hesitated to convict a white man on the unsupported testimony of an Indian.'[8] Colonel Macleod as magistrate had once ruled it illegal to arrest Indians at a sun dance, on the analogy of a church.[9] A few years later Superintendent Steele made the following report on the same subject.

I regret very much to say that permission has been granted to the Bloods and Piegans to hold a Sun Dance. It is a relic of barbarism that should be stamped out once and forever. I am convinced that the present generation of Indians have absorbed sufficient civilization and Christianity to render the ceremonies accompanying the Sun Dance a burlesque. It still, however, has power to excite the Indians and takes them away from their legitimate occupations of farming and inflames the young bucks with a desire for glory that can no longer be gratified, but finds vent in cattle killing and horse stealing.[10]

Logic was never one of Sam Steele's strong points but his report gives an indication of the shift in attitudes.

Examples of popular prejudice against the Indian could be multiplied many times. It is scarcely surprising that the attitudes of the police should have moved in the same direction. What is more significant is how few changes actually took place in relations between the police and the Indians. A strong element of sympathy along with the responsibility to uphold the law ensured that the force would maintain its role as protector of the tribes against the harsher manifestations of white civilization. The Indian Department in an effort to control the movements of their charges had made use of a system of passes issued by agents for Indians who wished to leave the reserve to visit the towns. The pass system was without legal foundation but the police had co-operated with the Indian Department in enforcing it as a matter of mutual convenience. In 1892, however, the subject came up in a conversation between Commissioner Herchmer and some of the Circuit Court judges. Herchmer was advised by the gentlemen of the bench that the pass system was illegal and that if the right of the police to enforce it was challenged in the courts, the police would surely lose. The commissioner at once informed the Indian Department that the police would no longer attempt to order Indians without passes back to their reserves. A legal opinion from the government's law officers was also requested.[11] The Indian Department urged the police to continue enforcing the pass regulations on the rather peculiar grounds that the moral responsibilities of the Indian Department transcended treaty obligations.[12] The advice of the law officers was unequivocally opposed to continuation of the practice. A circular immediately went out from Regina directing all officers to refrain from ordering Indians back to the reserves.[13] When the question came up again in later years the position of the force remained the same.[14]

The police were no more inclined after 1885 than they had ever been to give credence to ranchers and settlers who tried to blame the Indians for every missing cow. Complaints of this nature when investigated usually proved to be without foundation.[15] The police also continued to restrain those officials whose zeal to civilize the Indians sometimes outweighed their common sense. Investigating a small fire at the school on the Blood Reserve near Ft Macleod in 1895, Superintendent Steele discovered that the principal of the school was in the habit of locking his pupils in their dormitory at night to prevent them from escaping and returning to their parents. The principal was ordered to cease doing so immediately and was informed that if a child ever died in a fire in such circumstances he would be tried for manslaughter.[16]

The same approach can be seen even more clearly in an incident which took place on a different reservation the same year. An Indian by the name of Standing Buffalo removed his child, a boy named Dominick, from the Industrial School at Qu'Appelle because the child was ill. The principal of the school summoned a Mounted Police constable and asked him to bring the child back, by force if necessary. He also sought to have Standing Buffalo arrested as an example to others on a charge of stealing the boy's clothes, which technically belonged to the government. The constable refused to take any action without consulting his superior officer.[17] The officer, Inspector Charles Constantine, declined both of the principal's requests. After citing some legal grounds for leaving the boy with his parents he went on to say: 'Whether these reasons are good or not, it would have been an inhuman act to have taken the boy away, to say nothing of the criminality attached to it should the child have died after his having been taken out in such cold weather.'[18] This settled the particular case but not the principle involved. The issue eventually reached the prime minister, with the police arguing that care must be exercised in enforcing the education regulations. New regulations must be introduced gradually, Herchmer wrote, with the preservation of peace and order taking precedence over a narrow interpretation of the rules. 'In the case of the boy Dominick, it appears that he really is sick, and may die, and yet we are called upon to arrest him and send him back to the school, where though no doubt he would receive better attendance and food, yet I think the parents' wishes should be considered in such a case.'[19] The affair ended with the prime minister instructing the commissioner to use his discretion in cases of this nature.

In criminal cases involving Indians the police were quite as scrupulous as with any other group. Several instances exist of Indians suspected of murdering whites being released for lack of evidence.[20] When an Indian prisoner being held in a police guardroom managed to get his hands on a revolver and shoot himself, the sergeant responsible was reduced to the ranks and the constable actually guarding the prisoner received a month's hard labour.[21] Inevitably there were cases of discrimination against Indians which were not covered by the laws of the day. The police could not take direct action in such cases but they could and occasionally did bring informal pressure to bear, as in an incident at Calgary in 1898. The annual summer race meet was held that year at Springbank near the city. The committee in charge of organizing the races decided to exclude Indians from participation. Inspector J.O. Wilson reported:

I protested on behalf of the Indians, whom I considered to be very unjustly treated, and a most short-sighted policy on the part of the stock owners. The bills did not bar Indians or anyone so I could not see how they could deter them.

Public opinion, outside of the few horse owners who were no doubt afraid of being beaten, was with me in this matter.[22]

Wilson may well have been right about public opinion but the significant point was that he took the trouble to use his influence to bring it to bear.

However much their attitudes may have changed, the strategy of the police in dealing with the Indians remained constant. They consistently tried to demonstrate to the Indians that the actions of the police towards them were based on a rational system of laws which operated to the benefit of all. Superintendent Deane's approach to the problem of supervising the repatriation of a group of Canadian Crees from the United States illustrates the strategy perfectly. Some seven hundred Crees had been rounded up in Montana by the United States Army and put on trains to Canada. The Indian Department requested a police escort for the Indians on the grounds that the American officials considered it necessary to guard them with a troop of cavalry. Deane provided one man, Inspector Victor Williams, to perform this duty and sent him the following telegram:

Accompany Indians here on train tomorrow. It is said they are inclined to be troublesome. Remember we have no right to coerce them and the law will hold us responsible for the abuse of its powers. Make no display of force. Do nothing to irritate them. Keep them from leaving the train if possible, but take no step from which you may have to recede. For these reasons I wish you to come without other police.[23]

The inspector followed his instructions and conducted his charges to their destination without incident. In addition he spotted two suspected murderers in the group and arrested them. Deane, who was irritated by the attitude of the Indian Department to begin with, commented: 'The Indians must be duller than we take them for, if they cannot appreciate the difference between moral coercion under the Union Jack and physical force under the Stars and Stripes.'[24]

The Mounted Police employed some Indians and Métis as scouts and special constables. The name of the famous Métis scout, Jerry Potts, is known to anyone who has read anything of the history of the force. There were many others like him who served the police loyally for a pittance. These scouts and specials were strictly casual employees, even those like Jerry Potts who served continuously for twenty years or more. The police could not have done without these men and yet they received a fraction of the pay and none of the pensions or other privileges enjoyed by regular constables. In the early years scouts and interpreters were essential to maintain good relations with the Indians. In later years

Indian special constables were hired to perform routine tasks during periods in which there was a shortage of regular constables.

Sir John A. Macdonald had originally intended to recruit substantial numbers of Indians and Métis into the force on the model of the British Army in India.[25] This plan was abandoned, presumably because of the Métis part in the 1870 rebellion. Nothing further was heard about hiring either group as permanent members of the police until 1891, when the Deputy Superintendent-General of Indian Affairs, Lawrence Vankoughnet, wrote to White and suggested that more Indians be employed by the police. He pointed out that the United States Army had successfully made use of Indians as soldiers.[26] White rejected the suggestion on the grounds that the police had found the Indians unwilling to stay with a job over an extended period of time. Hiring Indians would also mean establishing their families in the vicinity of posts. 'The placing of a troop of Indians in the neighbourhood of a Police Post for drill and instruction, with their squaws, children, ponies, dogs and camp outfit, would be a source of much inconvenience and anxiety.'[27] The matter was dropped and did not come up again.

During the South African War a situation arose which indicated that there were additional unstated reasons for White's lack of enthusiasm for the idea. When the police were recruiting in the North-West for the Canadian contingents and later for the South African Constabulary, a considerable number of Métis wanted to serve.[28] Herchmer asked White's opinion about enlisting them and received the following reply:

This is a matter in which you must exercise your own discretion. You could not engage them as Half-Breeds, but any who are intelligent, educated and would pass as white men could be taken on the same as other applicants. It would be a mistake to accept men who would be known in the force as Half-Breeds; therefore only those who would be treated as equals by the rest of the Contingent should be engaged.[29]

The same considerations undoubtedly lay behind the reluctance of the police to recruit among the native peoples for their own service. Race was a factor to be considered because it correlated with the class ideas which were so important to the force.

Indian and Métis scouts and special constables continued to be used as the occasion demanded. They were unarmed and did not enjoy the same powers of arrest as regular constables.[30] On a few occasions Indians who were acquainted with or related to an Indian suspect were used by the police to detain or capture him so as to avoid arousing his suspicions. The murderer George Godin was captured in this way at Stony Plain in 1888 by four Indian special constables.[31] Bad

Young Man (or Charcoal), a Blood who murdered one of his own tribe and then killed Sergeant Wilde of the police, was apprehended by his two brothers in 1897.[32] On rare occasions when the police were very shorthanded Indian special constables were used to carry out regular patrols and even detachment duty.[33] This was a last resort, however, undertaken with great reluctance because the police, like almost everyone else, believed that Indians were unreliable and because the public disliked the idea.

European immigrants evoked a different set of responses from the police. Those European settlers who took up individual homesteads were treated by the police as part of the majority, that is they received no special attention. Those who settled in groups or colonies as they were called at the time usually had a police detachment established in their community as soon as it was founded. If possible the police would select a man who spoke the language for this duty; if none were available an interpreter was hired.[34] Sometimes these detachments were set up as a result of pressure from other settlers in the surrounding districts, who frequently harboured dire suspicions about anyone with a foreign accent. If no such request was forthcoming the police would establish a detachment anyway, since they were not themselves immune from these prejudices. As the great influx of settlers was beginning in the 1890s Herchmer raised the question in a letter to White. 'I would draw your attention to the very mixed nationalities of the other settlers now coming in, many of them from countries with very meagre ideas of right and wrong from our standpoint.'[35]

The detachments in the various colonies proved to have very little to do in the way of actual law enforcement. With one exception the police found European immigrants less prone to break the law than the general population.[36] Reports on German settlements were highly favourable.[37] The same was true of the Mennonites, who might have been suspect because of the resistance of some sects to public education. The Ukrainian settlers also impressed the police. Superintendent Sévère Gagnon, after visiting a Ukrainian settlement in Saskatchewan, reported that they were exceedingly poor and that many were having difficulty adapting to the farming techniques necessary on the prairies. 'They are, however, frugal, industrious and certainly the best workers in the country. It is believed by many that they will eventually form the best settlers of the District. They are anxious to learn the English language.'[38]

The fact that the police did establish detachments and get to know these groups at first hand proved a boon to all parties. In one case a settler near Qu'Appelle by the name of D. Henry Starr wrote an angry letter to the minister of the interior accusing some German colonists who lived nearby of stealing hay from him. Warming to his task, he went on to say that the Germans 'have turned out to be the very worst and lowest class of people under the sun, and who are considered quite a nuisance, and ought to be banished from the country otherwise they will be the means of driving every respectable settler out of the place.'[39] A corporal was dispatched at once to investigate and discovered that all Starr's ideas were based on hearsay; he had not talked to any of the Germans since their arrival in the community. After the corporal had finished his questioning Starr admitted that there was no shred of evidence to connect the Germans with the theft. In forwarding the report to Ottawa the officer in charge of the case appended his own views. 'I might add that our experience of German settlers in the different parts of the North West points to the fact that they are law-abiding and good citizens and cause the police little trouble.'[40]

A similar incident happened some years later at the Ukrainian settlement of Edna near Edmonton. The Member of Parliament for Edmonton, Frank Oliver, never one to be overly concerned with factual accuracy, wrote the police demanding that a detachment be established in the community at once. The English-speaking settlers were tired of the Ukrainians' thievery and would soon take the law into their own hands, Oliver said, adding that a smallpox epidemic had broken out in the community.[41] The police investigated at once. The smallpox epidemic turned out to be two cases of measles. No one could be found who had actually experienced theft from any source, but rumours of the larcenous propensities of the Ukrainians abounded. Inspector J.O. Wilson, who investigated the complaints, reported that both English-speaking and Ukrainian settlers were strongly in favour of a detachment being established. He urged that this be done at once to prevent rumour from getting out of hand in the future. For the Ukrainian settlers he had only praise as law-abiding and hard-working individuals.[42]

Police detachments established in new settlements like the one mentioned above spent the greater part of their time helping the settlers adjust to their new life. Many of the new arrivals were inadequately equipped and the police distributed relief supplies.[43] On at least one notable occasion concern for the welfare of an immigrant community brought the police into conflict with the Department of the Interior, whose immigration agents were responsible for the well-being of new settlers. The incident began with a report in August 1897 from a Mounted Police corporal stationed at a Ukrainian settlement east of Edmonton. The corporal reported truly terrible conditions among the newly arrived settlers there. Many of them were starving, sick, and unable to find work so that they could buy tools and seed grain. The corporal asked for permission to issue relief supplies.[44] The report was forwarded to the Department of the Interior in Ottawa. The Department demanded an immediate explanation from the local immigration agent. The agent visited the settlement, reported no sickness or deprivation, and accused the police of encouraging idleness among the settlers by offering relief supplies.[45] After some months this report was forwarded to police headquarters along with a not very subtle suggestion that they should mind their own business.

The police, who had no particular axe to grind, were stung by the implied assertion that a member of the force had falsified his report and was intent upon subsidizing laziness. Inspector P.C.H. Primrose was sent to recheck the situation. He submitted a report which was a model of clarity and circumstantial detail, as opposed to that of the immigration agent which was couched entirely in generalities. The inspector's report, based on interviews with all thirty-five destitute families mentioned in Corporal Butler's original report, is one of the best descriptions anywhere of the difficulties encountered by immigrant groups in the harsh environment of the Canadian West. It leaves no room for doubt about the accuracy of the original police report.

Primrose discovered that the immigration agent, Sutter, had visited only a few of the more well-to-do families in the settlement. Sutter had suggested that those who claimed to be starving were hiding their food but Primrose rejected this idea. The houses he found were invariably one-room sod huts which were simply too small to hide anything. Only two of these huts had floors and only four had stoves. A majority of the families had only the light summer clothing they wore on their backs, their baggage having been lost on the long journey to Canada. None of the families had blankets, only one had meat, and the most food Primrose found in any house was three bags of flour. The inspector did not say so but his description of the physical appearance of the children makes it clear that many were suffering from severe malnutrition. As for the accusation of idleness, Primrose found that all men who were able had worked during the fall but most had not been paid by the farmers who employed them. If any further proof were needed about the deplorable conditions in the settlement, six people out of the group of thirty-five families had died since Corporal Butler's report four months earlier.[46] One would be happy to be able to relate that the Department of the Interior admitted its error and corrected all the abuses, but this was not the case. Instead the police were ordered out of all Ukrainian settlements and did not get back in for several years.[47] Nevertheless, the mere existence of the police provided a valuable force for keeping nativist feelings among both government officials and the public in check.

It should be noted that the police attitudes described above applied to immigrants who settled on the land. Quite a different view of those in urban areas prevailed. In this period there was only one substantial urban group of European immigrants in the North-West Territories. Winnipeg was attracting thousands but it was outside the jurisdiction of the police. Only in Lethbridge, where there were large numbers of coal miners from eastern Europe, did recognizable immigrant groups exist in an urban setting. The miners were generally seen by the police as consisting of two groups: Hungarians and the blanket category of Slavs, or 'Sclavs' as Superintendent Deane insisted on spelling it. These people were regarded by the police solely as a problem in law enforcement, without any of the sympathy present in dealings with their rural counterparts. It was taken for granted that the Hungarians and Slavs would live in crowded, filthy conditions, get drunk often, and occasionally murder each other.[48] Evidence was difficult to acquire in such cases because of the clannishness of these groups and their unwillingness to talk to outsiders. The police made no special effort to penetrate these barriers except in one instance when a rumour arose that a secret society, similar to the Mafia, existed among the Hungarians. A constable who spoke Magyar was brought in but failed to uncover any further details.[49]

Generally speaking, relations between the police and European immigrants were healthy. The presence of the police and their positive attitude had a calming effect on the majority of the population. At the minimum the police prevented outright conflict between ethnic groups. In a substantial number of cases they offered the kind of assistance which made adjustment easier. One group, however, was an exception to this rule. The police could neither understand nor effectively come to terms with the radical Sons of Freedom sect of the Doukhobours. Nude parades and farm burning in the name of religion had no place in the mental equipment of the average Mounted Policeman. When the Doukhobours failed to respond to the same approach that succeeded with other European groups the police were at a loss. They could not come up with any creative solution to the problem of the Doukhobours and fell back on mass arrests of all who violated existing laws.[50] After several of these, one optimistic officer wrote: 'The Doukhobour question is now finally and satisfactorily settled and I fully believe that they will make excellent settlers.'[51] What he was witnessing was the beginning, not the end, of a series of confrontations between the sect and the Mounted Police which was to last for almost seventy years.

The police reacted to settlers from the United States in much the same manner as to European settlers but for different reasons. The prevailing attitudes to Americans were ambivalent. On the one hand they were regarded as the most desirable type of settler since they tended to be relatively well off and had no trouble adapting to the agricultural practices of the Canadian West.[52] On the other hand the police considered Americans to be even more in need of tutelage in the Canadian way of life than were Europeans. Americans were a more insidious threat simply because they adapted so easily. Although there is little evidence in the police records to support the belief, the police were convinced that all Americans were the potential bearers of anarchy, disorder, and violence. Commissioner Perry was merely expressing the view of the force as a whole when he wrote the following passage in a letter to White in 1903. 'I suppose that the peace of the Territories may seem assured to those who are in the East, and even to the people of the Territories who are accustomed to it. They little know of the reckless class of American outlaws to the South of us.'[53] This view prevailed in spite of many personal friendships between officers and Americans and constant friendly co-operation with United States law enforcement agencies. It was a fundamental part of the Canadian national myth and therefore not susceptible to rational analysis.[54]

The police arrived in the North-West with very definite ideas about Americans and American society. Early contacts were confined mainly to whisky traders and deserters from the United States Army; men who tended to reinforce the stereotypes. The police were constant and interested observers of the American scene across the border to the south. The only observations which registered, however, were those which provided opportunities to compare the quality of American life unfavourably with that of Canada. The police records are filled with lurid accounts of lynchings, mob violence, and general lawlessness garnered from American newspapers, hearsay, and observation of border towns. Sergeant G.W. Byrne, travelling in Montana on the trail of some cattle stolen in Canada, reported that he had been forced to pass himself off as a merchant because the town to which he traced the stolen cattle was controlled by a gang of thieves. 'I might state here that the town of Culbertson consists of two stores, two gambling saloons, one boarding house and a couple of houses of ill fame. There are about 20 cowboys or horse thieves and gamblers who take turns watching our every movement, and immediately one of us leaves the town scouts are sent out in all directions to give the alarm.'[55] Perhaps an even better illustration of police attitudes is to be found in the following comments by A. Bowen Perry, then a superintendent:

The detachment stationed at Sterling, the new town on the Boundary on the Soo R'way did good service in keeping the peace. The track laying gang on the American side was accompanied by a number of whisky sellers, gamblers and prostitutes. S/Sgt. McGinnis' report, which I have forwarded you, relates that great disorder prevailed on the American side; serious rows, drunkenness and debauchery. On our side there was no trouble of any kind.[56]

It followed from these assumptions that if disorder existed in the North-West Territories it was probably the work of American settlers. The police were not slow to draw this conclusion and on several occasions attributed disturbances to Americans on no better evidence than the presence of American settlers in the neighbourhood. When an angry crowd of trial spectators at Carlyle voiced their disapproval of a liquor conviction by shouting, 'To hell with the red coats,'

Superintendent J.O. Wilson offered the following explanation. 'The settlers and residents of Carlyle and Arcola are chiefly Americans, a large proportion of them being single men, who are imbued with the American western idea of law and order, and consequently will have to be taught that they cannot do as they like on this side of the line.'[57]

As Wilson's remarks imply, the remedy was as obvious to the police as the complaint. Commissioner Herchmer set forth the approach of the force to Canadianizing the Americans in a letter to White in 1892:

A very large immigration, as you are aware, took place last year into the Edmonton country, mostly from the Western States where law and order are not rigidly enforced, and I am credibly informed that the flow this year will greatly exceed all previous seasons, most of the immigrants being drawn from Oregon and Washington States, and it will be necessary to greatly increase our patrols in consequence as the opinion these people form of our administration of the laws on their first arrival, has the greatest possible effect on their future conduct, and inability on our part to impress them with the necessity of strictly obeying our laws, will, in my opinion, be certain to lead to heavy expenses later on in the administration of justice, the cost of which would greatly exceed that of laying a good moral foundation at the start, through the activity and vigilance of the police.[58]

The police reacted most strongly of all to the Mormon settlers who established themselves in southern Alberta in the late 1880s. It was one of the very few occasions upon which the actions of the police appear absurd in retrospect. No doubt it was the question of polygamy which aroused their animosity. Some of the reports indicate that part of the hostility derived from the fact that their religion made the Latter Day Saints more readily identifiable as Americans. When the Mormons arrived the police as was their custom checked out the new settlers. Superintendent Steele submitted a report on the Mormons which was so illogical that it can only be interpreted as the product of unvarnished prejudice. After confiding to Herchmer his suspicions that the Mormon settlers were continuing the practice of polygamy, Steele noted that the other settlers in the area disliked the new arrivals and continued:

The intelligence of the Mormons is far below the average of the settlers of any country; there are some sharp, shrewd men among them at the head of affairs but the remainder are, as a rule, steeped in ignorance and as perfect slaves to the Church and Elders as it is possible for any community to be.[59]

Without apparently realizing the contradiction, Steele then went on to state that the Mormons had the most prosperous and successful farms in the district.

After presenting this extraordinary collection of conflicting statements Steele suggested assigning a detective to spy on them. Herchmer was inclined to agree with Steele but fortunately cooler heads prevailed and White rejected the idea.[60] It is abundantly clear that Steele and Herchmer in this case were reflecting public opinion.[61] Public hostility was so much in evidence that a police corporal reporting on polygamy among the Latter Day Saints felt constrained to explain that he had obtained his information by winning the confidence of highly placed members of the church. 'I mention these facts as outsiders have at different times made statements that I was unnecessarily friendly, and I wish no action of mine to be misconstrued with regard to Mormons or Mormonism.'[62] Even Superintendent Deane, who got along well with the Mormons and regarded them as solid citizens, disliked the large role the church played in their life.[63]

The police continued to keep a wary eye on the Mormon settlements for years but that was the extent of their involvement. The Mormon communities generally had a member of the church as justice of the peace and ran their own affairs to a very large extent. When bad feeling between Mormons and other settlers surfaced in 1897 the latter asked a local magistrate for permission to carry guns. In spite of their suspicions the police quickly put an end to such notions. The settlers were warned that carrying firearms was illegal and would be punished with the utmost severity.[64] Perhaps because of public hostility the Mormons made a considerable display of celebrating Dominion Day every July first. The police regarded this phenomenon with curiosity since instead of making the Latter Day Saints less conspicuous it only made them more so. Canadians generally tended to be undemonstrative on the occasion. One officer commented: 'It is strange how those Mormons start in to celebrate our natal day.'[65] The police were more impressed by the fact that schools in Mormon communities made use of American textbooks, 'wherein, of course, a hatred of everything English is inculcated.'[66] This information was passed on to the Chairman of the Council of Public Instruction for the North-West Territories. Once the hierarchy of the Church of Jesus Christ of the Latter Day Saints suspended the practice of polygamy, public hostility died down but the police, at least until 1905, never accepted the Mormons as fully as they did other groups.

The final minority group to be discussed in this chapter, organized labour, presents a different set of problems than the ethnic minorities. Public attitudes toward labour have changed much more drastically in the last eighty years than toward any other minority. Nineteenth-century labour disputes are almost incomprehensible if approached with an assumption that people thought of them then as they do now. Attitudes to labour in the twentieth century have been polarized very strongly by a whole series of events. The Bolshevik Revolution in Russia and its repercussions elsewhere, for example, have planted the fear of class warfare among the middle and upper classes. On the other hand the successes of organized labour in raising the average standard of living in this century have convinced most union members and many others that the strike is almost entirely beneficial in its effects. These divergent views of labour and its place in society did not exist in nineteenth-century Canada outside of a tiny handful of individuals. Instead the whole question of labour-management relations was subsumed under existing concepts of class. The key phrase in 1890 was not labour-management relations but master-servant relations. This was the language of the law and of the public when they thought about the question at all.

Thus while the police spent much of their time dealing with problems which arose from labour disputes they did not think of it as a special problem apart from the other problems of maintaining peace and order. The police were not, as they often were to be in the twentieth century, forced to commit themselves morally to one side or another. It did not occur to any of the parties involved in labour disputes that the police by intervening could be considered to be helping one class exploit another class. Only one incident which happened at the end of the period under discussion showed the direction in which events were moving. The police were effectively neutral in almost all labour disputes. They acted as honest brokers to the general satisfaction of both sides and as often took the part of labour as of management.

Organized labour was very weak in the Canadian North-West around the turn of the century. Unions were confined almost exclusively to two industries, coal mining and the railways. Even in these industries many workers were unorganized. Strikes were usually local affairs concerned with local grievances. Strike funds and industry-wide bargaining were far in the future. The laws heavily favoured management and barely permitted unions to exist. In the case of an essential service like the railway it was taken for granted that, although the railway unions might strike, they had no right to interfere with strikebreakers hired by the company. During a strike by CPR engineers in 1883 the Mounted Police not only guarded railway property but operated engines when necessary to enable the company to put trains together.[67] Deserting employment was an offence which companies could and sometimes did insist that the police prosecute.[68] Those workers who legally left their jobs because of dissatisfaction with working conditions sometimes faced prosecution for vagrancy.[69] The general attitude of the police was summed up in a report by Commissioner Perry on police operations in connection with a CPR strike in 1901. The police had stepped in twice to prevent violence between scabs and strikers, Perry explained in a letter to White, then offered this comment: 'I know that it is difficult in such matters to please both parties. Without taking any part with the strikers it seems to me our duty to enable the railway company to continue its service.'[70]

On the whole, however, the police preferred to act as mediators and to prevent disputes from developing into potentially violent situations. In Lethbridge in 1894 the Alberta Railway and Coal Company closed down the mines, locked out the miners, and announced that only one hundred and thirty out of five hundred and eighty would be rehired and these at lower wages. The situation was very tense until Superintendent Deane persuaded the company to offer free transport to Great Falls, Montana, for those out of work. Deane felt the company had handled the situation very badly. He talked to the miners and reported: 'I mix freely with them and they will talk to me as one of themselves, in fact the only reliable information that Mr Galt [manager of the company] gets is from me. It is not always palatable, but I cannot help that.'[71] The situation eased at once. In his years at Lethbridge Deane settled many similar disputes by the use of such informal procedures, as did other officers at other locations.[72]

Probably the best description of the approach of the police to labour problems is to be found in the reports on police supervision of the construction of the Crow's Nest Pass branch of the CPR in 1897 and 1898. Some five thousand men were employed on the project and the company requested police aid.[73] Two inspectors, G.E. Sanders and A.R. Cuthbert, were assigned to the task along with eight non-commissioned officers and constables. Since part of the construction was in British Columbia, arrangements were made with the government of that province to have the officers appointed magistrates in British Columbia.[74] Sanders and Cuthbert soon found themselves inundated by work. By December 1897 Inspector Sanders was handling twenty to thirty complaints a day in his capacity as magistrate. He was forced to stop dealing with most of them through the court and resort to less formal methods of settling disputes.[75]

Since almost all the complaints were from employees, the police spent much of their time trying to pressure the CPR and its sub-contractors into improving working conditions and behaving reasonably toward the men. Most of the workers had been hired in eastern Canada, many under false pretences, as Inspector Sanders reported:

There is no doubt whatever that a great number of these men would never have come out here had they known they had to pay their fare, which from Ottawa here at a cent a mile is $22.49. These men have families in the East and when they discover that after working six weeks or two months there is not a cent coming to them, or more probably they are in debt to the contractors, that they have no money to send to their families and that they have nothing themselves, they as a rule leave that particular employer and wander around destitute, without blankets or even boots in some cases, looking for other work, and people have had to supply them with food and in some instances I have had to do so, also giving them a night's lodging.

Where the men have clearly understood their agreement in the East that they have had to pay their railway fare, we have endeavoured to make them stick to their contract. But where they were evidently brought up under false pretences we have, as Magistrates, when the cases came up before us discharged them from their contracts.[76]

The police did their best to prevent the CPR and the contractors from using the law to defraud the workers. On many occasions a contractor would simply refuse to pay wages owed. The men would then sue and usually won a favourable judgement from the magistrate. What happened next in one typical case was described by Sanders. The contractor immediately appealed the magistrate's ruling and the men had to wait, out of work and penniless. 'They could not hang around without money so we got another contractor, Mr. Buchanan, to employ them until Nov. 11.'[77] The CPR responded by pressuring Buchanan into firing them. Sanders was indignant. 'This proceeding, after everything had been arranged amicably pending the Judge's decision, and after the decision of the Magistrate's court, was, to say the least, certainly foolish on the part of the CPR, and practically meant interference with the course of justice.'[78] Sanders protested vigorously to the CPR officials, who grudgingly offered the men work:

The Management of Construction have been given to understand that we recognize the difficulties we have to contend with in controlling such a large body of men and the great necessity on their part to retain the upper hand, but at the same time it has been pointed out that any injustice or attempt to interfere with the due course of the law would be stopped.[79]

In addition to adjudicating countless other disputes, the police checked and reported on shortcomings in other areas such as the provision of housing and medical care.[80] There were no strikes on the Crow's Nest Pass construction project, a fact which even the CPR construction boss admitted was due almost entirely to the tact and influence of the police.[81]

In 1905 the police encountered a situation which indicated that the old order in labour relations was passing. Unions were beginning to use the law to fight back. This meant that a whole new set of problems was appearing which would make the old approach used by the police obsolete. The incident began with a letter to a member of parliament from a solicitor, L.P. Eckstein, acting on behalf of District Eighteen of the United Mine Workers of America. Eckstein asked for an investigation into reports that the Mounted Police had summarily evicted sixteen men from houses owned by the West Canadian Coal Company.[82] The investigation requested was held immediately by the police.

According to the report of Corporal S.J. Kemby, who was involved in the incident, he had received a telephone call from the mine manager asking for police assistance. The manager explained that he intended to fire eleven men and feared violence. The corporal and a constable went to the mine. Once there they were informed by the manager that he planned to evict the men from their company houses on two hours' notice. The corporal replied that he would have nothing to do with the eviction proceedings but would accompany the manager while he was paying the men off in case violence should materialize. None did and the police left soon after.[83]

Copies of the report were sent to Eckstein and the union agreed to drop the matter. The lawyer expressed himself satisfied but added a further comment on the case:

I suppose if the men had in the exercise of their lawful rights, refused to be thus ejected summarily by Williams, that the Police would have interfered. For my part, I know the record of the Police far too well to think that they would knowingly lend themselves to the commission of an act which was not lawful, and in this instance I must advise my clients that the Police are wholly blameless insofar as intention to offend was concerned.[84]

Comptroller White was pleased by this ending to the affair but he also grasped the wider implications. Discussing the case with the member of parliament to whom the complaint had been made, he wrote:

One of the most delicate parts of Police duty in the North West has been in deciding where their authority begins and ends. We have had many cases where efforts have been made to use the Police Force for the collection of debts recoverable by civil action. Also, as is apparent in the Lille case, an effort to use men in uniform, with all the semblance of the authority of the law, to awe those against whom proceedings have been taken.[85]

The reputation of the force had sustained it but the time would soon arrive when its disinterestedness would not be taken for granted.

The same could be said for all the techniques developed by the police to handle the problems created by minority groups. They were tailored to a society which had definite and strongly held beliefs about the place of minorities in the social order. Almost all these beliefs would be challenged in the decades after

1905. The genius of the Mounted Police lay precisely in the fact that they recognized the realities of their time and place and strove to meet them in a humane way. With few exceptions the police reacted to the difficulties they faced as human beings confronted by human problems. They could do so only because they were entirely confident of their own position in society.

12

Conclusion:
An idea whose time had come

The NWMP were uniquely a product of Canada's first period of nation-building under the leadership of Macdonald. Apart from that marriage of federalism with the parliamentary system that the BNA Act represented, the Mounted Police were the first major Canadian institution not derived from abroad. There was a superficial resemblance to British police forces in Ireland and India that Macdonald emphasized to reassure a parliament which was still very colonial in its outlook, but in fact the force developed in response to local conditions almost entirely without reference to outside models. Canadians in general outside the North-West Territories and the federal government in particular were slow to recognize the indigenous character of the Mounted Police but outsiders noticed it immediately. When parliament belatedly came to realize what it had done in creating the Mounted Police, the initial reaction was to repudiate this dangerous innovation as quickly as possible.

In a debate that lasted over twenty years, Canadian legislators pondered the ultimate fate of the force. By 1905 a majority of both political parties had been forced to the conclusion that the Mounted Police or at least some sort of centrally controlled police force was a necessity for a modern state. Until that happened the Mounted Police and their supporters were prophets without honour in their own country.

The most striking feature of the debate in the period from 1882 to 1905 was the transformation of the attitude of the Liberal party toward the Mounted Police. Although the government of Alexander Mackenzie had carried through Macdonald's plans for sending the force west and had maintained it there, the Liberals in opposition after their defeat in 1878 became increasingly hostile to the Mounted Police. Under the leadership of Edward Blake the Liberals consistently opposed any change in the legislation governing the Force that could be considered a move in the direction of permanence. As minister of justice in the Mackenzie government, Blake had for a short time been responsible for the Mounted Police. His unsympathetic attitude at that time had led to the resignation of Commissioner French and presaged his later outright opposition to the existence of the force.

Blake's distrust of the Mounted Police was firmly rooted in some of his most basic principles. A federal police force violated the idea of local autonomy. The Mounted Police were undeniably expensive. At bottom, Blake believed that any police force above the municipal level was a threat to individual liberties. Since the Mackenzie government had made use of the Force there was little that Blake could say at first. But in 1882 when the Conservative government decided to increase the strength of the Force from 300 to 500 men, the Liberal leader objected. The time had come, he felt, to begin replacing the NWMP with Militia units in the Territories.[1] Macdonald agreed that this would have to be done eventually but stated that the time was not yet ripe. Local magistrates and the Militia could not be trusted to take the long view in their dealings with the Indians.[2]

Three years later during the 1885 Rebellion the size of the force was once again increased, this time to 1000 men. The Liberals mounted a vigorous attack in the House of Commons, with Blake castigating Macdonald for going back on what Blake took to be his promise of 1882 that the government would strictly limit the size of the force. Blake argued, correctly, that a principle of the utmost importance was involved. What was at stake was the very character of the Canadian West. Was the region to adopt the eastern Canadian model of law enforcement, or did the government intend to keep on expanding this costly and sinister institution indefinitely? Why was the government deliberately hampering the organization of Militia units when the residents of the Territories wanted them?[3]

Macdonald was not yet prepared to admit that the Mounted Police were more than a temporary expedient. Whether or not he really believed this, his political instincts were undoubtedly sound. A permanent federal police force was a long step in the direction of direct government involvement in the life of the citizen that we accept as normal, but which was widely feared in the nineteenth century. The government therefore ignored Blake's challenge and turned the debate into one on the specifics of Militia organization in the North-West Territories.[4] In the atmosphere created by the Rebellion, the Liberal objections to increasing the size of the Force were easily overcome.

Eventually, of course, the question would have to be faced. Every year that passed made it more difficult to uphold the fiction that the Mounted Police would soon disappear. In 1889 a turning point of sorts was reached when the government introduced a bill to provide pensions for members of the force.[5] This amounted to an admission that they had no intention of doing away with the Police in the immediate future. The Opposition recognized the significance of the move and countered with a resolution demanding that the force be reduced by 100 men a year until it was completely phased out.[6] Fortunately for the government and the Mounted Police, Blake had left the Liberal leadership by this time and David Mills, who conducted the Opposition attack, failed to make the most of his opportunity. Seizing on a statement by Macdonald that the pensions were intended to keep good men in the Force longer, Mills launched into a lengthy discourse on the harmful moral and economic effects of Mounted Police life on the individual unfortunate enough to join.[7] This had the effect of lifting the debate to a philosophical plane several stages removed from the concerns of the average member of parliament and the pension bill passed without further difficulty.

The government's defence of the Mounted Police in 1889 was made easier by the fact that the Territories were now represented in parliament and the Territorial members had unanimously and vocally supported the force. But the political victory of 1889 proved shortlived. Within two years the force was the object of renewed Opposition attacks. Two events in particular brought about the change. The most important was the death of Macdonald, who had always used his parliamentary skill and authority to defend the Police. A temporary breakdown in the solidarity of Territorial support for the force provided the opening. Nicholas Flood Davin's personal vendetta against Commissioner Herchmer, which he brought to the floor of the House, touched off a bitter squabble within the Conservative party. The Liberals pounced gleefully on this opportunity and their criticisms of the force became increasingly extravagant. G. Landerkin of South Grey said that it was absurd to keep the Police any longer. 'The Indians would be perfectly quiet if they were not constantly harrassed by an army of Mounted Policemen.'[8]

The Conservatives hastily closed ranks in the face of this attack but the Opposition sensed that the government was weakening on the question and pressed home their advantage the following year. Once again, as in 1885, the Liberals succeeded in making the Mounted Police the focal point of an assault on the government's overall policy of western development. J. McMullen of North Wellington linked the force to land policy, claiming that ranchers needed the protection of the Police but settlers did not. If the government would abandon its leasing policy, the Mounted Police could go too.[9] Several MPs held that the very existence of the force was an admission of the failure of government policy. Landerkin fumed, 'I say it is a standing shame and a disgrace upon the civilization of this country that we have to keep 1000 men to preserve the peace in this Christian country, in this noonday of the nineteenth century.'[10] David Mills argued that any effort to interpose the police between Indians and settlers was a grave error since it violated natural law. 'The doctrine of survival of the fittest is a necessary law of human existence, but we make an effort to frustrate the operations of that law, so far as we can by supporting a population that the ministers, in their own defence when pressed on account of expenditure, declare are incorrigibly idle...'[11]

Laurier, taking part in a debate on the Mounted Police for the first time, was more temperate than his followers but his conclusion was basically the same. He praised the Police for good work in the past but said that the coming ascendancy of the settler over the rancher meant that the usefulness of the Force was at an end: 'the hon. gentleman must remember that the force was not established to remain permanent and perennial. It was understood that one day it should cease.'[12] under this pressure the government retreated. Sir John Thompson said that the government was not opposed to reducing the size of the force. It was, in fact, 100 men below its authorized strength and further reductions would be made as circumstances permitted.[13] This promise was kept and the force shrank gradually to 750 men by the time the Conservatives were defeated in 1896.

The new Liberal government of Wilfrid Laurier took power in 1896 with a seemingly clear-cut policy toward the Mounted Police. Shortly after the new parliament had assembled, M.C. Camerson of West Huron, a long-time opponent of the force, asked if the government would be examining the possibility of doing away with the Police. Laurier replied with apparent surprise, 'Up to the present time it had never occurred to me that there should be an investigation into the question of reducing the force. I took it for granted that the force should not be reduced, that it is not more than adequate for the requirements of the country.' If Cameron felt very strongly an investigation might be held. 'But I tell him frankly that the opinion that comes to us from all parts of the North-west is that the force is not too large.'[14] It would be difficult to say who was the more astonished; Cameron and the other critics of the Police or its supporters. Davin, never at a loss for words, recovered first, complimenting the government and assuring Laurier of the undying gratitude of the people of the Territories.[15]

In spite of this hopeful change of direction the Liberal government could not immediately abandon its commitment to phase out the force. In 1897 Clifford Sifton announced that the strength of the Mounted Police would be reduced by 250 men. He was immediately assailed by the western MPs, including his fellow Liberal, Frank Oliver.[16] Their fears for the future of the Mounted Police proved groundless. Sifton had merely discovered a face-saving way to make it appear that the government was cutting back without actually eliminating a single man. The 250 men serving in the Yukon at this time were simply separated from the rest of the force for bookkeeping purposes and given their own item in the estimates.

It is a measure of the disarray of the Conservative opposition that it took them four years to discover this subterfuge. In 1901 the following exchange took place between Laurier and G.W. Fowler, a New Brunswick Conservative, during the debate on the Police estimates:

Mr Fowler: Has the force been kept up to its usual strength?
The Prime Minister: There were 700 men when we took office. We have reduced the number to 500.
Mr Fowler: You have 250 additional men in the Yukon?
The Prime Minister: Yes.
Mr Fowler: That makes 750 men altogether?
The Prime Minister: Yes.
Mr Fowler: So that instead of the force being reduced it has been increased by 50 men?
The Prime Minister: No, my hon. friend will remember that the Yukon was not in existence at that time. We take one appropriation for the force in the North-West Territories and for the force in the Yukon we take another appropriation.
Mr Fowler: Yes, but they are all Mounted Police?
The Prime Minister: Yes, all Mounted Police.[17]

By 1904 the government had abandoned its efforts to conceal its continued support of the force. In that year an increase in strength of 100 men was announced. When some Conservatives ventured to object, they received a stern lecture from Sifton on the vital role of the Mounted Police. The Police were particularly important in attracting settlers from the western United States, Sifton said, where the Mounted Police were widely admired. No 'paltry considerations of economy' could be allowed to stand in the way of their efficiency. Furthermore, if the honourable members thought that provincial autonomy would alter the status of the Force they were mistaken. 'If the hon. gentleman were to submit to the people of the Northwest Territories that they should be given provincial autonomy conditional on the Northwest Mounted Police Force being abolished, he would not find in the Territories five hundred people out of four hundred thousand to vote in favour of his proposition.'[18] The final evidence of the government's conversion came later in the same year when the Police were granted their first pay increase in thirty years.[19]

The fundamental change in the Liberal government's attitude to the Mounted Police was to some extent the result of political pressure from below. But there was a good deal more to it than that. From the government's point of view the Police were too useful to abandon. They performed such a wide range of duties apart from their law enforcement activities that to govern without them by 1905 would have meant a difficult and expensive reorganization of other government departments.

Still, there is an air of inevitability about the survival of the Mounted Police that cannot be fully explained by either political pressure or general administrative usefulness. Had the force not been outstandingly successful in its main function, law enforcement, it would now be a distant memory. The fact was that the society of the North-West Territories differed from that of eastern Canada in one crucial respect. The population was much more transient and mobile than that of the older parts of the country. This meant that the old institutions of law enforcement, premised as they were on a relatively stable population, would not serve in the West. The Militia, an essential element in the law enforcement system in eastern Canada, could not be maintained in the Territories in this period. In the 1880s it had been discovered that so many volunteers moved within a year that units often disappeared completely.[20] The local constable, whose jurisdiction ended at the town limits, could not cope with the lawbreaker who drifted in, committed a crime, and left, indistinguishable from the other faceless transients who were constantly coming and going.

In this sense the North-West Territories, although it was largely rural and thinly populated, shared certain important social characteristics that urbanization and industrialization were beginning to create elsewhere. A society of strangers, where few men knew their neighbours well, required a police force with comprehensive powers and wide jurisdiction. Frank Oliver made this point in a debate on the Mounted Police in 1909. Eastern Canada, he said, was not as law-abiding as many MPs complacently assumed. 'Let me point out further that in this fair province of Ontario where law and order have been known for generations, there have been committed this last few years, most deplorable and most terrible murders, the perpetrators of which have gone undiscovered and unwhipt of justice. This cannot be said of the Territories, where the rule is that if murder is committed the murderer is discovered and punished for his crime.' The difference was due to the Mounted Police and Ontario would do well 'to adopt some such system of police as prevails in the Northwest Territories, for the protection of its innocent children from the murderer and the reprobate.'[21] Oliver's remarks were prophetic. Within 25 years the rest of the country had followed the example of the North-West.

The NWMP was an institution very much in tune with its times; innovative enough to be effective but with sufficient of the traditional to be widely accepted. Much of the credit for its success must go to Sir John A. Macdonald, who created it and presided over its later development. But the force rapidly outgrew the expectations of its creator and became a vastly more significant institution than Macdonald could have imagined in 1873. To the end of his life Macdonald retained, publically at least, a narrowly defined and temporary conception of the role of the Police. Most of the credit for the development of the force belongs to its officers and men, who, left largely to themselves, did what they thought was necessary to build a just and orderly society. Parliament followed, ratifying after the fact, and usually with great reluctance, practices that had originated in the West.

Notes

PREFACE

1 *Annual Report of the RNWMP*, 1906, 19

CHAPTER 1: INTRODUCTION

1 Oliver Knight, *Following the Indian Wars* (Norman, Oklahoma 1960) 13
2 PAC, Macdonald Papers, vol. 252, Morris to Macdonald, 17 January 1873
3 S.W. Horrall, 'Sir John A. Macdonald and the Mounted Police Force for the Northwest Territories,' *Canadian Historical Review* LIII (June 1972) 179-200
4 PAC, MG 29, F-4, Diary of Constable James Finlayson, 12-15
5 Dale C. Thomson, *Alexander Mackenzie: Clear Grit* (Toronto 1960) 249
6 The only piece of writing on the Mounted Police which does raise the question is Lorne and Caroline Brown, *An Unauthorized History of the RCMP* (Toronto 1973) 1. The authors of this work raise the question but do not answer it, except by implying that the police were thrust upon unwilling provincial governments by the federal government, an assertion which has no foundation in fact.
7 Tessier, Thouin, Fourgeroux de Bondary, *et al., Encyclopédie méthodique,* t. dixième, *Jurisprudence, la police et les municipalités* (Paris 1791) 637

CHAPTER 2: THE ORIGINS
OF THE NORTH-WEST MOUNTED POLICE

1 Paul F. Sharp, *Whoop-Up Country: The Canadian-American West, 1865-1885* (Minneapolis 1955; reprinted 1973)
2 Alvin C. Gluek, *Minnesota and the Manifest Destiny of the Canadian North-West: A Study in Canadian-American Relations* (Toronto 1965)
3 PAC, Macdonald Papers, vol. 516, Macdonald to Cameron, 21 December 1869
4 PAC, Macdonald Papers, vol. 258, Sir John Rose to Macdonald, 7 February 1870
5 Norman Gash, *Mr Secretary Peel: The Life of Sir Robert Peel to 1830* (Cambridge 1961) 186; Sir Charles Jeffries, *The Colonial Police* (London 1952) 30; Charles Stuart Parker, *Sir Robert Peel from His Private Papers* (London 1891) I 145
6 PAC, Macdonald Papers, vol. 516, Macdonald to William McDougall, 12 December 1869
7 The Red River rising of 1869-70 has been thoroughly studied in most of its aspects. The best works are the volumes by A.C. Gluek, cited above; G.F.G. Stanley, *The Birth of Western Canada* (Toronto 1960), and *Louis Riel* (Toronto 1963); and several works by W.L. Morton, especially his introduction to Alexander Begg's *Red River Journal* (Toronto 1956).
8 Alexander Begg and Walter R. Nursey, *Ten Years in Winnipeg: A Narration of the Principal Events in the History of the City of Winnipeg, from the Year A.D. 1870 to the Year A.D. 1879 Inclusive* (Winnipeg 1879) 15
9 Toronto *Globe*, 26 January 1871
10 *Ibid.* 39
11 PAC, Macdonald Papers, vol. 518, Macdonald to Cartier, 16 June 1871
12 PAC, Macdonald Papers, vol. 519, Macdonald to Gilbert McMicken, 24 October 1871. McMicken is one of the most enigmatic and intriguing figures in Canadian public life in the last half of the nineteenth century. Born in Scotland, he emigrated to Canada in 1832 and quickly established a successful business. He was an MP for a time in the 1850s and then magistrate at Windsor during the troubled times of the Fenian raids in the 1860s. McMicken in fact organized and ran the Canadian government's spy network in the US, which kept track of the brotherhood and warned of forthcoming raids. After Confederation McMicken organized the Dominion police and was employed by Macdonald on a number of important confidential missions. Although he was ostensibly Dominion Lands Agent in Winnipeg in 1873, Macdonald used him to direct the extradition of the Cypress Hills Massacre suspects. After

retiring from government service, McMicken was elected to the Manitoba legislature in 1879 and ended his career as Speaker of the Legislative Assembly. McMicken was exceedingly self-effacing and even his confidential reports reveal nothing of his own personality or ideas. W.M. Cochrane, ed., *The Canadian Album. Men of Canada; or Success by Example* (Brantford 1894) III 18; J.P. Robertson, *A Political Manual of the Province of Manitoba and the North-West Territories* (Winnipeg 1887); W.S. Wallace, *The Dictionary of Canadian Biography* (Toronto 1945) II 425

13 Toronto *Globe*, 22 April 1872. 'The Chief of Police attempted to interfere but was intimidated by the crowd.'

14 PAC, Macdonald Papers, vol. 246, McMicken to Macdonald, 12 July 1872

15 Canada, House of Commons, *Debates*, 14 June 1872

16 PAC, Macdonald Papers, vol. 521. On 22 July 1872, Macdonald wrote to L.W. Herchmer, a future commissioner of the NWMP, and offered him a commission in the force to be established in the fall. A month later he had evidently changed his mind because on 28 August he wrote to another applicant, a Captain Hilliker of Toronto: 'It has not been settled yet that such a force is to be raised.'

17 Alexander Morris, *Nova Britannia; or Our New Canadian Dominion Foreshadowed* (Toronto 1884). This book originally appeared before Confederation and is a collection of Morris's speeches and writings on the subject

18 PAC, Macdonald Papers, vol. 252, Morris to Macdonald, nd, August 1872

19 PAC, Macdonald Papers, vol. 252, Morris to Macdonald, 5 September 1872

20 Begg and Nursey, *Ten Years in Winnipeg* 11; Toronto *Globe*, 23 September 1872; Toronto *Mail*, 30 September 1872

21 PAC, Macdonald Papers, vol. 521, Macdonald to Morris, 11 October 1872

22 PAC, Macdonald Papers, vol. 252, Morris to Macdonald, 16 November 1872

23 PAC, Macdonald Papers, vol. 252, Morris to Macdonald, 17 January 1873

24 PAC, Alexander Campbell Papers, S.L. Tilley to Campbell, 3 December 1872. 'The Adjutant-General was with Sir John this morning giving him the result of his observations in passing through the North West and British Columbia. He proposes to establish some men at different points on the frontier for the protection of life and property and the preservation of peace. He suggests these men should also look after the revenue and put a stop to illicit trade. Sir John suggested that he prepare a written report and have it printed for the use of Council, this will bring the whole question up.'

25 W.F. Butler, *The Great Lone Land: A Narrative of Travel and Adventure in the North-West of America* (London 1873). The book had gone through seventeen editions by 1910. Butler's report is printed as an appendix to the 1873 edition, 357-80.

26 *Ibid.* 378-9. It is difficult to understand the recommendation for unmounted police, who would have been entirely useless given the vast distances of the prairies.

27 Canada, *Sessional Papers*, Report on the State of the Militia of the Dominion of Canada, 1873, 'Reconnaissance of the North West Provinces and Indian Territories of the Dominion of Canada and Narrative of a Journey through Canadian Territory to British Columbia and Vancouver Island,' cvii-cxxvi

28 The Act when passed was entitled An Act respecting the Administration of Justice, and for the Establishment of a Police Force in the North-West Territories, *Statutes of Canada*, 1873, 36 Vic., c 35

29 Public Archives of Manitoba [PAM], Alexander Morris Papers (Lieutenant-Governor's Collection), Walter J.S. Traill to Morris, 7 July 1873

30 PAM, Morris Papers (Ketcheson Collection), Campbell to Morris, 8 September 1873

31 PAM, Morris Papers (Ketcheson Collection), Morris to Macdonald, 20 September 1873

32 PAC, Dufferin Papers, real A-460, Dufferin to Macdonald, 13 September 1873

33 PAC, Macdonald Papers, vol. 523, Macdonald to Dufferin, 24 September 1873

34 *Ibid.*

35 PAC, RCMP Papers [RG 18] Comptroller's Office Official Correspondence Series [A-1], vol. III; copies of diplomatic correspondence, US Secretary of the Interior to Hamilton Fish, 29 November 1873; Sir Edward Thornton to Lord Dufferin, 3 December 1873

36 PAC, Dufferin Papers, reel A-406, Dufferin to Kimberley, 24 December 1873

37 *Ibid.*

38 Desmond Morton, 'Aid to the Civil Power: The Canadian Militia in Support of Social Order, 1867-1914,' *Canadian Historical Review* LI (December 1970) 407-25

39 Michael S. Cross, 'The Shiner's War: Social Violence in the Ottawa Valley in the 1830s,' *Canadian Historical Review* LIV (March 1973) 1-26; Orlo Miller, *The Donnellys Must Die* (Toronto 1962)

40 Dale and Lee Gibson, *Substantial Justice: Law and Lawyers in Manitoba, 1670-1970* (Winnipeg 1972); Roy St George Stubbs, *Four Recorders of Rupert's Land* (Winnipeg 1967)

41 PAC, Macdonald Papers, vol. 517, Macdonald to Rose, 23 February 1870

42 PAC, Macdonald Papers, vol. 252, Morris to Macdonald, 25 September 1872

43 PAC, Macdonald Papers, vol. 252, Morris to Macdonald, 1 October 1872

44 PAC, Macdonald Papers, vol. 252, Morris to Macdonald, 12 March 1873

CHAPTER 3: THE BENEVOLENT DESPOTISM
OF THE MOUNTED POLICE 1874-85

1 The great bulk of the police records for the period up to 1885 were destroyed by a fire in the Parliament Buildings in 1897. Many scattered documents from the period survive but they are insufficient to permit a systematic
study of the day-to-day activities of the force. See E.C. Morgan, 'The North-
West Mounted Police, 1873-1883' (unpublished MA thesis, University of
Saskatchewan 1970). The author of this thesis has done an excellent job of
finding and using the available documents.

2 The first headquarters of the force after it left Ft Garry in 1874 was the
Boundary Commission post at Dufferin on the Red River near the Manitoba-
North Dakota border. Headquarters were supposed to be located at Swan
River, the site chosen as the temporary seat of government for the North-
West Territories. This location was apparently chosen because it was on the
proposed main line of the CPR. Certainly it had little else to recommend it.
Commissioner French refused to spend the winter of 1874-5 there and returned to Dufferin instead. In the spring of 1875 headquarters was moved
to Swan River, where it remained for a year and a half until transferred to
Ft Macleod in the fall of 1876. In May 1878 it was moved again, this time
to Ft Walsh in the Cypress Hills. Finally in 1882 the headquarters post was
moved to Regina, where it remained until the NWMP became the RCMP in
1919, when it was moved to Ottawa.

3 PAC, RG 18, Commissioner's Office Letterbooks [B-3], vol. 48, 342-5

4 The rather clumsy rank designations for both commissioned officers and
other ranks were changed within a few years. Inspectors became superintendents and sub-inspectors became inspectors. The more familiar titles of staff
sergeant, sergeant, and corporal replaced chief constable, constable, and acting constable. The rank of subconstable was changed to constable.

5 Small detachments were left at Dufferin and the Hudson's Bay Company
post of Ft Ellice.

6 Commissioner French's diary is summarized in the *Annual Report* for 1875.
This report was not printed but a copy in typescript exists at the RCMP Museum, Regina. Sub-Inspector Sévère Gagnon kept a diary which is preserved
in PAC, RG 18, A-1, vol. 3, no. 18. The other ranks are represented by trumpeter Fred Bagley, whose diary is in the Glenbow-Alberta Institute Archives,
Calgary, and by Constable James Finlayson, cited below.

7 PAC, MG 29, F-4, Diary of Constable James Finlayson, 12, 14, and 15

8 RCMP Museum, *Annual Report of the Commissioner for 1875* (unprinted) 6

9 PAC, RG 18, A-1, vol. 1, no. 6, French to minister of justice, 14 November 1873

10 Sharp, *Whoop-Up Country* 90-1

11 The government commissioned John McDougall to perform this task. He also claims to have warned the whisky traders at Ft Whoop-Up that the police were coming. McDougall, *On Western Trails* 174-90

12 Sharp, *Whoop-Up Country* 27-51. Sharp states, with little exaggeration, that the arrival of the police prevented the complete destruction of the Blackfoot.

13 Hugh A. Dempsey, *Crowfoot: Chief of the Blackfeet* (Edmonton 1972)

14 PAC, RG 18, A-1, vol. 8, no. 490. Copy of a letter from US Indian agent W.H. Alderson, Fort Peck Agency, to Edwin P. Smith, Commissioner of Indian Affairs, 1 March 1875

15 PAC, RG 18, A-1, vol. 4, no. 98. Statement of I.G. Baker, 25 February 1875

16 NWMP, *Annual Report* 1876, 24; 1878, 27; 1881, 8; 1884, 66

17 Canada, *Sessional Papers* 1882, 'Annual Report of the Minister of the Interior for the year ended 30th June, 1881,' Part II, North-West Mounted Police Force, Report of the Commissioner, 1881, 8

18 When the police arrived in the North-West, for example, a regulation forbidding the Indians to purchase repeating rifles was on the books. They soon discovered it was neither necessary nor enforceable and recommended that it be dropped. The government complied at once. PAC, RG 18, A-1, vol. 9, no. 69, memo by Frederick White, 6 October 1876

19 PAC, RG 18, A-1, vol. 6, no. 249, copies of diplomatic correspondence on the question of the transfer of stolen horses across the international boundary, April-October 1875; also RG 18, B-3, vol. 48, 365, Superintendent J.H. McIlree to Commissioner Irvine, 15 February 1882

20 There is a massive literature on the Hudson's Bay Company. For the missionaries see Frits Pannekoek, 'Protestant Agricultural Missions in the Canadian West to 1870' (unpublished MA thesis, University of Alberta 1970).

21 PAC, RG 18, A-1, vol. 7, no. 429, French to minister of justice, 13 October 1875

22 PAC, Macdonald Papers, vol. 210, 89546, Wadsworth to E.T. Galt (assistant Indian commissioner) 25 July 1881

23 PAC, Macdonald Papers, vol. 290, 132763, Vankoughnet to Macdonald, 3 January 1884

24 PAC, RG 18, A-1, vol. 26, no. 43, correspondence between the commissioner and the High River Branch, Alberta Stock Grower's Association, November 1888-January 1889

25 PAC, Macdonald Papers, vol. 209, 88785, Laird to Macdonald, 30 June 1879

26 PAC, RG 18, Orders and Regulations, 1880-1954 [B-4], vol. 8, General Order

No. 901 (Old Series), 1883. Police to give 'every possible assistance' in removing squatters from reserves when requested by Indian agents

27 PAC, RG 18, Comptroller's Office Letterbooks 1883-1919 [A-2], vol. 1, 135, Fred White (comptroller) to deputy minister of the interior, 18 October 1883

28 Most recently by Gary Pennanen, 'Sitting Bull: Indian Without a Country,' *Canadian Historical Review* LI (June 1970) 123-40

29 PAC, Lorne Papers, 186, Macdonald to Lorne, 24 November 1879

30 PAC, RG 18, B-3, vol. 47, 7, Macleod to Walsh, 1 January 1878

31 PAC, Lorne Papers, 195-6, Macdonald to Lorne, 25 January 1881

32 Apparently this book was never published. The mss are in PAM, James Morrow Walsh Papers.

33 This question is considered in detail in chapter 4 below.

34 Liquor offences were 26 per cent of the total number of cases in 1880 and 1883, 35 per cent in 1884. NWMP *Annual Report*, 1881 and 1884

35 There was a loophole which was to become important later. Permits to import specified quantities of liquor for medicinal purposes could be granted by the lieutenant-governor. D.M. McLeod, 'Liquor Control in the North-West Territories: The Permit System, 1870-1891,' *Saskatchewan History* XVI (Spring 1963)

36 PAC, MG 29, F-52, Diary of Constable R.N. Wilson, 1881-8

37 The best account of this incident is in Sharp, *Whoop-Up Country*, chapter 4.

38 The exception was Ft Calgary, built on contract by I.G. Baker and Co.

39 PAC, RG 18, A-1, vol. 5, no. 211, French to minister of justice, 6 April 1875

40 PAC, RG 18, A-1, vol. 8, no. 18, French to minister of justice, 21 December 1875

41 At Dufferin and Swan River in February 1875 and at Ft Macleod in April. PAC, RG 18, A-1, vol. 4, no. 84 and no. 150

42 PAC, RG 18, A-1, vol. 150, no. 199, Guernsey to Oliver, 10 February 1898

43 PAC, RG 18, A-1, vol. 9, no. 59, French to minister of justice, 20 January 1876

44 There are references to the distribution of relief as early as 20 January 1876

45 PAC, RG 18, A-1, vol. 57, no. 794, White to minister of interior, 18 November 1891

46 PAC, RG 18, A-1, vol. 58, no. 44, White to Commissioner L.W. Herchmer, 8 February 1892

47 W.P. Ward, 'The Administration of Justice in the North-West Territories, 1870-1887' (unpublished MA thesis, University of Alberta 1966)

48 PAC, RG 18, A-1, vol. 19, no. 249, 3 February 1888

49 PAC, RG 18, B-3, vol. 47, 253, Macleod to deputy minister of the interior, 23 December 1878
50 Sharp, *Whoop-Up Country* 99

CHAPTER 4: THE ORGANIZATION MAN:
COMMISSIONER L.W. HERCHMER'S REFORMS

1 PAC, RG 18, A-1, vol. 10, no. 118, French to minister of justice, 28 April 1876
2 *Ibid.*, French to deputy minister of justice, 30 March 1876
3 Macleod was not born in Canada but must have left his native Scotland as a child because all his contemporaries considered him a Canadian.
4 Glenbow-Alberta Institute Archives, Calgary [GAI], W.M. Herchmer Papers, clipping of an anonymous letter to the editor of the Toronto *Globe* dated Swan River, 10 October 1876. Superintendent W.M. Herchmer was the brother of Commissioner L.W. Herchmer and was an original member of the force.
5 PAC, Macdonald Papers, vol. 524, 291, Macdonald to Macleod, 23 June 1879
6 PAC, Macdonald Papers, vol. 209, Macleod to Macdonald, 15 March 1879; also RG 18, B-3, vol. 47, 263, Macleod to Thomas White, MP, 16 January 1879; and 267, Macleod to Macdonald, 18 January 1879
7 The comptroller was in fact a deputy minister although the position did not formally attain that rank until 1883.
8 PAC, RG 18, A-1, vol. 12, no. 20. Some of the police reports were so accurate in predicting the outbreak that judicious editing was necessary before they were included in the parliamentary papers on the rebellion. See also PAC, Macdonald Papers, vol. 105, Sgt H. Keenan to Supt L.N.F. Crozier, 25 September 1884. Several paragraphs of this report are crossed out and marked, 'Not sent to the House,' among them the following: 'The crops here are almost a total failure and everything indicates that the Half-breeds are going to be in a very straitened condition before the end of the coming winter, which of course will make them more discontented and will probably drive them to an outbreak, and I believe that trouble is almost certain before the winter ends unless the government extends some aid to the Half-breeds during the coming winter.'
9 GAI, Edgar Dewdney Papers, vol. 3, Macdonald to Dewdney, 20 November 1885. Macdonald states his intention to get rid of Irvine as soon as possible.
10 Melgund was later, as the Earl of Minto, governor-general of Canada. Hutton later commanded the Canadian Militia. PAC, Macdonald Papers, vol. 85, Melgund to Macdonald, 22 May 1885; and vol. 86, Marquis of Lansdowne to Macdonald, 2 February 1886

11 PAC, Macdonald Papers, vol. 402, Smith to Macdonald, 2 April 1884
12 GAI, Sir Alexander Campbell Papers, Macdonald to Campbell, 8 March 1886
13 PAC, Macdonald Papers, vol. 521, Macdonald to L.W. Herchmer, 22 July 1872. The letter refers to the elder Herchmer as, 'my school fellow and long life friend...'
14 *Ibid.*
15 Biographical details are from a memorandum outlining Herchmer's career in PAC, Macdonald Papers, vol. 43.
16 PAC, RG 18, B-4, vol. 8, General Order No. 22 (New Series), 10 April 1886
17 A rough draft of the handbook is in PAC, RG 18, A-1, vol. 32, no. 217. There is a copy of the finished product, published as *Regulations and Orders for the Government and Guidance of the North-West Mounted Police* (Ottawa 1889), in the RCMP Museum, Regina.
18 NWMP, *Annual Report*, 1884, 14
19 PAC, Macdonald Papers, vol. 212, Dewdney to Macdonald, 22 August 1884
20 NWMP, *Annual Report*, 1883, 8-10
21 NWMP, *Annual Report*, 1884, 20
22 NWMP, *Annual Report*, 1886, 1
23 NWMP, *Annual Report*, 1885, 1 and 1887, 129
24 PAC, RG 18, A-1, vol. 42, no. 495, Calgary patrol reports, April-June 1890
25 PAC, RG 18, A-1, vol. 82, no. 378, Superintendent Steele to Herchmer, 19 April 1893
26 The police were brought into Manitoba at the request of the Customs Department to enforce customs laws and prevent Americans from crossing the border to cut timber. Although permanent detachments were only stationed in the area for the summer of 1888, it was patrolled from Estevan for another ten years. PAC, RG 18, A-1, vol. 31, no. 200, minister of the interior to White, 30 July 1888. In 1887 the British Columbia government requested federal aid in controlling the Kootenai Indians. An entire division of seventy-nine men under Superintendent Sam Steele was sent to the district and was so successful in settling the differences between Indians and settlers that they were able to withdraw after a year. PAC, RG 18, A-1, vol. 24, no. 655, White to Herchmer, 21 June 1888
27 PAC, RG 18, A-1, vol. 72, no. 864, memo by White, 1892
28 PAC, RG 18, B-4, vol. 8, Circular Memorandum, 12 April 1890
29 PAC, RG 18, A-1, vol. 96, no. 499, W.B. Ives (president of the Privy Council) to White, 18 June 1894
30 PAC, RG 18, A-1, vol. 147, no. 102, estimates for the fiscal year 1898-9
31 GAI, Diary, Nanton Detachment NWMP, 1899
32 PAC, RG 18, A-1, vol. 75, no. 125, patrol report of Inspector D'Arcy Strickland, January 1892

33 Hugh Dempsey, 'The "Thin Red Line" in the History of the Canadian West,' *The American West* VII (January 1970) 24-30

34 PAC, RG 18, B-4, vol. 8, Circular Memorandum, 12 April 1890

35 PAC, RG 18, Commissioner's Office Miscellaneous Correspondence [B-10], vol. 3, no. 6

36 PAC, RG 18, B-4, vol. 8, General Order No. 2786 (New Series), 13 July 1888

37 PAC, RG 18, B-4, vol. 9, General Order No. 1875 (New Series), 8 October 1887

38 PAC, RG 18, A-1, vol. 86, no. 679, White to Herchmer, 3 November 1893

39 PAC, RG 18, A-1, vol. 104, no. 131, Lethbridge Monthly Reports, 1895

40 PAC, RG 18, A-1, vol. 181, no. 163, Ft Macleod Monthly Reports, 1900. The telephone enabled Superintendent Deane to leave one detachment in the sole charge of an Indian scout, Piegan Frank. 'He was delighted to report every day by telephone that "Everything is all right" and the people round there tell me that he does his patrols and work religiously.'

41 L.H. Thomas, *The Struggle for Responsible Government in the North-West Territories, 1870-97* (Toronto 1956) 254; H.A. Robson, 'Sir Frederick Haultain,' *Canadian Bar Review* XXII (October 1944) 648

42 PAC, RG 18, A-1, vol. 198, no. 799, memorandum for the minister of the interior by White, 8 January 1900

43 In 1905 a survey revealed that there were only forty-seven local police in the whole of the North-West Territories. The largest municipal force was that of Calgary, which boasted six constables. PAC, RG 18, A-1, vol. 301, no. 622

44 PAC, RG 18, A-1, vol. 22, no. 383, White to Macdonald, 24 August 1887

45 NWMP, *Annual Report*, 1887, 8

46 PAC, RG 18, A-1, vol. 82, no. 370, White to L. Pereira (Department of the Interior), 27 April 1895

47 PAC, RG 18, A-1, vol. 94, no. 258, White to Herchmer, 19 March 1894

48 PAC, RG 18, A-1, vol. 219, no. 889, Inspector W.S. Casey to Assistant-Commissioner J.H. McIlree, 30 October 1901

49 PAC, RG 18, A-1, vol. 141, no. 632, White to Herchmer, 17 December 1897

50 Detachments were sent into Edmonton in 1889 and 1892, into Calgary in 1890 and 1892, and into Prince Albert in 1890. PAC, RG 18, A-1, vol. 35, no. 480; vol. 68, no. 505; vol. 43, no. 660; vol. 49, no. 615; and vol. 43, no. 692

51 PAC, RG 18, A-1, vol. 147, no. 102

52 PAC, RG 18, A-1, vol. 160, no. 64, Herchmer to White, 4 January 1899

53 PAC, RG 18, A-1, vol. 198, no. 799, White to Commissioner A. Bowen Perry, 2 November 1900

54 *Ibid.*, White to Sifton, 8 January 1900

55 PAC, Macdonald Papers, vol. 395, Dewdney to Macdonald, 24 August 1883
56 PAC, Macdonald Papers, vol. 397, Davin to Macdonald, 8 November 1883
57 GAI, Dewdney Papers, vol. 3, Macdonald to Dewdney, 24 August 1883
58 Deane was an intelligent and competent officer whose temperament made a clash with Herchmer almost inevitable. His reports were written in a light, humorous style which enraged Herchmer, who considered Deane's attitude flippant and irresponsible. PAC, RG 18, A-1, vol. 45, no. 945, Herchmer to White, December 1890
59 Ft Macleod *Gazette*, 12 September 1889; Regina *Leader*, 5 November 1889
60 PAC, RG 18, A-1, vol. 71, no. 720, memorandum by White, 8 October 1892
61 PAC, RG 18, A-1, vol. 79, no. 241, 36
62 *Ibid.*, White to Dewdney, 10 October 1892
63 PAC, RG 18, A-1, vol. 176, no. 751, Laurier to White, 3 December 1899
64 PAC, Sir Wilfrid Laurier Papers, vol. 164, Laurier to Sir Richard Cartwright, 27 July 1900

CHAPTER 5: COMMISSIONER A. BOWEN PERRY AND THE SURVIVAL OF THE NORTH-WEST MOUNTED POLICE 1900-5

 1 PAC, RG 18, A-1, vol. 299, no. 466, White to Premier Walter Scott, 26 May 1905
 2 PAC, Laurier Papers, vol. 35, Oliver to Laurier, 25 January 1897
 3 PAC, Laurier Papers, vol. 19, Walsh to Laurier, 15 September 1896
 4 PAC, Minto Papers, vol. 2, conversation with Laurier, 24 October 1902
 5 See chapter 8.
 6 PAC, Laurier Papers, vol. 39, memo by White, 5 March 1897
 7 PAC, RG 18, A-1, vol. 166, no. 206, clipping from Ft Macleod *Gazette*, 22 September 1899. Letter to the editor from Commissioner Herchmer explaining details of the proposed organization
 8 PAC, Laurier Papers, vol. 318, Laurier to White, 18 May 1904
 9 Regina *Standard*, 7 August 1901, an editorial entitled, 'Playing Soldier'
10 The police operations in the Yukon are beyond the scope of this study and will be treated only in so far as they affected the main body of the force in the North-West Territories.
11 PAC, RG 18, A-1, vol. 151, no. 253, supplementary estimates, 1897-8
12 White was aware of the long term implications of the move into the Yukon. When a Department of the Interior report recommended sending in the police, White agreed it could be done but added this warning: 'If the Mounted Police formally take possession of the District, will not the Government be committed to keep them there permanently, and, if necessary, in-

crease their strength no matter what the cost may be?' PAC, RG 18, A-1, vol. 100, no. 17, memo by White, 2 May 1894

13 The cost in the Territories was $700.00/year/man, in the Yukon it was $1400.00/year/man. PAC, RG 18, A-1, vol. 147, no. 102, estimates 1898-9

14 PAC, RG 18, A-1, vol. 145, no. 56, letter introducing CPR construction manager M.J. Haney and instructing the commissioner to provide assistance, White to Herchmer, 10 June 1897; RG 18, A-1, vol. 233, no. 227, Commissioner reports sending a detachment to supervise construction on the Canadian Northern, Perry to White, 19 January 1901

15 PAC, RG 18, A-1, vol. 141, no. 577, F.W. McNeill to Stewart, 20 September 1897

16 Ibid., White to Stewart, 23 October 1897

17 Other typical examples of business pressure are to be found in PAC, RG 18, A-1, vol. 141, no. 580, E.T. Galt (manager of the Alberta Railway and Coal Company, Lethbridge) to Laurier, 17 September 1897; and PAC, Laurier Papers, vol. 194, R.G. Matthews (Secretary, Western Stock Growers Association) to Laurier, 19 April 1901

18 PAC, Laurier Papers, vol. 45, Oliver to Laurier, 12 May 1897

19 PAC, Laurier Papers, vol. 65, Oliver to Laurier, 5 February 1898; RG 18, A-1, vol. 124, no. 512, Oliver to Laurier, 10 September 1898; and vol. 197, no. 765, Oliver to White, 20 December 1898. There were many more in later years.

20 PAC, RG 18, A-1, vol. 136, no. 268, T.O. Davis, MP, to White, 31 March 1897; vol. 168, no. 269, J.M. Douglas, MP, to White, 28 January 1899; and Laurier Papers, vol. 105, Douglas to Laurier, 27 March 1899

21 PAC, Laurier Papers, vol. 21, A.E. Forget to Laurier, 27 September 1896

22 PAC, RG 18, A-1, vol. 137, no. 349, Herchmer to White, 17 May 1897

23 PAC, RG 18, A-1, vol. 174, no. 594, Perry was sent on orders from Sifton. Memo by White, 24 August 1899

24 PAC, RG 18, A-1, vol. 180, no. 114, telegram, Herchmer to White, 27 December 1899

25 PAC, RG 18, A-1, vol. 193, no. 573, Sifton to White, 6 March 1900

26 PAC, RG 18, A-1, vol. 187, no. 291

27 PAC, RG 18, A-1, vol. 187, no. 288, White to ex-Superintendent A.C. Macdonell, 6 February 1900

28 PAC, RG 18, A-1, vol. 193, no. 573, Sifton to White, 6 March 1900

29 PAC, RG 18, A-1, vol. 528, no. 108, White to Laurier, 27 March 1905

30 The number of NCOs was the same for seven hundred and fifty men in 1902 as it had been for a thousand in 1890. PAC, RG 18, A-1, vol. 242, no. 915, Perry to White, 24 June 1902

31 PAC, RG 18, A-1, vol. 273, no. 315, White to Perry, 1 June 1901

32 PAC, RG 18, A-1, vol. 202, no. 64, Perry to White, 3 January 1901

33 PAC, RG 18, A-1, vol. 273, no. 315, Perry to White, 7 April 1902

34 PAC, RG 18, A-1, vol. 253, no. 304, Superintendent J.O. Wilson to Assistant Commissioner McIlree, 3 March 1903

35 PAC, RG 18, A-1, vol. 285, no. 24, Perry to Superintendent A.H. Griesbach, 11 May 1903

36 PAC, RG 18, A-1, vol. 250, no. 177, Lethbridge Monthly Report for October 1903

37 PAC, RG 18, A-1, vol. 272, no. 438

38 PAC, RG 18, A-1, vol. 208, no. 213, Lethbridge Monthly Report for May 1901

39 PAC, RG 18, A-1, vol. 217, no. 723, Perry to White, 20 August 1901; D.H. Breen, 'Plain talk from Plain Western Men,' *Alberta Historical Review* XVIII (Summer 1970) 8-13

40 Rouleau made comments to this effect in the case of King vs Leitinger in March 1901. PAC, RG 18, A-1, vol. 214, no. 513, Inspector H.S. Casey to Perry, 30 March 1901

41 Calgary *Herald*, 27 June 1901, an editorial entitled 'Trouble Ahead'

42 PAC, RG 18, A-1, vol. 219, no. 933, White to Sifton, 11 December 1901

43 Judge E.L. Wetmore, for example, took the opposite position in King vs Thornhill. PAC, RG 18, A-1, vol. 214, no. 513

44 PAC, RG 18, A-1, vol. 219, no. 933, White to Sifton, 11 December 1901

45 PAC, RG 18, A-1, vol. 175, no. 680, Sifton to White, 21 November 1899

46 PAC, RG 18, A-1, vol. 288, no. 121, Sifton to White, 12 February 1904

47 PAC, RG 18, A-1, vol. 272, no. 279, Sifton to Laurier, 25 January 1904

48 PAC, Sifton Papers, vol. 148, Senator L.G. Power to Sifton, 21 August 1903

49 C.C. Lingard, *Territorial Government in Canada* (Toronto 1946) 117

50 PAC, RG 18, A-1, vol. 528, no. 108, Perry to White, 8 December 1905

51 At this crucial juncture strong pressure was exerted for the retention of the police by the powerful ranching interests of southern Alberta. George Lane, Pat Burns, and E.A. Cross made their views known to Laurier in no uncertain terms. GAI, E.A. Cross Papers, George Lane to E.A. Cross, 5 February 1906; M.S. McCarthy to E.A. Cross, 19 March 1906. I am indebted to Dr D.H. Breen for drawing these documents to my attention.

52 PAC, RG 18, A-1, vol. 528, no. 108, Laurier to Scott and Rutherford, 7 February 1906

CHAPTER 6: 'THE FEELINGS AND MANNERS OF A
GENTLEMAN': SOCIAL CLASS IN THE NORTH-WEST
MOUNTED POLICE

1 The phrase used in the title comes from a report on a candidate for commissioned rank recommended by Colonel Macleod. 'He has given every satisfaction as a non-commissioned officer and possesses also those qualities
which are very desirable in an officer – the feelings and manners of a gentleman.' PAC, RG 18, A-1, vol. 9, no. 30, Macleod to Hewitt Bernard, 16
December 1875

2 Medical personnel varied from three in the early years to eight in the years
when the force numbered a thousand. NWMP *Annual Report*, 1892

3 PAC, Macdonald Papers, vol. 292, D.R. Girard, MD, to L. Vankoughnet,
23 November 1887

4 PAC, RG 18, A-1, vol. 96, no. 413; and vol. 100, no. 886

5 PAC, RG 18, A-1, vol. 96, no. 413

6 The best book on the subject is Carl Berger's *The Sense of Power: Studies
in the Ideas of Canadian Imperialism 1867-1914* (Toronto 1970). Berger's
view of imperialism as a form of nationalism is challenged by Douglas L.
Cole, 'Canada's "Nationalistic" Imperialists,' *Journal of Canadian Studies*
(August 1970) 44-9, but Cole's case is not very convincing. All the evidence
concerning the Mounted Police supports Berger's interpretation.

7 Ottawa *Free Press*, 16 February 1888

8 PAC, Laurier Papers, vol. 19, memo by White on Davin's bill to amend the
Police Act, 14 September 1896; RG 18, A-1, vol. 137, no. 348, copy of
Davin's bill to amend the Police Act, 1897; and vol. 187, no. 283, copy of
Davin's bill to amend the Police Act, 1900

9 *Canadian Military Gazette*, 1 March 1894

10 PAC, RG 18, A-1, vol. 94, no. 322, clipping from the Toronto *Telegram*,
no date

11 PAC, RG 18, Comptroller's Office Letterbooks [A-2], vol. 1, 208, White to
H.H. Warren, 29 October 1883

12 PAC, RG 18, A-1, vol. 12, no. 199, Confidential Report on Officers

13 PAC, RG 18, A-1, vol. 205, no. 110

14 PAC, RG 18, A-1, vol. 260, no. 763

15 PAC, Macdonald Papers, vol. 209, Macleod to Macdonald, 15 March 1879

16 PAC, RG 18, A-1, vol. 9, no. 30, French to minister of justice, 29 November
1875

17 PAC, RG 18, A-1, vol. 242, no. 915, Sifton to White, 4 December 1902

18 PAC, RG 18, A-1, vol. 96, no. 413

19 PAC, Bowell Papers, vol. 9, McDonagh to Costigan, 4 March 1895
20 PAC, Macdonald Papers, vol. 226, Sir Hector Langevin (minister of public works) to Macdonald, 5 October 1873; and vol. 229, L.F.R. Masson (minister of militia and defence) to Macdonald, 30 May 1880; RG 18, A-1, vol. 82, no. 339, White to Herchmer, 6 March 1894
21 PAC, RG 18, A-1, vol. 3, no. 18, typed copy of Gagnon's diary
22 PAC, RG 18, A-1, vol. 45, no. 957, Herchmer to White, 9 April 1890
23 PAC, RG 18, A-1, vol. 299, no. 450, Sanders to Perry, 1 May 1905
24 *Ibid.*, White to Perry, 17 May 1905
25 PAC, RG 18, A-1, vol. 134, no. 163, Herchmer to White, 4 February 1897
26 PAC, Laurier Papers, vol. 186, J.M. Skelton to Laurier, 1 February 1901
27 PAC, RG 18, A-1, vol. 8, no. 29
28 PAC, RG 18, B-4, vol. 8, General Order 4397, 2 November 1889. Pay of officer's servant set at an extra five dollars per month
29 PAC, RG 18, A-1, vol. 361, no. 490
30 *Ibid.*, White to Perry, 22 September 1908
31 GAI, Gilbert E. Sanders Papers, vol. 1
32 PAC, RG 18, A-1, vol. 8, no. 29, Major-General Smyth's report, 8
33 PAC, RG 18, A-1, vol. 22, no. 413; and vol. 118, no. 76
34 PAC, RG 18, B-3, vol. 46, French to Hewitt Bernard, 17 December 1875
35 PAC, RG 18, A-2, vol. 2, 626-9, memo by White, 25 February 1884
36 PAC, RG 18, A-1, vol. R-10, letter number 36, 21 November 1878
37 *Ibid.*, letter number 18, January 1878
38 PAC, RG 18, A-1, vol. 26, no. 209
39 PAC, Laurier Papers, vol. 387, White to Laurier, 11 November 1905
40 PAC, RG 18, A-1, vol. 186, no. 274, Inspector W.S. Morris to White, 4 May 1900
41 PAC, RG 18, A-1, vol. 252, no. 284, Superintendent J.O. Wilson to Perry, 18 April 1903
42 PAC, RG 18, B-3, vol. 47, 298, Commissioner Macleod to J.S. Ross, MP, submits list of qualified applicants from Dundas County and asks him to list in order of priority those he would like to see appointed
43 PAC, RG 18, A-2, vol. I, 146, White to William Macdonald, MP, 18 October 1883
44 PAC, RG 18, A-1, vol. 252, no. 284, White to Perry, 7 March 1903
45 GAI, Frederick A. Bagley, 'The '74 Mounties' (unpublished MS, 1938)
46 PAC, RG 18, A-1, vol. 8, no. 29
47 PAC, RG 18, A-1, vol. 1, no. 2, French to Minister of Justice, 14 January 1874
48 PAC, RG 18, B-4, vol. 10, 19 January 1874

49 *Regulations and Orders for the Government and Guidance of the North-West Mounted Police, 1889* (Ottawa 1889) 4

50 Inspector W.R. Routledge, *Hand Book of Ready Reference: Police Duties for Non-Commissioned Officers and Constables of the North-West Mounted Police, Yukon Territory* (Dawson 1904) 8

51 PAC, RG 18, A-1, vol. 4, no. 84, inspectors J. Walker (Dufferin) and A.H. Griesbach (Ft Saskatchewan) to French, 3 February 1875

52 PAC, RG 18, A-1, vol. 8, no. 484, Macleod to Hewitt Bernard, 11 October 1875; and RG 18, B-1, vol. 2, no. 121, Superintendent W.M. Herchmer to Commissioner Irvine, 10 February 1883

53 PAC, RG 18, A-2, vol. 2, 2

54 GAI, Papers of Mrs Jessie De Geer, invitations (engraved) to police annual balls, 1884 and 1885

55 GAI, Frederick Davis Shaw Papers, 1856-1926

56 GAI, William John Redmond, 'History of the Southwestern Saskatchewan Old-Timer's Association' (unpublished MS, 1932)

57 *Ibid.*

CHAPTER 7: PATRONAGE AND PUBLIC SERVICE: THE MOUNTED POLICE AND POLITICS

1 In 1903, for example, the deputy attorney-general of the North-West Territories complained that the liquor regulations in Calgary were not being enforced by city authorities. A Mounted Police investigation revealed that this was true but the commissioner declined to intervene. PAC, RG 18, A-1, vol. 254, no. 340, Horace Harvey to Perry, 19 March 1903

2 PAC, RG 18, A-1, vol. 68, no. 521, Inspector A.R. Cuthbert to Herchmer, 5 July 1892

3 PAC, RG 18, A-1, vol. 69, no. 616, Herchmer to White, 17 December 1892

4 PAC, RG 18, A-1, vol. 71, no. 664, Cuthbert to Herchmer, 12 August 1892

5 PAC, RG 18, A-1, vol. 218, no. 815, Sergeant Camies to Superintendent Howe, 7 December 1900

6 *Ibid.*, Howe to Perry, 12 December 1900

7 *Ibid.*, Perry to Howe, 13 December 1900

8 PAC, RG 18, A-1, vol. 85, no. 620, G.W. Greene (lawyer for the Rev. Leonard Gaetz) to White, 9 August 1893; and vol. 97, no. 632, H.H. Gaetz to White, 31 August 1894

9 *Ibid.*, Nolan to Herchmer, 6 September 1894

10 PAC, RG 18, A-1, vol. 93, no. 211, Ft Saskatchewan Monthly Report for September 1894

11 PAC, RG 18, A-1, vol. 146, no. 86, Senator W.D. Perley to Herchmer, 5 January 1898

12 PAC, RG 18, A-1, vol. 153, no. 356, Resolution of the Legislative Assembly, 10 November 1897

13 R.B. Deane, *Mounted Police Life in Canada: A Record of Thirty-One Years' Service* (London 1916) 64-6

14 PAC, Macdonald Papers, vol. 263, 119719-20; vol. 395, 189133-5; vol. 405, 195420-1; vol. 417, 202381-3, 202511-3, 202663-4; vol. 430, 210880-2; vol. 442, 219466-7; vol. 229, 98707-8

15 PAC, RG 18, A-1, vol. 82, no. 339 and no. 385, correspondence regarding Ives's instructions concerning promotions to commissioned rank of several non-commissioned officers, 12 March 1893 to 6 March 1894; PAC, MG 26, E, Bowell Papers, vol. 9, correspondence regarding the appointment of Inspector F.J. Horrigan, March 1895

16 PAC, RG 18, A-1, vol. R-2, Blake to French, 3 March 1875

17 PAC, RG 18, A-1, vol. 133, no. 146, White to Herchmer, 21 January 1897

18 The first two officers appointed were Superintendent J.M. Walsh, a personal friend of Sifton's, and Inspector F.L. Cartwright, son of Laurier's minister of trade and commerce, Sir Richard Cartwright. PAC, RG 18, A-1, vol. 148, no. 137

19 PAC, RG 18, A-1, vol. 171, no. 392; vol. 174, no. 594; and vol. 242, no. 915

20 PAC, RG 18, A-1, vol. 174, no. 594, memo by White, 24 August 1899

21 PAC, RG 18, A-1, vol. 71, no. 751

22 PAC, RG 18, A-1, vol. 42, no. 395, Scarth to White, 27 November 1890

23 PAC, RG 18, A-1, vol. 160, no. 64, White to Herchmer, 26 June 1899

24 PAC, Laurier Papers, vol. 72, White to Laurier, 14 April 1898

25 PAC, RG 18, A-1, vol. 224, no. 78, White to Perry, 17 October 1902

26 PAC, Sifton Papers, vol. 150, White to Sifton, 23 November 1903

27 PAC, RG 18, A-2, vol. 2, 561-2, White to G.A. Kirkpatrick (speaker of the House of Commons), 13 February 1884; PAC, Macdonald Papers, vol. 433, Herchmer to White, 2 January 1887; and PAC, MG 26, D, Sir John Thompson Papers, White to Thompson, 17 June 1893

28 PAC, RG 18, A-1, vol. 298, no. 371, Frank Oliver to White, 5 April 1905

29 PAC, Sifton Papers, vol. 150, Sifton to A.P. Collier (Sifton's private secretary), 2 December 1903

30 PAC, RG 18, A-1, vol. 193, no. 579, instructions from Sifton regarding hotels for billetting, March 1900

31 PAC, RG 18, A-1, vol. 98, no. 686, Herchmer to White, 7 October 1894

32 *Ibid.*, Herchmer to White, 16 October 1894

33 PAC, Macdonald Papers, vol. 256, R.H. Pope, MP, to Macdonald, 30 April 1891

34 PAC, Laurier Papers, vol. 29, J.M. Skelton to Sifton, 5 December 1896
35 PAC, RG 18, A-1, vol. 174, no. 594, telegram, Sifton to White, 22 November 1899; and vol. 205, no. 110, White to Perry, 19 January 1901
36 PAC, Sifton Papers, vol. 257, Sifton to Oliver, 12 April 1904
37 PAC, Bowell Papers, vol. 9, 4984-6, 6000-1, 6004-6, 6007, 6009, 6013, 6014, 6041, 6047, 6058-9, 6060-3, 6121-2, 6213-14
38 PAC, Bowell Papers, vol. 13, John Costigan (minister of fisheries) to Bowell, 28 December 1894
39 PAC, RG 18, A-1, vol. 240, no. 831, Perry to White, 25 October 1902
40 PAC, RG 18, A-1, vol. 260, no. 702, White to Dr T.S. Sproule, MP, 20 October 1903. The letter explains why police personnel at Ft Saskatchewan were not permitted to take part in the annual Orange parade.
41 Norman Ward, 'Electoral Corruption and Controverted Elections,' *Canadian Journal of Economics and Political Science* (July 1949)
42 Davin's majority amounted to three hundred and twenty-seven votes in the election; C.B. Koester, 'The Parliamentary Career of Nicholas Flood Davin, 1887-1900' (unpublished MA thesis, University of Saskatchewan 1964) 108-12. There were two hundred and forty-four Mounted Police in the constituency; NWMP *Annual Report*, 1891, 112
43 PAC, RG 18, A-1, vol. 50, no. 198, Herchmer to White, 2 June 1891
44 PAC, RG 18, A-1, vol. 297, no. 388, Inspector J.H. Heffernan to Superintendent J.O. Wilson, 5 April 1905
45 PAC, RG 18, A-1, vol. 133, no. 146, White to Herchmer, 21 January 1897
46 PAC, Laurier Papers, vol. 154, Scott to Laurier, 9 May 1900
47 Calgary *Herald*, 22 and 23 December 1896 and 1 and 25 February 1897
48 Ft Macleod *Gazette*, 19 February 1897
49 Edmonton *Bulletin*, 28 January 1897

CHAPTER 8: THE MILITARY TRADITION
IN THE MOUNTED POLICE

1 PAC, RG 18, A-1, vol. 19, no. 260, memo by White recommending that the claim be paid, 9 January 1888
2 GAI, Edgar Dewdney Papers, vol. 3, Macdonald to Dewdney, 2 September 1884
3 J.P. Turner, *The North-West Mounted Police 1873-1893* (Ottawa 1950) II, 221
4 PAC, RG 18, A-1, vol. 12, no. 20, White to Sir David Macpherson (minister of the interior), 22 October 1884
5 A.L. Haydon, *The Riders of the Plains* (London 1910) 147-9
6 PAC, RG 18, A-1, vol. 121, no. 297, Herchmer to White, 16 April 1896

7 PAC, RG 18, A-1, vol. 175, no. 669, White to Herchmer, 23 October 1899
8 It was more convenient for the commissioner to list the seven officers who did not volunteer than those who did. PAC, RG 18, A-1, vol. 180, no. 114, telegram, Herchmer to White, 31 December 1899
9 PAC, RG 18, A-1, vol. 165, no. 193, Ft Saskatchewan Monthly Report for December 1899
10 The word came directly from Clifford Sifton, who handled this as he did other patronage matters at the start. PAC, RG 18, A-1, vol. 175, no. 702, White to Herchmer, 31 October 1899
11 The first battalion shortly became the Royal Canadian Dragoons, so that the second battalion, the Mounted Police battalion, went to South Africa as the First Battalion, Canadian Mounted Rifles.
12 PAC, RG 18, A-1, vol. 180, no. 114, telegram, White to Herchmer, 19 December 1889
13 PAC, RG 18, A-1, vol. 202, no. 57
14 PAC, RG 18, A-1, vol. 187, no. 303, Ft Saskatchewan Monthly Report for January 1900. Some who missed the quota for the Edmonton district went to Calgary and enlisted there.
15 PAC, Minto Papers, Letterbooks vol. 1, Minto to Roberts, 31 December 1899
16 This hostility was undoubtedly a motivating factor in Middleton's criticisms of the police in 1885. In 1896 a man who was making a collection of Canadian military crests and mottoes wrote to White asking for that of the Mounted Police. White sent it to him but warned, 'I would not suggest your including it in your design of a Military trophy for all arms in Canada, for the reason that the Police force is not a military organization, and I know from experience that many Militia officers object to having the Mounted Police included in anything as being part of the Military organization of the country.' PAC, RG 18, A-1, vol. 121, no. 303, White to T.S. Hay, 16 April 1896
17 The original name was Strathcona's Rangers, PAC, RG 18, A-1, vol. 180, no. 138. The name was later repatriated and given to a permanent Canadian regiment, now an armoured regiment, with a long and distinguished record.
18 *Ibid.*, Nominal Roll, Strathcona's Horse, 2 April 1900. In addition to Steele and his second-in-command, two of the three majors and two of the three captains were police officers.
19 *Ibid.*, White to Assistant Commissioner McIlree, 27 January 1900
20 PAC, RG 18, A-1, vol. 202, no. 57
21 Haydon, *Riders of the Plains* 251
22 *Ibid.* 256
23 PAC, RG 18, A-1, vol. 180, no. 114
24 *Ibid.*, memo by White, 19 December 1899

25 PAC, RG 18, A-1, vol. 180, no. 138, White to Assistant Commissioner McIlree, 30 January 1900

26 For the third contingent, for example, the North-West Territories quota was eighty men of whom twenty might be police. PAC, RG 18, A-1, vol. 221, no. 12, White to Perry, 2 December 1901

27 PAC, RG 18, A-1, vol. 10, no. 118, minister of justice (Edward Blake) to French, 6 April 1876

28 PAC, RG 18, A-1, vol. 4, no. 84, reports from Inspector James Walker, 3 February 1875 and paymaster W.G. Griffiths, 6 February 1875

29 PAC, RG 18, A-1, vol. 8, no. 18, French to Minister of Justice, 21 December 1875

30 PAC, RG 18, B-4 vol. 10 (General Orders, Swan River Barracks), 18 July 1876

31 PAC, RG 18, B-3, vol. 47, Macleod to minister of the interior, 4 February 1876

32 PAC, RG 18, A-2, vol. 1, White to J.G. Colmer (High Commissioner's Office, London), 16 November 1883

33 PAC, RG 18, A-1, vol. 237, no. 545, Perry to White, 2 June 1902

34 PAC, MG 29, F-53, Diary of R. Burton Deane, 1883

35 PAC, RG 18, B-4, vol. 8, General Order No. 22, 10 April 1886

36 PAC, RG 18, A-1, vol. 141, no. 622, Perry to Herchmer, 13 November 1897

37 PAC, RG 18, A-1, vol. 205, no. 110, Perry to White, 4 December 1900

38 PAC, RG 18, A-1, vol. 274, no. 392, Perry to White, 24 March 1904

39 This was the substance of a memorandum written by White for Laurier on the consequences of a reduction in the force, 5 March 1897; PAC, RG 18, A-1, vol. 144, no. 42. There were numerous complaints from superintendents that they were unable to carry out drill due to shortages of men. See, for example, PAC, RG 18, A-1, vol. 208, no. 223, Ft Saskatchewan Monthly Report for December 1901.

40 PAC, RG 18, A-1, vol. 102, no. 46, Ft Macleod Monthly Report for September 1895

41 PAC, RG 18, A-1, vol. 113, no. 8, Regina Monthly Report for June 1896

42 PAC, RG 18, A-1, vol. 325, no. 353, White to Perry, 26 April 1902

43 Ibid., Perry to White, 5 May 1907

44 PAC, Macdonald Papers, vol. 229, Masson to Macdonald, 10 June 1885

45 Ibid., vol. 85, Lansdowne to Macdonald, 11 November 1885

46 Ibid., vol. 482, Boulton to Macdonald, 15 February 1890

47 PAC, RG 18, A-1, vol. 2, no. 141½, memo by Hewitt Bernard, 2 June 1874

48 PAC, RG 18, A-1, vol. 11, no. 242, Hewitt Bernard to Minister of Justice, April 1876

49 PAC, RG 18, A-1, vol. 8, no. 29, 8

50 PAC, RG 18, A-1, vol. 120, no. 235 and vol. 150, no. 199
51 Visitors were invariably impressed by Mounted Police escorts. One Chinese official by the name of Kang Yu-wei even requested that the Mounted Police sergeant assigned to escort him across Canada be allowed to accompany him to England. PAC, RG 18, A-1, vol. 170, no. 339, White to Herchmer, 18 May 1899
52 In 1901, for example, a request for the musical ride by the manager of the Winnipeg Fair was refused on these grounds on orders from Clifford Sifton. PAC, RG 18, A-1, vol. 217, no. 666, White to Perry, 16 July 1901
53 S.B. Steele, *Forty Years in Canada* (Toronto 1915) 156

CHAPTER 9: CRIME AND CRIMINALS
IN THE NORTH-WEST TERRITORIES 1873-1905

1 PAC, RG 18, A-1, vol. 18, no. 225, Ft. Saskatchewan Monthly Reports for January and December 1888
2 PAC, RG 18, A-1, vol. 126, no. 2, Regina Monthly Report for March 1897
3 PAC, RG 18, A-1, vol. 49, no. 192, Lethbridge Monthly Report for April 1891
4 PAC, RG 18, A-1, vol. 239, no. 672, Calgary Crime Reports, 1902
5 PAC, RG 18, A-1, vol. 230, no. 159, Calgary Monthly Report for March 1902
6 PAC, RG 18, A-1, vol. 18, no. 255, Ft Saskatchewan Monthly Report for January 1888; and vol. 49, no. 140, Regina Monthly Report for December 1891
7 PAC, RG 18, A-1, vol. 126, no. 2, Regina Monthly Report for June 1897
8 PAC, RG 18, A-1, vol. 121, no. 270, Inspector A.C. Macdonell to Superintendent Perry, 9 April 1896
9 PAC, RG 18, A-1, vol. 181, no. 163, Ft Macleod Monthly Report for June 1900
10 PAC, RG 18, A-1, vol. 113, no. 8, Regina Monthly Report for December 1896
11 PAC, RG 18, A-1, vol. 65, no. 313, Superintendent Steele to Herchmer, 2 April 1892. Similar cases may be found in vol. 88, no. 729; vol. 93, no. 200; vol. 105, no. 147; vol. 114, no. 24; and vol. 124, no. 480
12 PAC, RG 18, A-1, vol. 230, no. 159, Calgary Monthly Report for March 1902. Similar cases may be found in vol. 74, no. 63; vol. 93, no. 215; vol. 127, no. 20; and vol. 143, no. 17
13 PAC, RG 18, A-1, vol. 93, no. 215, Superintendent Perry to Herchmer, 17 February 1894

14 PAC, RG 18, A-1, vol. 126, no. 2, Regina Monthly Report for May 1897

15 The Cashel case is reported in several places: PAC, RG 18, A-1, vol. 270, no. 240, Calgary Monthly Reports for 1904; GAI, G.E. Sanders Papers and the Reminiscences of A.C. Bury. There is also an article on the case by a former policeman, Constable T.E.G. Shaw, 'The Cashel Case,' *Alberta Historical Review* VIII (Winter 1960) 17.

16 PAC, RG 18, A-1, vol. 123, no. 447, Griesbach to Herchmer, 7 August 1896

17 PAC, RG 18, A-1, vol. 114, no. 26, Ft Saskatchewan Monthly Report for August 1896

18 PAC, RG 18, A-1, vol. 69, no. 615, Inspector A.R. Cuthbert to Herchmer, 3 August 1892

19 PAC, RG 18, A-1, vol. 68, no. 521, Cuthbert to Herchmer, 19 August 1892

20 PAC, RG 18, A-1, vol. 69, no. 615, Cuthbert to Herchmer, 9 August 1892

21 PAC, RG 18, A-1, vol. 70, no. 664, White to Herchmer, 26 August 1892

22 PAC, RG 18, A-1, vol. 104, no. 131, Lethbridge Monthly Report for February 1895

23 *Ibid.*

24 *Ibid.*, Lethbridge Monthly Reports for June and July 1895

25 PAC, RG 18, A-1, vol. 114, no. 25, Lethbridge Monthly Report for December 1896

26 PAC, RG 18, A-1, vol. 107, no. 218, D.H. MacDowall, MP, to Mackenzie Bowell, 16 February 1895 and Inspector D'Arcy Strickland to Herchmer, 4 March 1895

27 PAC, RG 18, A-1, vol. 47, no. 34, Superintendent John Cotton to Herchmer, 10 May 1890

28 PAC, RG 18, A-1, vol. 130, no. 76, Herchmer to White, 29 November 1896

29 PAC, RG 18, A-1, vol. 44, no. 775; vol. 98, no. 671; and vol. 107, no. 220

30 The postmaster, Campbell by name, fled in March 1893 and was arrested in Chicago 29 September of the same year. PAC, RG 18, A-1, vol. 98, no. 671

31 PAC, RG 18, A-1, vol. 140, no. 493

32 PAC, RG 18, A-1, vol. 147, no. 549

33 PAC, RG 18, A-1, vol. 214, no. 452, Superintendent G.E. Sanders to Herchmer, 5 May 1899

34 PAC, RG 18, A-1, vol. 217, no. 723, Deane to Perry, 24 August 1901

35 *Ibid.*, Perry to White, 20 August 1901. The same complaint was voiced by Inspector A.R. Cuthbert, vol. 207, no. 210, Prince Albert Monthly Report for October 1901.

36 Calgary *Herald*, 27 June 1901. See also the Moose Jaw *Times*, 24 October 1902 and Superintendent Deane's comments on cattle rustling in PAC, RG 18, A-1, vol. 183, no. 202, Lethbridge Monthly Report for January 1900.

37 PAC, RG 18, A-1, vol. 216, no. 651, Perry to White, 4 July 1901
38 PAC, RG 18, A-1, vol. 273, no. 315, Perry to White, 28 August 1901; and vol. 300, no. 510, Perry to White, 12 June 1905
39 PAC, RG 18, A-1, vol. 22, no. 383, Constantine to Herchmer, 14 August 1887
40 For the former see PAC, RG 18, A-1, vol. 114, no. 24, Calgary Monthly Report for October 1896; and vol. 125, no. 586. For the latter see vol. 91, no. 148, Lethbridge Monthly Reports for April and May 1894
41 PAC, RG 18, A-1, vol. 249, no. 154, Calgary Monthly Report for February 1903; and vol. 271, no. 241, Calgary Monthly Report for July 1904
42 PAC, RG 18, A-1, vol. 24, no. 711
43 PAC, RG 18, A-1, vol. 43, no. 660, Herchmer to White, 1 September 1890
44 PAC, RG 18, A-1, vol. 104, no. 25, Lethbridge Monthly Report for February 1896
45 GAI, Diaries of Sergeant S. Hetherington, 1 June 1899
46 PAC, RG 18, A-1, vol. 52, no. 369
47 PAC, RG 18, A-1, vol. 128, no. 44, Constable A.F. Glend to Superintendent Perry, 29 December 1896
48 PAC, RG 18, A-1, vol. 58, no. 37, Superintendent Deane to Herchmer, 22 October 1891 and Sir Julian Pauncefote to Lord Stanley, 5 January 1892
49 PAC, RG 18, A-1, vol. 74, no. 73, Lethbridge Monthly Report for October 1893
50 PAC, RG 18, A-1, vol. 91, no. 148, Lethbridge Monthly Report for July 1894
51 PAC, RG 18, A-1, vol. 143, no. 17, Lethbridge Monthly Report for September 1898
52 PAC, RG 18, A-1, vol. 167, no. 215, Calgary Monthly Report for January 1899
53 PAC, RG 18, A-1, vol. 279, no. 579, Perry to Inspector J.V. Begin, 11 June 1904
54 Calgary *Herald*, 6 February 1905; and PAC, RG 18, A-1, vol. 297, no. 323, White to Perry, 21 March 1905
55 In 1894, for example, the Regina Town Council applied for a Mounted Police detachment, 'To maintain law and order and especially enforce those by-laws pertaining to licences, gambling, and the suppression of vice and immorality.' PAC, RG 18, A-1, vol. 94, no. 258, John Secord (Regina Town Clerk) to Herchmer, 28 February 1894. The request was refused by the police. White to Herchmer, 10 March 1894
56 See, for example, PAC, RG 18, A-1, vol. 131, no. 202, Regina Monthly Reports for 1899, in which sentences for vagrancy range from a fine of one dollar to three months in jail.

57 PAC, RG 18, A-1, vol. 112, no. 190, Calgary Monthly Report for June 1894
58 PAC, RG 18, A-1, vol. 49, no. 192, Lethbridge Monthly Report for April 1891
59 PAC, RG 18, A-1, vol. 126, no. 2, Regina Monthly Report for April 1897
60 For example see, PAC, RG 18, A-1, vol. 229, no. 156, Prince Albert Monthly Reports, 1902; and vol. 247, no. 101, Regina Monthly Reports, 1903
61 PAC, RG 18, A-1, vol. 107, no. 215, Ft Saskatchewan Monthly Reports for 1895; and vol. 143, no. 20, Prince Albert Monthly Reports for 1898
62 PAC, RG 18, A-1, vol. 247, no. 101, Regina Monthly Report for October 1903
63 PAC, RG 18, A-1, vol. 102, no. 54, Regina Monthly Report for January 1895
64 PAC, RG 18, A-1, vol. 30, no. 130, Lethbridge Monthly Report for April 1889

CHAPTER 10: THE ENFORCEMENT OF THE LIQUOR LAWS: THE IDENTITY CRISIS OF THE MOUNTED POLICE

1 PAC, MG 30, E-6, Papers of Corporal Alfred Spearman, a newspaper entitled *The Fool*, published at Prince Albert, 18 December 1890. This seems to have been the first and only issue.
2 The question of the authorship of this interesting piece is not within the scope of this study. Perhaps it was the local newspaper editor. It might also have been the poet, Charles Mair, who was living in Prince Albert at the time and who had had a brush with the Mounted Police previously over the enforcement of the liquor laws. PAC, RG 18, A-1, vol. 13, no. 2, report on a public meeting organized by Mair, 8 December 1886, which protested police methods of enforcing the liquor laws.
3 Peter B. Waite, *Canada 1874-1896: Arduous Destiny* (Toronto 1971) 3-5
4 Public Archives of Saskatchewan [PAS], Diary of William Wallace Clarke, 1875. Clarke's waggons were searched several times on his way to the Touchwood Hills in that year.
5 PAC, MG 29, F-52, Diary of Constable R.N. Wilson 1881-8, 20 February 1882
6 PAC, RG 18, A-1, vol. 18, no. 230, Maple Creek Monthly Reports for 1888
7 For public opinion see the editorial and letters to the editor in the *Ft Macleod Gazette*, 2 October 1890. For the police reaction to the potential effects of the new liquor legislation on the native population, see PAC, RG 18, A-1, vol. 72, no. 798, Herchmer to Lieutenant-Governor Joseph Royal, 17 November 1892.

8 PAC, RG 18, A-1, vol. 278, no. 531, Perry to Morris, 23 May 1904

9 Public Archives of Manitoba [PAM], James Morrow Walsh Papers, journal
   while acting commanding officer, 1 October 1873

10 PAC, RG 18, A-1, vol. 1, no. 22, memo by Superintendent J.M. Walsh,
   30 October 1873

11 PAC, RG 18, A-1, vol. 10 (General Orders, Lower Ft Garry), 13 December
   1873

12 *Ibid.*, 8 January 1874

13 PAC, RG 18, A-1, vol. 9, no. 82, French to minister of justice, 1 February
   1876

14 *Ibid.*

15 PAC, RG 18, B-1, vol. 1, no. 52, Superintendent A. Shurtliff to Irvine,
   28 December 1882

16 PAC, RG 18, B-4, vol. 8, General Order No. 100 (Old Series), 12 April 1881

17 PAC, RG 18, A-1, vol. 2, no. 168, French to Minister of Justice, 15 January
   1875

18 Deane, *Mounted Police Life in Canada* 58

19 PAC, RG 18, A-1, vol. 39, no. 137, Lethbridge Monthly Report for April
   1890

20 Manitoba *Free Press*, 10 April 1890, records a resolution to that effect by
   the Regina Board of Trade.

21 PAC, RG 18, A-1, vol. 63, no. 247, Lethbridge Monthly Report for September
   1892

22 PAC, RG 18, A-1, vol. R-2, Letter No. 405, 20 September 1875

23 GAI, Edgar Dewdney Papers, vol. 6, S.E. Clarke to Dewdney, 17 December
   1883

24 PAC, Macdonald Papers, vol. 227, Langevin to Macdonald, 6 June 1884

25 *Ibid.*, vol. 421, telegram, George Murdock (Mayor of Calgary) to Macdonald,
   10 November 1885

26 PAC, Macdonald Papers, vol. 526, Macdonald to Murdock, 11 November 1885

27 Toronto *Mail*, 18 November 1887, reprint of part of Bleecker's submission
   to the Council

28 PAC, RG 18, A-1, vol. 15, no. 34, Bleecker to Superintendent W.M. Herchmer,
   6 December 1887

29 *Ibid.*, Superintendent W.M. Herchmer to Commissioner Herchmer,
   8 December 1887

30 PAC, RG 18, A-1, vol. 17, no. 163, Superintendent Perry to Herchmer,
   27 March 1888

31 PAC, RG 18, A-1, vol. 25, no. 843, Superintendent Perry to Herchmer,
   2 October 1888

32 PAC, RG 18, A-1, vol. 17, no. 204, Superintendent W.M. Herchmer to Commissioner Herchmer, 25 January 1888
33 PAC, RG 18, A-1, vol. 34, no. 107, Superintendent McIlree to Herchmer, 13 January 1890
34 *Ibid.*
35 Medicine Hat *Times*, 10 September 1887
36 PAC, RG 18, A-1, vol. 44, no. 741, White to Herchmer, 27 September 1890
37 *Ibid.*, Herchmer to White, 11 September 1890
38 *Ibid.*, McIlree to Herchmer, 5 September 1890
39 See especially McIlree's report on the liquor situation in Calgary in PAC, RG 18, A-1, vol. 17, no. 145, McIlree to Herchmer, 29 December 1888
40 PAC, RG 18, A-1, vol. 44, no. 809, R.B. Gordon (Secretary to the Lieutenant-Governor) to Herchmer, 20 October 1890
41 PAC, RG 18, B-4, vol. 8, Circular Memorandum, 9 December 1890
42 The Assembly had proposed a plebiscite on the liquor question in 1888 but the federal government vetoed this idea after consulting their legal experts. Thomas, *The Struggle for Responsible Government* 167 and 207-8
43 PAC, RG 18, A-1, vol. 71, no. 720, Herchmer to Prime Minister J.J.C. Abbott, 6 August 1891
44 PAC, RG 18, A-1, vol. 91, no. 148, Lethbridge Monthly Report for June 1894
45 PAC, RG 18, A-1, vol. 94, no. 258, reply to a request from the Regina Town Council, 19 March 1894; and vol. 109, no. 441, reply to a Department of the Interior request for police in Banff National Park, 29 November 1894
46 PAC, RG 18, A-1, vol. 126, no. 2, Regina Monthly Report for March 1897
47 PAC, RG 18, A-1, vol. 233, no. 227
48 PAC, RG 18, A-1, vol. 49, no. 192, Lethbridge Monthly Report for February 1891. Superintendent Deane noted that the prohibition faction had been victorious in the municipal elections of that year.

CHAPTER 11: THE MOUNTED POLICE
AND MINORITY GROUPS

1 This phenomenon in the relations between whites and non-whites in the British Empire generally is explored at length in Christine Bolt, *Victorian Attitudes to Race* (Toronto 1971)
2 PAC, RG 18, B-4, vol. 7, General Order No. 4640 (new series), 21 January 1890
3 RCMP Museum, Regina, *Revised General Orders for the North-West Mounted Police*, 1895, 17
4 PAC, RG 18, A-1, vol. 25, no. 900, Herchmer to Commissioner of Indian Affairs, 12 November 1888

5   PAC, RG 18, A-1, vol. 256, no. 410

6   PAS, Diary of William Wallace Clarke, 1875

7   PAC, RG 18, A-1, vol. 24, no. 667, Superintendent P.R. Neale to Herchmer, 17 July 1888

8   PAC, RG 18, A-1, vol. 181, no. 163, Ft Macleod Monthly Report for November 1900

9   PAC, RG 18, A-1, vol. 36, no. 817, Superintendent Steele to Herchmer, 12 August 1889

10 PAC, RG 18, A-1, vol. 55, no. 586, Steele to Herchmer, 23 June 1891

11 PAC, RG 18, A-1, vol. 218, no. 763, White to Herchmer, 20 May 1893

12 *Ibid.*, Hayter Reed to L. Vankoughnet (Deputy Superintendent of Indian Affairs), 5 June 1893

13 *Ibid.*, Steele to Herchmer, 19 June 1893

14 *Ibid.*, White to James A. Smart (Deputy Superintendent of Indian Affairs), 17 September 1901; and vol. 273, no. 303, Superintendent J.O. Wilson to Corporal Dubuque, 28 May 1904

15 PAC, RG 18, A-1, vol. 73, no. 6; and vol. 84, no. 505

16 PAC, RG 18, A-1, vol. 112, no. 665, Steele to Herchmer, 5 October 1895

17 PAC, RG 18, A-1, vol. 103, no. 63, Father J. Hugonnard (Principal) to Indian Commissioner, 19 December 1894

18 *Ibid.*, Constantine to Superintendent Perry, 8 January 1895

19 *Ibid.*, Herchmer to White, 22 February 1895

20 PAC, RG 18, A-1, vol. 15, no. 28; and vol. 113, no. 8, Regina Monthly Report for July 1896

21 PAC, RG 18, A-1, vol. 98, no. 679, Herchmer to White, 21 September 1894

22 PAC, RG 18, A-1, vol. 143, no. 18, Calgary Monthly Report for July 1898

23 PAC, RG 18, A-1, vol. 114, no. 25, Lethbridge Monthly Report for June 1896

24 *Ibid.*

25 PAC, Macdonald Papers, vol. 516, Macdonald to William McDougall, 12 December 1869

26 PAC, RG 18, A-1, vol. 61, no. 170, Vankoughnet to White, 12 December 1891

27 *Ibid.*, White to Vankoughnet, 18 February 1892

28 PAC, RG 18, A-1, vol. 179, no. 106, Inspector F.J.A. Demers (Battleford) to Herchmer, 12 January 1900; vol. 180, no. 114, White to Herchmer, 29 December 1899; and vol. 207, no. 210, Prince Albert Monthly Report for January 1901

29 PAC, RG 18, A-1, vol. 180, no. 114, White to Herchmer, 27 December 1899

30 PAC, RG 18, A-1, vol. 261, no. 888, White to F. Bopp (German Consul at Ottawa), 28 December 1903

31 PAC, RG 18, A-1, vol. 26, no. 48

32 PAC, RG 18, A-1, vol. 127, no. 20

33 PAC, RG 18, A-1, vol. 125, no. 605, Herchmer to White, 4 November 1896; and vol. 181, no. 63, Ft Macleod Monthly Report for May 1900

34 PAC, RG 18, A-1, vol. 74, no. 68; vol. 126, no. 6; vol. 165, no. 193; vol. 167, no. 224; and vol. 257, no. 512

35 PAC, RG 18, A-1, vol. 74, no. 68, Herchmer to White, 13 January 1893

36 The exception was the Sons of Freedom sect of the Doukhobours, whose defiance of the law was religiously inspired and consisted of destroying their own property and parading in the nude.

37 PAC, RG 18, A-1, vol. 41, no. 339, report on a German colony near Medicine Hat

38 PAC, RG 18, A-1, vol. 172, no. 426, Gagnon to Herchmer, 15 May 1899

39 PAC, RG 18, A-1, vol. 97, no. 587, Starr to F.M. Daly (minister of the interior), 17 July 1894

40 Ibid., Superintendent McIlree to White, 16 August 1894

41 PAC, RG 18, A-1, vol. 172, no. 438, Frank Oliver to White, 1 and 8 June 1899

42 Ibid., Wilson to Superintendent Griesbach, 21 June 1899

43 PAC, RG 18, A-1, vol. 141, no. 545, White to Secretary of Department of the Interior, 5 October 1897

44 PAC, RG 18, A-1, vol. 146, no. 96, Corporal Butler to Superintendent Griesbach, 28 August 1897

45 Ibid., C.W. Sutter (immigration agent, Edmonton) to C.W. McCreary (Department of the Interior), 27 September 1897

46 Ibid., Primrose to Superintendent Griesbach, 7 January 1898

47 The police did not have a detachment in this particular settlement again until 1901. PAC, RG 18, A-1, vol. 208, no. 213, Ft Saskatchewan Monthly Report for June 1901. The incident is described in more detail in Vladimir J. Kaye, Early Ukrainian Settlements in Canada 1895-1900 (Toronto 1964) 322-37

48 PAC, RG 18, A-1, vol. 49, no. 192, Lethbridge Monthly Report for February 1892

49 PAC, RG 18, A-1, vol. 63, no. 247, Lethbridge Monthly Report for February 1892

50 PAC, RG 18, A-1, vol. 295, no. 263

51 PAC, RG 18, A-1, vol. 247, no. 101, Regina Monthly Report for February 1903 (Inspector A.R. Cuthbert)

52 PAC, RG 18, A-1, vol. 229, no. 156, Prince Albert Monthly Report for April 1902. Refers to American settlers as 'the best class obtainable'

53 PAC, RG 18, A-1, vol. 274, no. 353, Perry to White, 17 October 1903

54 The best discussion of this phenomenon is in S.F. Wise and Robert Craig Brown, Canada Views the United States: Nineteenth Century Political Attitudes (Seattle 1967)

55 PAC, RG 18, A-1, vol. 168, no. 241, Sergeant Byrne to Superintendent Howe, 12 March 1899

56 PAC, RG 18, A-1, vol. 76, no. 161, Regina Monthly Report for August 1893

57 PAC, RG 18, A-1, vol. 253, no. 304, Wilson to Assistant Commissioner McIlree, 28 February 1903

58 PAC, RG 18, A-1, vol. 74, no. 68, Herchmer to White, 13 January 1893

59 PAC, RG 18, A-1, vol. 41, no. 250, Steele to Herchmer, 4 December 1889

60 *Ibid.*, memo by White, 16 December 1899

61 For unfavourable press reaction to the LDS see the Calgary *Herald*, 12 December 1889 and 5 January 1890; and the Ft Macleod *Gazette*, 6 February 1890.

62 PAC, RG 18, A-1, vol. 169, no. 305, Corporal Bolderson to Superintendent Deane, 11 March 1899

63 PAC, RG 18, A-1, vol. 181, no. 163, Ft Macleod Monthly Report for September 1900

64 PAC, RG 18, A-1, vol. 126, no. 3, Ft Macleod Monthly Report for January 1897

65 PAC, RG 18, A-1, vol. 250, no. 177, Lethbridge Monthly Report for June 1903 (Inspector J.V. Begin)

66 PAC, RG 18, A-1, vol. 104, no. 131, Lethbridge Monthly Report for July 1895

67 PAC, Diary of Inspector R. Burton Deane, 4 October to 30 December 1883

68 PAC, RG 18, A-1, vol. 64, no. 248, Regina Monthly Reports for September and October 1892

69 PAC, RG 18, A-1, vol. 113, no. 8, Regina Monthly Report for February 1896

70 PAC, RG 18, A-1, vol. 217, no. 723, Perry to White, 28 August 1901

71 PAC, RG 18, A-1, vol. 91, no. 148, Lethbridge Monthly Report for February 1894

72 PAC, RG 18, A-1, vol. 127, no. 5; vol. 209, no. 235; vol. 225, no. 84

73 PAC, RG 18, A-1, vol. 145, no. 56, G. Drinkwater (secretary of CPR) to White, 7 September 1897

74 *Ibid.*, White to Drinkwater, 14 September 1897

75 PAC, RG 18, A-1, vol. 126, no. 3, Ft Macleod Monthly Report for December 1897

76 PAC, RG 18, A-1, vol. 145, no. 56, Sanders to Superintendent Deane, 23 October 1897

77 *Ibid.*, Sanders to Deane, 30 October 1897

78 *Ibid.*

79 *Ibid.*

80 PAC, RG 18, A-1, vol. 143, no. 17, Ft Macleod Monthly Report for January 1898

81 PAC, RG 18, A-1, vol. 156, no. 3, M.J. Haney to Herchmer, 31 October 1898
82 PAC, RG 18, A-1, vol. 300, no. 517, L.P. Eckstein to W.A. Galliher, MP, 9 June 1905
83 *Ibid.*, Corporal S.J. Kemby to Inspector Primrose, 14 June 1905
84 *Ibid.*, Eckstein to Galliher, 24 June 1905
85 *Ibid.*

CHAPTER 12: CONCLUSION

 1 *Debates of the House of Commons*, 24 March 1882, 545
 2 *Ibid.*
 3 *Debates*, 9 June 1885, 2403-13
 4 *Ibid.*, 2412-15
 5 *Debates*, 21 March 1889, 769
 6 *Debates*, 15 April 1889, 1277
 7 *Debates*, 21 March 1889, 770
 8 *Debates*, 1 September 1891, 4819
 9 *Debates*, 16 May 1892, 2672
10 *Ibid.*, 2696
11 *Ibid.*, 2689
12 *Ibid.*, 2684
13 *Ibid.*, 2686
14 *Debates*, 25 September 1896, 2041
15 *Ibid.*, 2042
16 *Debates*, 14 June 1897, 4078-81
17 *Debates*, 19 April 1901, 3445
18 *Debates*, 2 February 1905, 464
19 *Ibid.*
20 *Debates*, 9 June 1885, 2412-13
21 *Debates*, 6 May 1904, 2701-3

Bibliography

MANUSCRIPT COLLECTIONS

Glenbow-Alberta Institute. Archives, Frederick A. Bagley Papers and Diary
A very useful collection since Bagley was not only an original member of the force who participated in the 1874 march west but was one of the most articulate of the non-commissioned ranks to leave any record of his service in the Mounted Police. The papers include an unpublished manuscript, 'The '74 Mounties.'
- James W. and David L. Brereton Diaries
- A.C. Bury Diary and Reminiscences
These papers contain an interesting and useful account of Constable Bury's participation in the Cashel case.
- Cochrane Ranch Diary and Letterbook
- Mrs Jessie De Gear Papers
- Edgar Dewdney Papers
These papers are an important source of information since Dewdney was lieutenant-governor of the North-West Territories and a confidant of Sir John A. Macdonald. He worked closely with commissioners Irvine and Herchmer.
- F.W.G. Haultain Correspondence
- W.M. Herchmer Papers
- Sergeant S. Hetherington Diary
- W.M. Jarvis Papers
- Dr Augustus Jukes Papers
Dr Jukes was senior surgeon of the NWMP for many years.

- Eleanor Luxton Papers
- James F. Macleod Papers
  These papers are disappointingly brief and consist mostly of copies of official records available elsewhere along with a few details of Commissioner Macleod's personal finances.
- Frederick Davis Shaw Papers
- Superintendent Samuel B. Steele Letters
- Frank White Diary
- Superintendent James Walker Papers
- C.E.D. Wood Correspondence
Public Archives of British Columbia. John Henry McIlree Papers
Public Archives of Canada. Governor-General Sir John Campbell Hamilton Gordon, seventh Earl of Aberdeen Papers
- Edward Blake Papers
  As minister of justice in the Mackenzie government, Blake was responsible for the NWMP from 1875 to 1877.
- Sir Mackenzie Bowell Papers
  Bowell was prime minister from 1894 to 1896. He took a personal interest in the Mounted Police and his papers contain a good deal of interesting material, much of it dealing with patronage in the force.
- Sir Alexander Campbell Papers
  Campbell held various cabinet posts under Sir John A. Macdonald between 1867 and 1885. His papers contain some essential material concerning the origins of the Mounted Police.
- Sir Adolphe Caron Papers
- Superintendent Charles Constantine Diary
  This diary is a great disappointment. Constantine was brought into the Mounted Police from the Manitoba Provincial Police to organize a detective branch and subsequently handled many of the most difficult and interesting assignments the force had to offer. The diary consists almost entirely of routine daily observations on the weather.
- Superintendent R. Burton Deane Diary
  A useful supplement to Deane's official reports and his autobiography.
- Governor-General Frederick Temple, first Marquis of Dufferin and Ava Papers
  These papers, microfilm copies of the originals in the Public Record Office of Northern Ireland, are probably the most useful of any of the Governor-General's Records. Dufferin held the office at the time of the formation of the Mounted Police and took a personal interest in the formation and early development of the police.
- Constable James Finlayson Diary
- Sir Wilfrid Laurier Papers

These papers are essential to any serious study of the history of the Mounted Police. They are very extensive and contain material on every aspect of Mounted Police policies and operations.

- Governor-General Sir John Douglas Sutherland Campbell, Marquis of Lorne Papers
- Sir John A. Macdonald Papers
  The Macdonald papers are almost as important to the historian of the Mounted Police as the RCMP Records. The Mounted Police were in a very real sense the invention of Sir John A. Macdonald and he guided their development for most of the first twenty years of their existence.
- Alexander Mackenzie Papers
- Governor-General Sir Gilbert John Elliot, fourth Earl of Minto Papers
  Minto was offered the command of the Mounted Police in the 1880s but turned the post down. His interest in the force continued after he was appointed governor-general in 1898 and he subsequently became honorary commissioner. Minto had a good deal to do with police participation in the South African War.
- Alexander Morris Papers
  As chief justice and later lieutenant-governor of Manitoba and the North-West Territories from 1872 to 1877, Morris was one of the key figures in the formation of the Mounted Police. This collection must be supplemented by other Morris papers in the Public Archives of Manitoba and Queen's University Library.
- Royal Canadian Mounted Police Records
  The RCMP Records are the chief documentary source for this book, as they must be of any serious study of the history of the Mounted Police. Most of the records for the period 1873-85 were destroyed by a fire in the Parliament Buildings in 1897 but after 1885 they provide complete and very detailed documentation for every aspect of police operations from policy decisions to the care of horses. The records are so extensive, amounting to over three thousand volumes for the period to 1920, that it would be impossible to examine all of them in detail. The difficulties of selection are eased to a considerable extent by the fact that most of the records are financial or deal with routine administrative matters. Many of the other records are repetitive to a large extent: the Commissioner's Office correspondence, for example, is to a large degree duplicated in the Comptroller's Office correspondence.

As will be evident from the footnotes, this study relies most heavily on the Comptroller's Office Official Correspondence Series (RG 18, A-1). From 1880 until 1919 the comptroller was the most important link between the police and their political superiors. This series contains correspondence dealing with policy decisions at all levels of importance and reports from the field on every matter which the leadership of the force considered worthy of Ottawa's attention. The series also includes the monthly divisional reports which are the most comprehensive and useful summaries of day-to-day police activities. While the Official Correspondence Series of the Commissioner's Office (RG 18, B-1) is largely duplicated in the records of the Comptroller's Office, except for the years before 1880, three other series emanating from the Commissioner's Office contain essential material not to be found elsewhere. The letterbooks of some of the early commissioners (RG 18, B-3) help fill the gaps left by the destruction of the correspondence series by fire. The Orders and Regulations series (RG 18, B-4) provides material which gives a good deal of insight into the thinking of the officers of the force and the internal problems they encountered. Personnel Records, Men (RG 18, B-8) is the most important source of information about the background of recruits. The Division and Detachment Records (RG 18, C-1-13) are very routine records of daily events, summarized in any case in the monthly divisional reports.

- Corporal Alfred Spearman Papers
- Sir Clifford Sifton Papers
  Sifton was Laurier's minister of the interior and chief political organizer. Laurier informally delegated many of the policy decisions concerning the police to Sifton.
- Sir John Thompson Papers
- Constable R.N. Wilson Diary
Public Archives of Manitoba. Adams G. Archibald Correspondence
  Archibald was lieutenant-governor of Manitoba 1870-3 and was responsible for sending Captain William F. Butler on his reconnaissance of the NWT.
- Alexander Morris Papers
- James Morrow Walsh Papers
  These papers are important because they contain Walsh's version of the Sitting Bull incident.
Public Archives of Saskatchewan. J.E. Ashton Reminiscences
- William Wallace Clark Diary
- N. Cowan Reminiscences
- Robert Noltby Diary
- Stanley Rackham Diary
- Robert K. Thompson Diary
Queen's University. Archives, Sir Alexander Campbell Papers
- Alexander Morris Papers
RCMP Museum, Regina. Commissioner G.A. French's Diary of the 1874 expedition
- A.G. Irvine Papers
University of Alberta. Archives, C.A. Magrath Papers

- William Pearce Papers
- A. Rutherford Papers

GOVERNMENT DOCUMENTS

Canada. Parliament. *Canada Parliamentary Debates*, Debates reported by newspapers, 1873-4

Canada. Parliament. House of Commons. *Debates*; official reports, 1875-1905

Canada. Parliament. *Sessional Papers* (House of Commons), 1871, IV, vol. 5, no. 120, 'Return: Instructions to the Honorable A. Archibald'

- 1873, VI, vol. 5, no. 9, 'Report on the State of the Militia of the Dominion of Canada'
- 1876, IX, vol. 8, no. 70, 'North-West Territories, Laws and Ordinances'
- 1877, X, vol. 7, no. 9, 'Report of the Secretary of State of Canada for the Year ended 31st December, 1876.' Appendix D, North-West Mounted Police

    The annual report for 1876 was the first to be published in the Sessional Papers. The reports for every succeeding year with the exceptions of 1877 and 1879 were published both separately and in the Sessional Papers. The annual reports of the force were issued as appendices of various government departmental reports until 1884 when they began to be issued as separate sessional papers. The reports for the period considered in this study are lengthy and detailed summaries of all police activities in the North-West Territories.

- 1879, XII, vol. 9, no. 52, 'Report of the Secretary of State of the Dominion of Canada for the Year ended 31st December, 1878.' Appendix D, North-West Mounted Police
- 1880-1, XIV, vol. 3, no. 3, 'Annual Report of the Department of the Interior for the Year ended 31st December, 1880,' Part II, North-West Mounted Police, Commissioner's Report 1880
- 1882, XV, vol. 8, no. 18, 'Annual Report of the Minister of the Interior for the Year ended 30th June, 1881,' Part II, North-West Mounted Police Force, of the Commissioner 1881
- 1883, XVI, vol. 10, no. 23, 'Annual Report of the Minister of the Interior for the Year ended 30th June, 1882,' Part II, North-West Mounted Police Force, Report of the Commissioner 1882
- 1884, XVII, vol. 11, no. 125, 'Report of the Commissioner of the North-West Mounted Police Force 1883'
- 1885, XVIII, vol. 13, no. 153a, 'Report of the Commissioner of the North-West Mounted Police Force 1884'
- 1886, XIX, vol. 6, no. 8a, 'Report of the Commissioner of the North-West Mounted Police Force 1885'

- 1887, xx, vol. 6, no. 7a, 'Report of the Commissioner of the North-West Mounted Police Force 1886'
- 1888, xxi, vol. 17, no. 28, 'Report of the Commissioner of the North-West Mounted Police Force 1887'
- 1889, xxii, vol. 13, no. 17, 'Report of the Commissioner of the North-West Mounted Police Force 1888'
- 1890, xxiii, vol. 10, no. 13, 'Report of the Commissioner of the North-West Mounted Police Force 1889'
- 1891, xxiv, vol. 15, no. 19, 'Report of the Commissioner of the North-West Mounted Police Force 1890'
- 1891, xxiv, vol. 17, no. 69, 'Departmental Report on Charges Preferred against the Commissioner of the North-West Mounted Police'
- 1892, xxv, vol. 10, no. 15, 'Report of the Commissioner of the North-West Mounted Police Force 1891'
- 1893, xxvi, vol. 9, no. 15, 'Report of the Commissioner of the North-West Mounted Police Force 1892'
- 1894, xxvii, vol. 11, no. 15, 'Report of the Commissioner of the North-West Mounted Police Force 1893'
- 1895, xxviii, vol. 9, no. 15, 'Report of the Commissioner of the North-West Mounted Police Force 1894'
- 1896, xxix, vol. 11, no. 15, 'Report of the Commissioner of the North-West Mounted Police Force 1895'
- 1896, xxix, vol. 11, no. 15a, 'Supplementary Report of the Commissioner of the North-West Mounted Police Force 1895'
- 1897, xxxi, vol. 11, no. 15, 'Report of the Commissioner of the North-West Mounted Police Force 1896'
- 1898, xxxii, vol. 12, no. 15, 'Report of the Commissioner of the North-West Mounted Police Force 1897'
- 1899, xxxiii, vol. 12, no. 15, 'Report of the Commissioner of the North-West Mounted Police Force 1898'
- 1900, xxxiv, vol. 12, no. 15, 'Report of the Commissioner of the North-West Mounted Police Force 1899'
- 1901, xxxv, vol. 11, no. 28 and 28a, 'Report of the North-West Mounted Police 1900'
- 1902, xxxvi, vol. 12, no. 28, 'Report of the North-West Mounted Police 1901
- 1903, xxxvii, vol. 12, no. 28, 'Report of the North-West Mounted Police 1902'
- 1904, xxxviii, vol. 11, no. 28, 'Report of the North-West Mounted Police 1903'
- 1905, xxxix, vol. 12, no. 28, 'Report of the North-West Mounted Police 1904'

- 1906, xl, vol. 13, no. 28, 'Report of the North-West Mounted Police 1905'
Great Britain. Parliament. *Parliamentary Papers* (House of Commons), 1854,
vol. x, 53, 'Minutes of Evidence taken before the Select Committee on extending the Functions of the Constabulary in Ireland to the Suppression of Illicit
Distillation'
- 1866, vol. 34, 3685, 'Report of the Commission on the Present State of the
Constabulary Force of Ireland'
- 1873, vol. 22, c.831, 'Report of the Commission on the Civil Service (Ireland):
Royal Irish Constabulary'

NEWSPAPERS AND PERIODICALS

Calgary *Herald*
Edmonton *Bulletin*
Fort Macleod *Gazette*
Medicine Hat *Times*
Regina *Leader*
RCMP *Quarterly*
   The *Quarterly* has been published since 1934 as a house organ of the Mounted
Police. It contains a good many articles dealing with the history of the force.
These must be used with caution and checked against contemporary reports
where they are available.
Scarlet and Gold
   This magazine has been published since 1919 by the RCMP Veterans' Associa-
tion. It contains much the same sort of material as the *Quarterly* and the same
strictures apply to the use of articles found in it.
Toronto *Globe*
Toronto *Mail*
Winnipeg *Free Press*

SECONDARY WORKS ON THE MOUNTED POLICE

Atkin, Ronald *Maintain the Right: The Early History of the North-West
Mounted Police, 1873-1900* Toronto 1973
Chambers, Ernest J. *The Royal North-West Mounted Police: A Corps History*
Montreal 1906
   This was the first attempt at a history of the force. Chambers's account of the
origins of the police is still the most accurate in print.
Constantine, C.P. *I Was a Mountie: The Adventures of a Trooper of Canada's
Famed Mounted Police* New York 1958

D'Artigue, Jean *Six Years in the Canadian North-West* Toronto 1882

Deane, R. Burton *Mounted Police Life in Canada: A Record of Thirty-One Years' Service* London 1916

Deane was one of the most articulate police officers and this is one of the best autobiographical accounts. The book is unfortunately marred by a tendency to ramble and forget details and by Deane's bitterness at being passed over for commissioner or assistant commissioner.

Dempsey, Hugh 'The "Thin Red Line" in the Canadian West,' *American West* VII (January 1970)

– ed. *Men in Scarlet* Calgary 1974

– ed. *William Parker: Mounted Policeman* Edmonton 1974

Denny, Sir Cecil E. *The Law Marches West* Toronto 1939

Donkin, John G. *Trooper and Redskin in the Far North-West: Recollections of Life in the North-West Mounted Police, Canada, 1884-1888* London 1899

Douthwaite, L. Charles *The Royal Canadian Mounted Police* London 1939

Fetherstonhaugh, R.C. *The Royal Canadian Mounted Police* New York 1938

Fitzpatrick, F.J. *Sergeant 331* New York 1921

Harvison, Clifford W. *The Horsemen* Toronto 1967

Haydon, A.L. *The Riders of the Plains: A Record of the Royal North-West Mounted Police of Canada 1873-1910* London 1910

Horrall, S.W. 'Sir John A. Macdonald and the Mounted Police Force for the North-West Territories,' *Canadian Historical Review* 2 (1972) 179-200

Kelly, Nora *The Men of the Mounted* Toronto 1949

Kelly, Nora and William *The Royal Canadian Mounted Police: A Century of History* Edmonton 1973

Kemp, Vernon A.M. *Scarlet and Stetson: The Royal North-West Mounted Police on the Prairies* Toronto 1964

– *Without Fear, Favour or Affection: Thirty-Five Years with the Royal Canadian Mounted Police* Toronto 1958

Longstreth, T. Morris *The Scarlet Force* New York 1953

– *The Silent Force* New York 1927

Macbeth, R.G. *Policing the Plains: Being a Real-life Record of the Famous Royal North-West Mounted Police* London 1922

Montague, Sydney R. *Riders in Scarlet* Evanston 1941

Morgan, Edwin Charles 'The North-West Mounted Police, 1873-1883,' unpublished MA thesis, University of Saskatchewan 1970

Morris, Edmund 'Lt-Col Irvine and the North-West Mounted Police,' *The Canadian Magazine* XXXVII 6 (1911)

Neuberger, Richard L. 'The Royal Canadian Mounted Police,' *Harper's Magazine* (July 1934)

Steele, Harwood 'The Mounties Take the West,' *The Canadian Magazine*
(July 1934)
Steele, Samuel B. *Forty Years in Canada: Reminiscences of the Great North-West with Some Account of His Service in South Africa* Toronto 1915
Stegner, Wallace 'The Mounties at Fort Walsh,' *Atlantic* (July 1958)
Turner, John Peter *The North-West Mounted Police 1873-1893* Ottawa 1950
Turner's two volumes are the most serious attempt so far at a detailed history of the force. Although Turner was a journalist and spent some forty years on the work it is not easy to read. It is organized with a chapter for each year and goes into great detail on such things as armaments, uniforms, and saddlery. As a reference book it is quite useful, although the lack of footnotes makes it less reliable then it might otherwise have been. The book contains almost nothing in the way of historical interpretation, being little more than a chronicle of events. Like the other histories of the force it is laudatory and uncritical throughout, concentrating on the achievements of the police to the exclusion of any of their difficulties or shortcomings. Turner's notes for the book are still in the possession of the Mounted Police and the official historian of the force, S.W. Horrall, has informed me that Turner relied almost entirely on interviews with former members of the police for his information. With the exception of the annual reports, Turner paid little attention to documentary sources.
- 'When the Mounted Police Went West,' *Canadian Geographical Journal* x 2 and 3 (1935)
Walker, James 'My Life in the North-West Mounted Police,' *Alberta Historical Review* viii 1 (1960)
Young, Delbert A. *The Mounties* (Toronto 1968)

Index